THE PASS

Life stories that converge, entangle, entwine, and enchain. How lucky when your own crosses paths with exceptional people. People who give everything at every moment, freely and without complaint. People with the gift to turn your daily routine into a thing of wonder.

They share their lust for life, their art of living, with you. They make you strong. For all that, I thank them for being there.

I thank a father, a grandfather, a beautiful individual who gave everything to his little guy, his "meccutt." Thank you for helping him to this day to become in turn . . . a good person.

K, Espé's wife

writing & illustrations   ESPÉ

colors   Aretha BATTISTUTTA

THE PASS

Some stories are invented, others are told. . .

graphic mundi

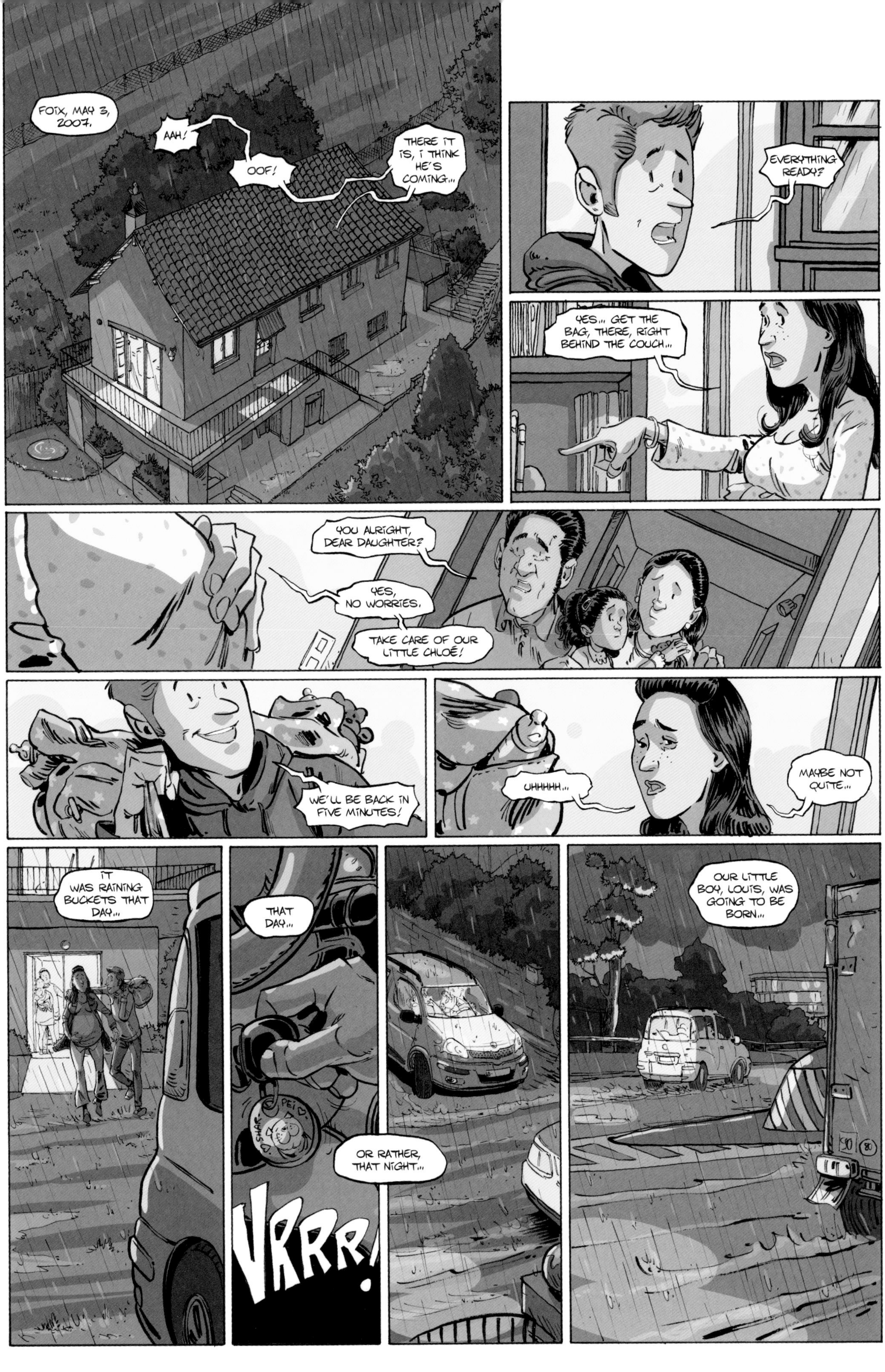
FOIX, MAY 3, 2007.
AAH!
OOF!
THERE IT IS, I THINK HE'S COMING...
EVERYTHING READY?
YES... GET THE BAG, THERE, RIGHT BEHIND THE COUCH...
YOU ALRIGHT, DEAR DAUGHTER?
YES, NO WORRIES.
TAKE CARE OF OUR LITTLE CHLOÉ!
WE'LL BE BACK IN FIVE MINUTES!
UHHHHH...
MAYBE NOT QUITE...
IT WAS RAINING BUCKETS THAT DAY...
THAT DAY...
OR RATHER, THAT NIGHT...
VRRR!
OUR LITTLE BOY, LOUIS, WAS GOING TO BE BORN...

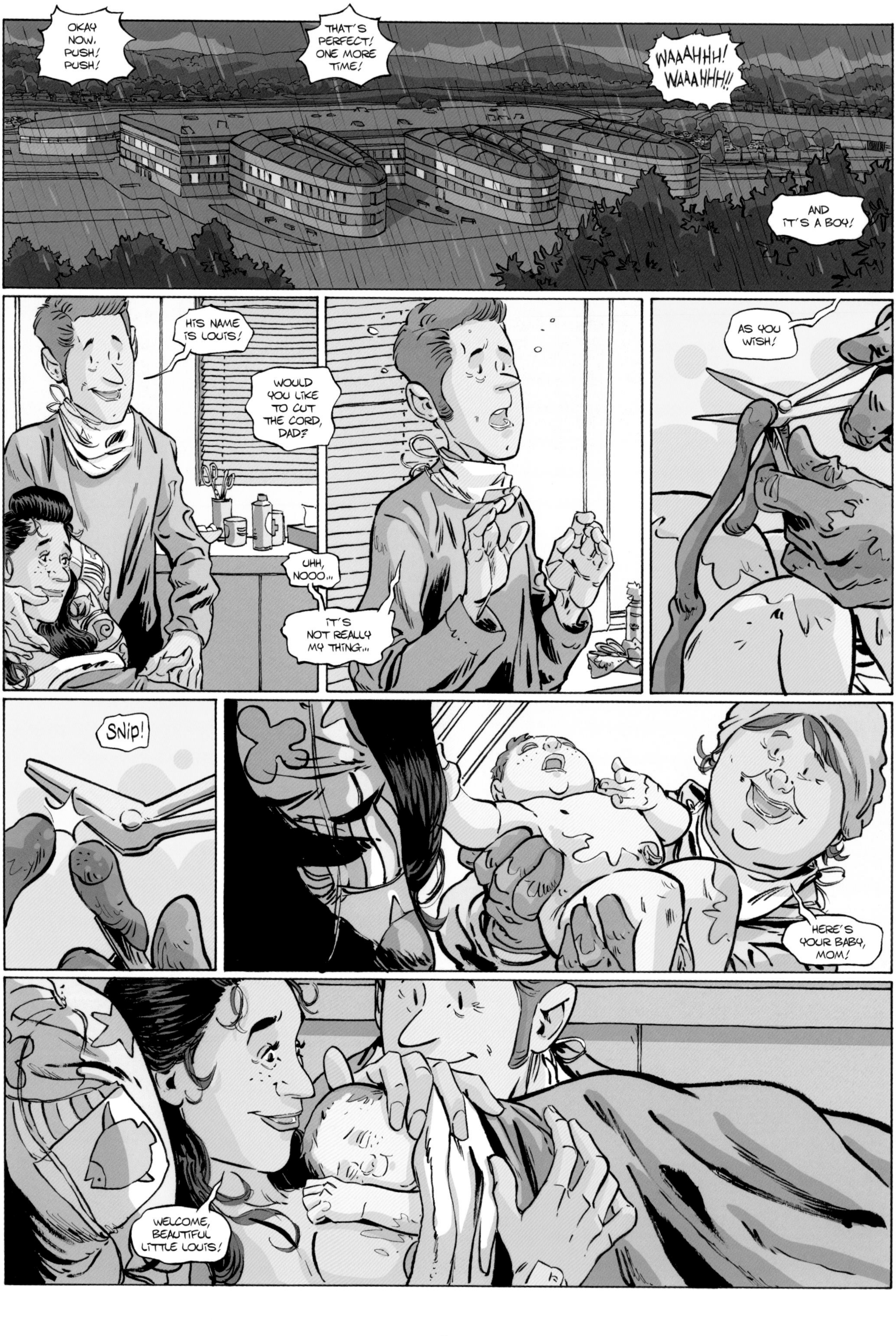
OKAY NOW. PUSH! PUSH!
THAT'S PERFECT! ONE MORE TIME!
WAAAHHH! WAAAHHH!!
AND IT'S A BOY!
HIS NAME IS LOUIS!
WOULD YOU LIKE TO CUT THE CORD, DAD?
UHH, NOOO...
IT'S NOT REALLY MY THING...
AS YOU WISH!
SNIP!
HERE'S YOUR BABY, MOM!
WELCOME, BEAUTIFUL LITTLE LOUIS!

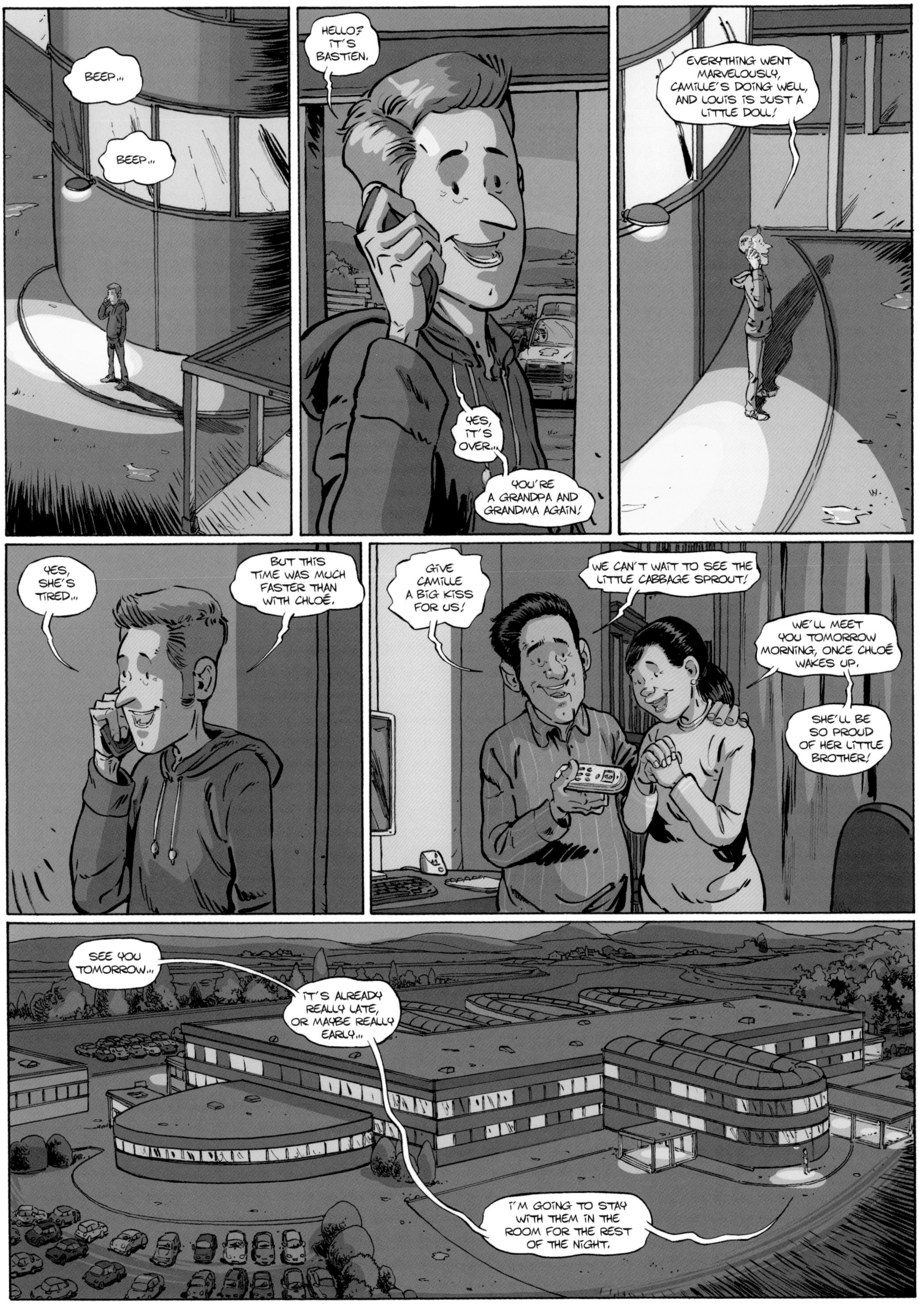
BEEP...
BEEP...
HELLO? IT'S BASTIEN.
YES, IT'S OVER...
YOU'RE A GRANDPA AND GRANDMA AGAIN!
EVERYTHING WENT MARVELOUSLY, CAMILLE'S DOING WELL, AND LOUIS IS JUST A LITTLE DOLL!
YES, SHE'S TIRED...
BUT THIS TIME WAS MUCH FASTER THAN WITH CHLOÉ.
GIVE CAMILLE A BIG KISS FOR US!
WE CAN'T WAIT TO SEE THE LITTLE CABBAGE SPROUT!
WE'LL MEET YOU TOMORROW MORNING, ONCE CHLOÉ WAKES UP.
SHE'LL BE SO PROUD OF HER LITTLE BROTHER!
SEE YOU TOMORROW...
IT'S ALREADY REALLY LATE, OR MAYBE REALLY EARLY...
I'M GOING TO STAY WITH THEM IN THE ROOM FOR THE REST OF THE NIGHT.

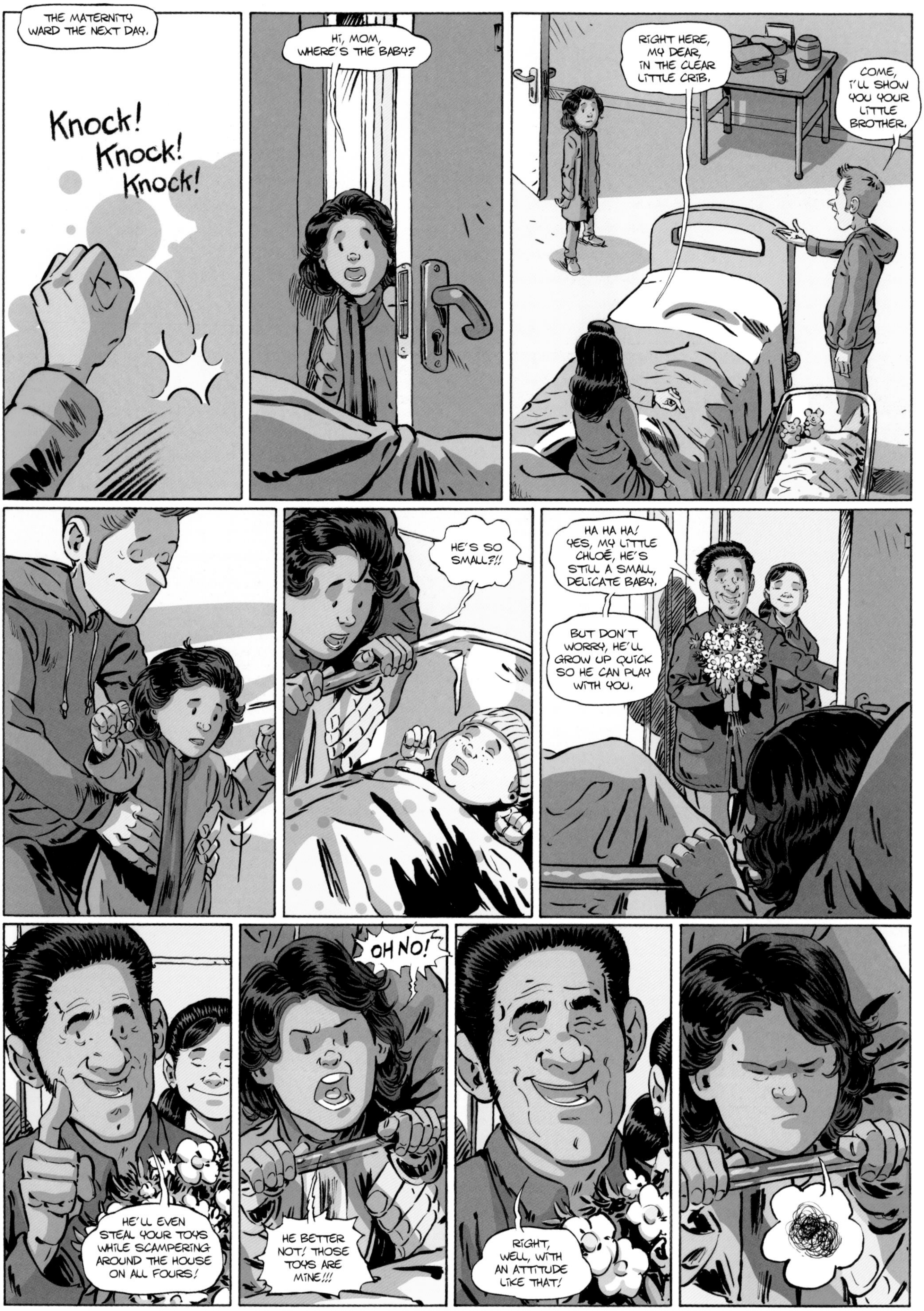
THE MATERNITY WARD THE NEXT DAY.
Knock! Knock! Knock!
HI, MOM, WHERE'S THE BABY?
RIGHT HERE, MY DEAR, IN THE CLEAR LITTLE CRIB.
COME, I'LL SHOW YOU YOUR LITTLE BROTHER.
HE'S SO SMALL?!!
HA HA HA! YES, MY LITTLE CHLOÉ, HE'S STILL A SMALL, DELICATE BABY.
BUT DON'T WORRY, HE'LL GROW UP QUICK SO HE CAN PLAY WITH YOU.
HE'LL EVEN STEAL YOUR TOYS WHILE SCAMPERING AROUND THE HOUSE ON ALL FOURS!
OH NO!
HE BETTER NOT! THOSE TOYS ARE MINE!!!
RIGHT, WELL, WITH AN ATTITUDE LIKE THAT!

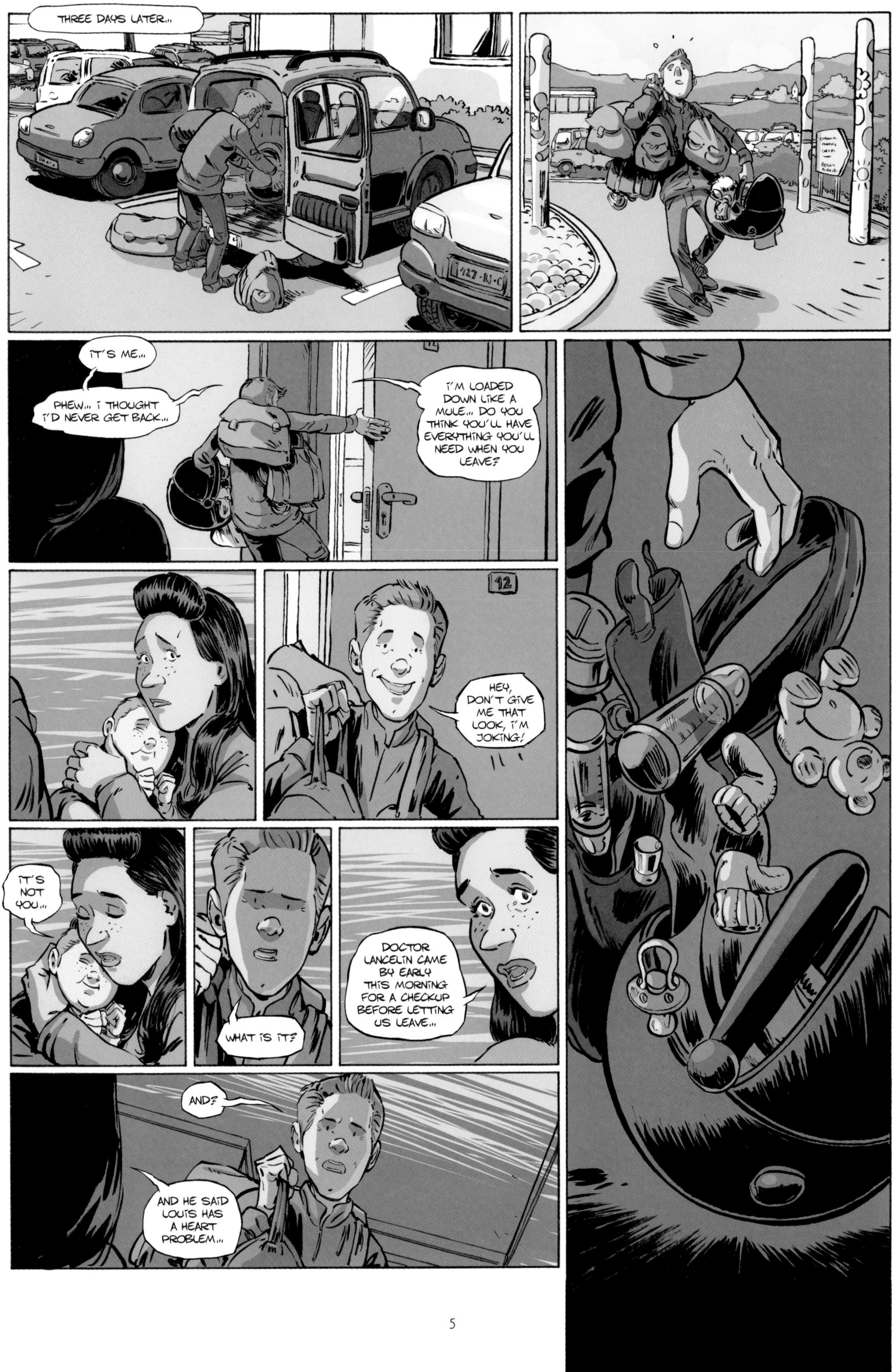
THREE DAYS LATER...
IT'S ME...
PHEW... I THOUGHT I'D NEVER GET BACK...
I'M LOADED DOWN LIKE A MULE... DO YOU THINK YOU'LL HAVE EVERYTHING YOU'LL NEED WHEN YOU LEAVE?
12
HEY, DON'T GIVE ME THAT LOOK, I'M JOKING!
IT'S NOT YOU...
WHAT IS IT?
DOCTOR LANCELIN CAME BY EARLY THIS MORNING FOR A CHECKUP BEFORE LETTING US LEAVE...
AND?
AND HE SAID LOUIS HAS A HEART PROBLEM...

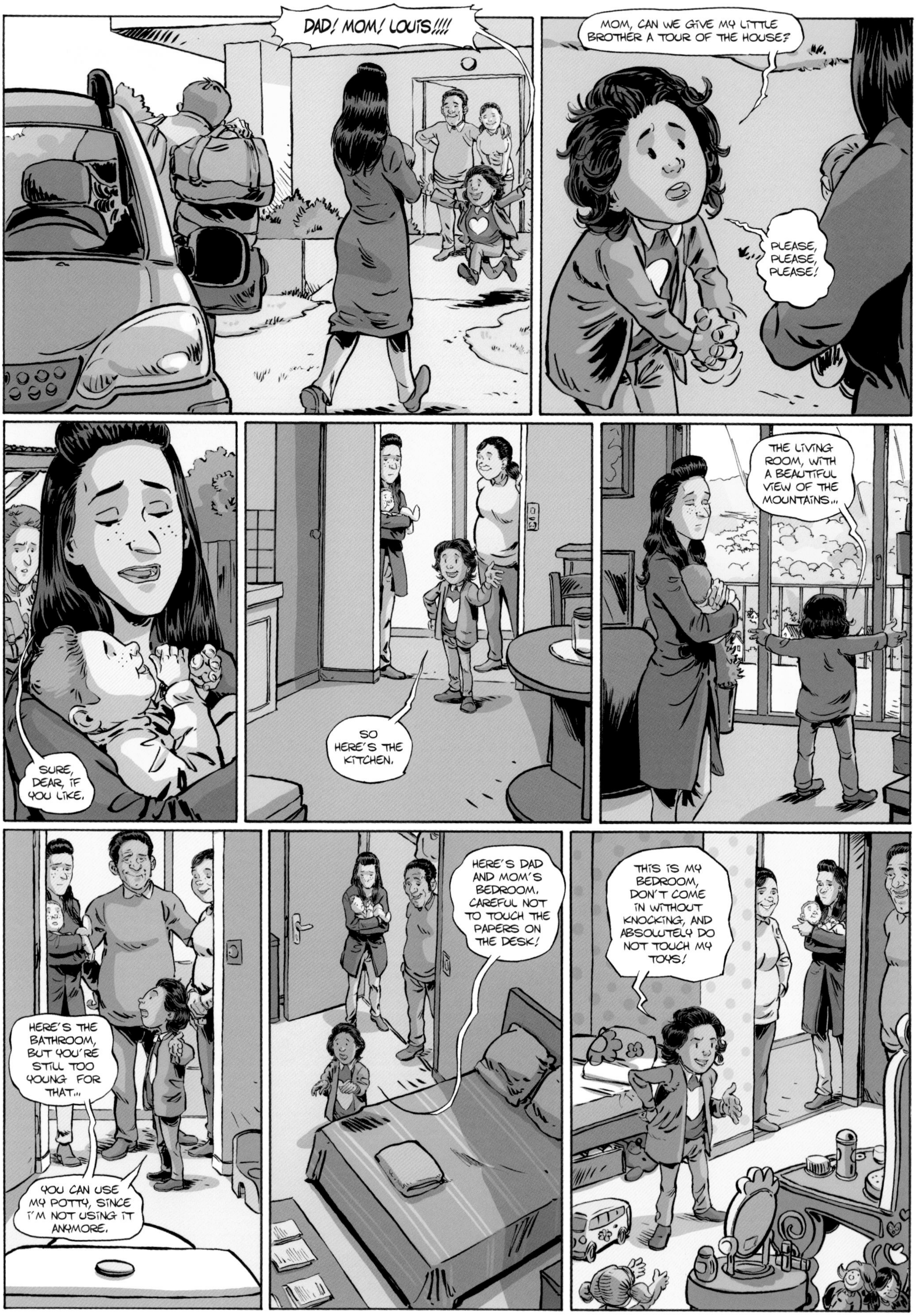
DAD! MOM! LOUIS!!!!
MOM, CAN WE GIVE MY LITTLE BROTHER A TOUR OF THE HOUSE?
PLEASE, PLEASE, PLEASE!
SURE, DEAR, IF YOU LIKE.
SO HERE'S THE KITCHEN.
THE LIVING ROOM, WITH A BEAUTIFUL VIEW OF THE MOUNTAINS...
HERE'S THE BATHROOM, BUT YOU'RE STILL TOO YOUNG FOR THAT...
YOU CAN USE MY POTTY, SINCE I'M NOT USING IT ANYMORE.
HERE'S DAD AND MOM'S BEDROOM, CAREFUL NOT TO TOUCH THE PAPERS ON THE DESK!
THIS IS MY BEDROOM, DON'T COME IN WITHOUT KNOCKING, AND ABSOLUTELY DO NOT TOUCH MY TOYS!

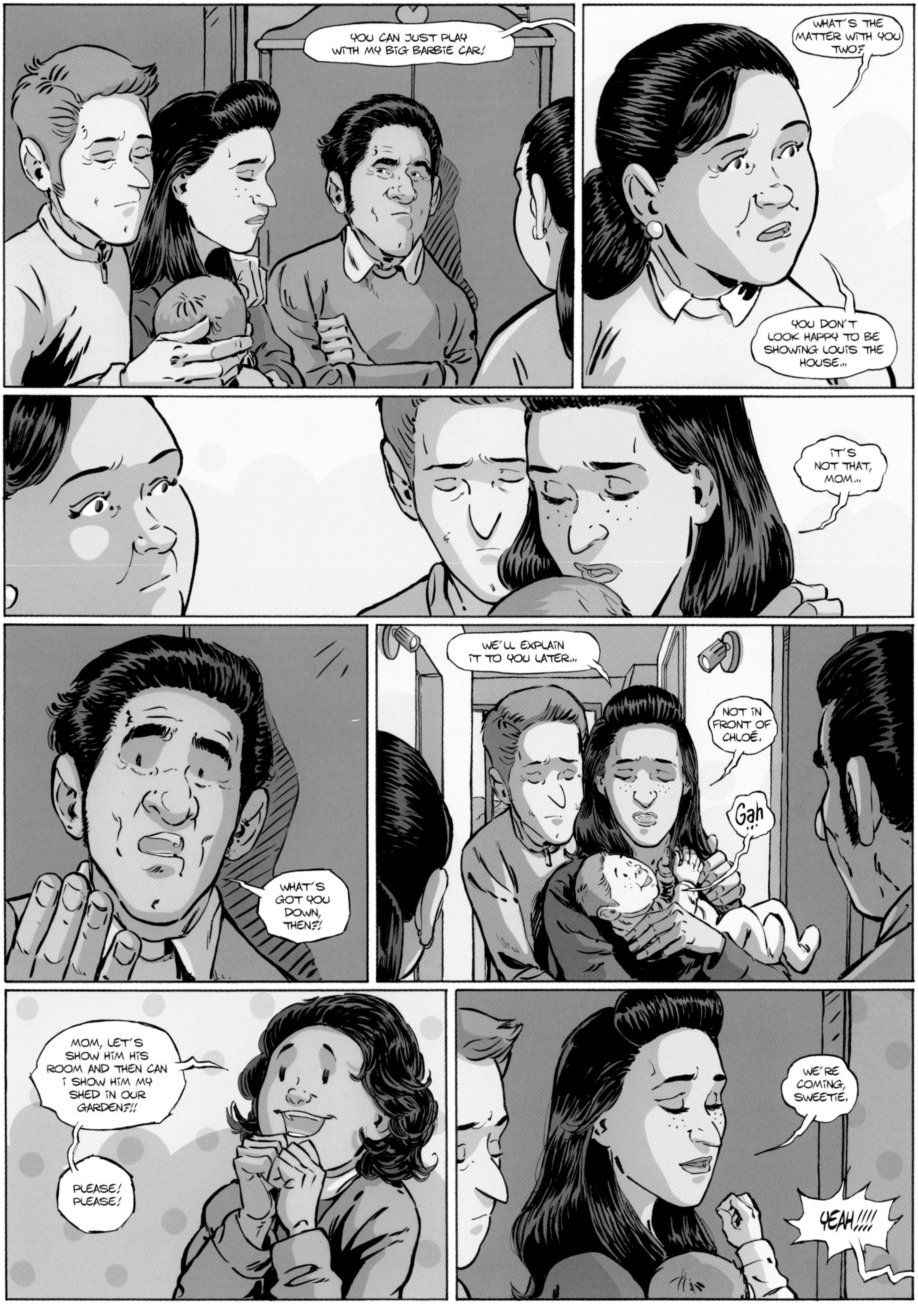
YOU CAN JUST PLAY WITH MY BIG BARBIE CAR!
WHAT'S THE MATTER WITH YOU TWO?
YOU DON'T LOOK HAPPY TO BE SHOWING LOUIS THE HOUSE...
IT'S NOT THAT, MOM...
WHAT'S GOT YOU DOWN, THEN?!
WE'LL EXPLAIN IT TO YOU LATER...
NOT IN FRONT OF CHLOÉ.
Gah
MOM, LET'S SHOW HIM HIS ROOM AND THEN CAN I SHOW HIM MY SHED IN OUR GARDEN?!!
PLEASE! PLEASE!
WE'RE COMING, SWEETIE.
YEAH!!!!

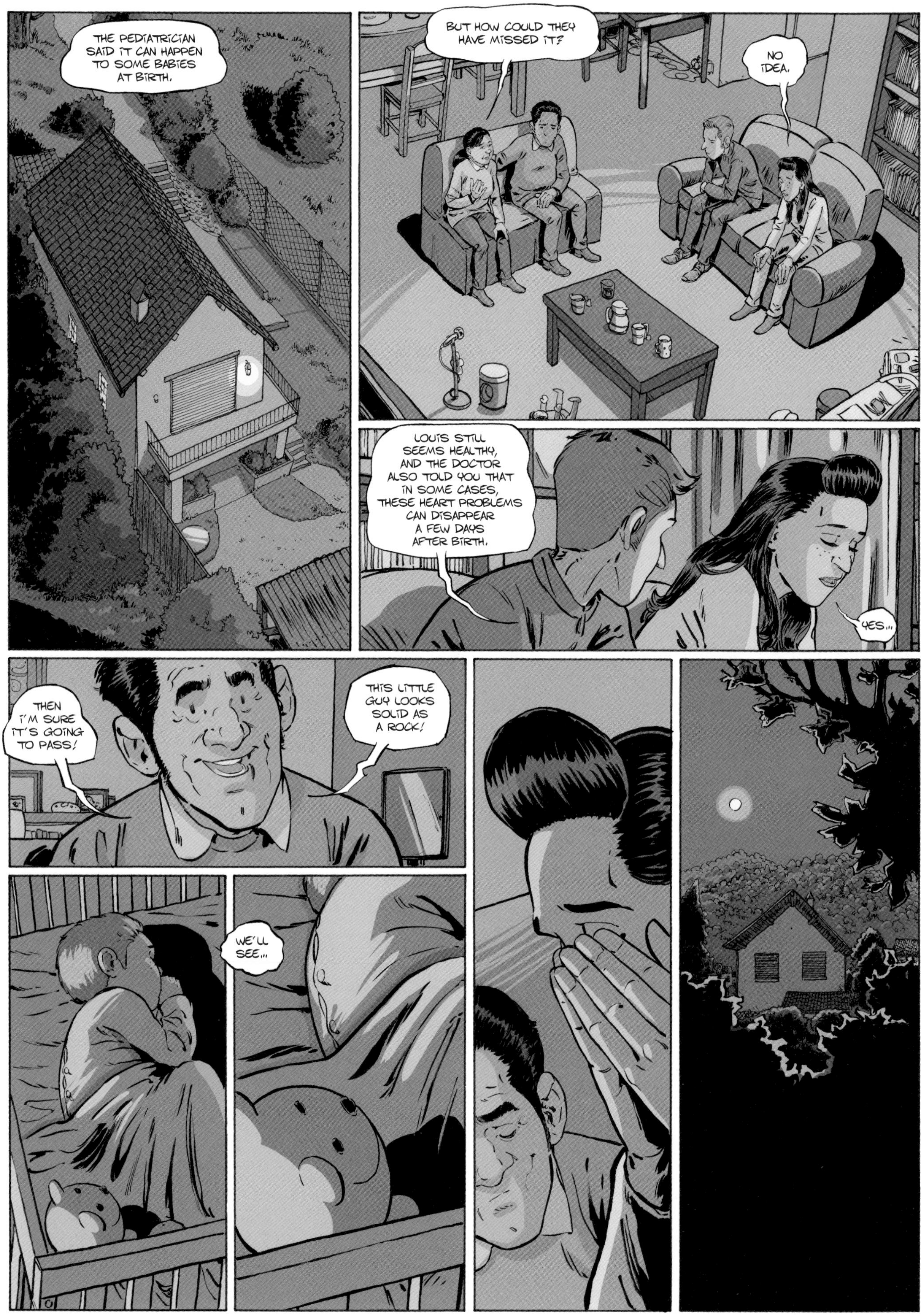

THE PEDIATRICIAN SAID IT CAN HAPPEN TO SOME BABIES AT BIRTH.
BUT HOW COULD THEY HAVE MISSED IT?
NO IDEA.
LOUIS STILL SEEMS HEALTHY, AND THE DOCTOR ALSO TOLD YOU THAT IN SOME CASES, THESE HEART PROBLEMS CAN DISAPPEAR A FEW DAYS AFTER BIRTH.
YES...
THEN I'M SURE IT'S GOING TO PASS!
THIS LITTLE GUY LOOKS SOLID AS A ROCK!
WE'LL SEE...

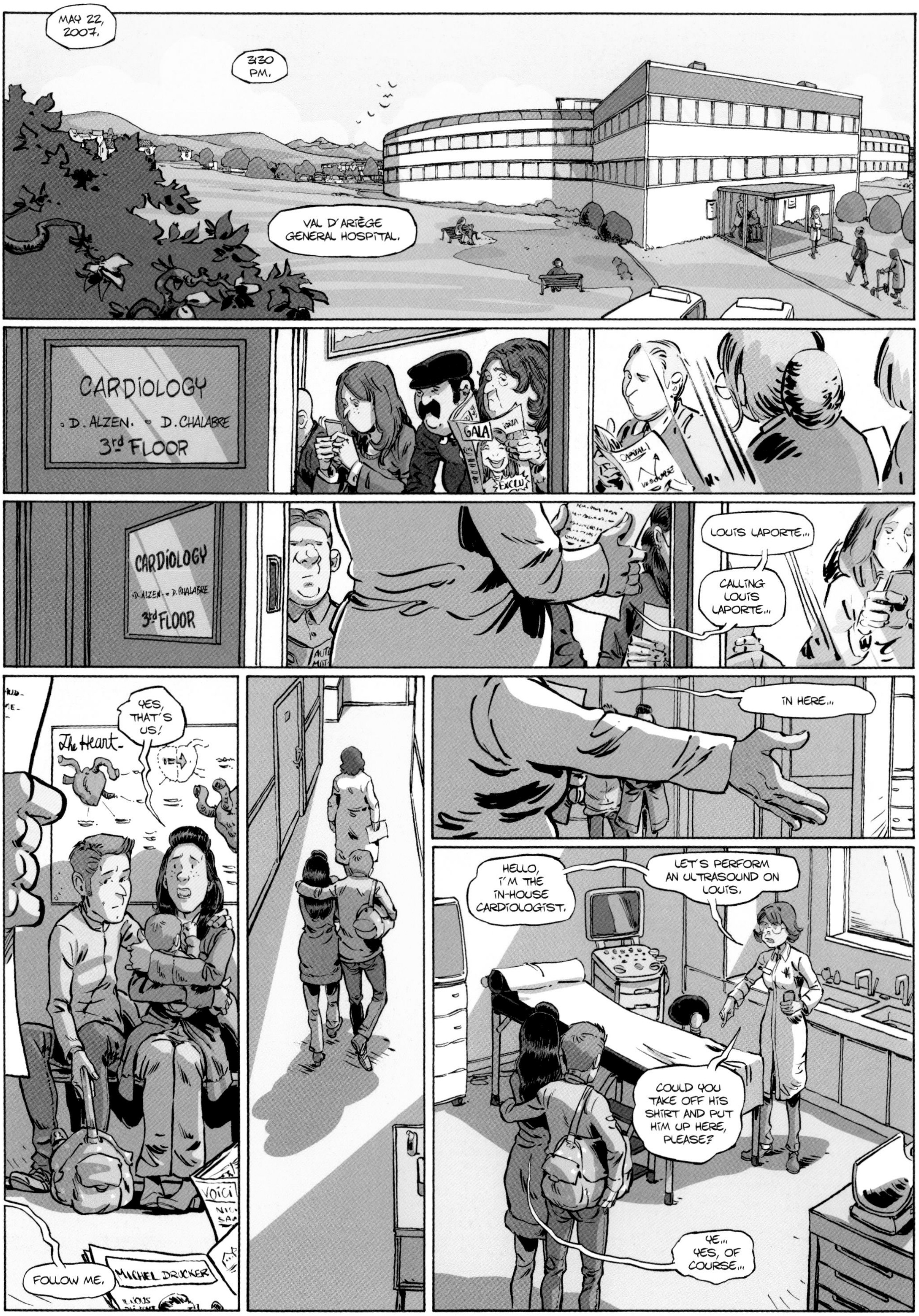
MAY 22, 2007.
3:30 PM.
VAL D'ARIÈGE GENERAL HOSPITAL.
CARDIOLOGY
D. ALZEN. D. CHALABRE
3rd FLOOR
GALA
CARDIOLOGY
D. ALZEN. D. CHALABRE
3rd FLOOR
LOUIS LAPORTE...
CALLING LOUIS LAPORTE...
YES, THAT'S US!
The Heart
FOLLOW ME.
MICHEL DRUCKER
VOICI
IN HERE...
HELLO, I'M THE IN-HOUSE CARDIOLOGIST.
LET'S PERFORM AN ULTRASOUND ON LOUIS.
COULD YOU TAKE OFF HIS SHIRT AND PUT HIM UP HERE, PLEASE?
YE... YES, OF COURSE...

THUMP!

THUMP!

THUMP!

THUMP!

THUMP!

THUMP!

YES...

THERE'S DEFINITELY SOMETHING...

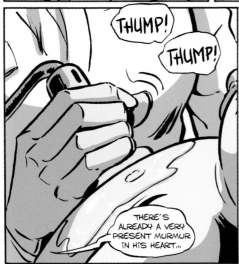

THUMP!

THUMP!

THERE'S ALREADY A VERY PRESENT MURMUR IN HIS HEART...

THUMP!

THUMP!

THAT CONFIRMS HIS CARDIAC ISSUE...

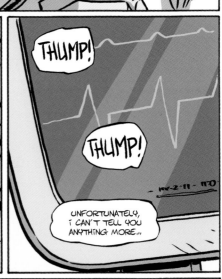

THUMP!

THUMP!

UNFORTUNATELY, I CAN'T TELL YOU ANYTHING MORE...

THE MACHINES HERE IN FOIX AREN'T POWERFUL ENOUGH...

YOU'LL HAVE TO GO TO TOULOUSE, TO THE PASTEUR CLINIC. I DID MY RESIDENCY THERE WITH PROFESSOR HALTS, ONE OF THE GREATEST SPECIALISTS IN CHILD CARDIOLOGY...

I'LL REFER YOU TO HIM ASAP. HE'LL KNOW HOW TO FIND OUT WHAT'S GOING ON. I CAN CONTACT HIM DIRECTLY, IF YOU'D LIKE, THAT'LL BUY YOU SOME TIME...

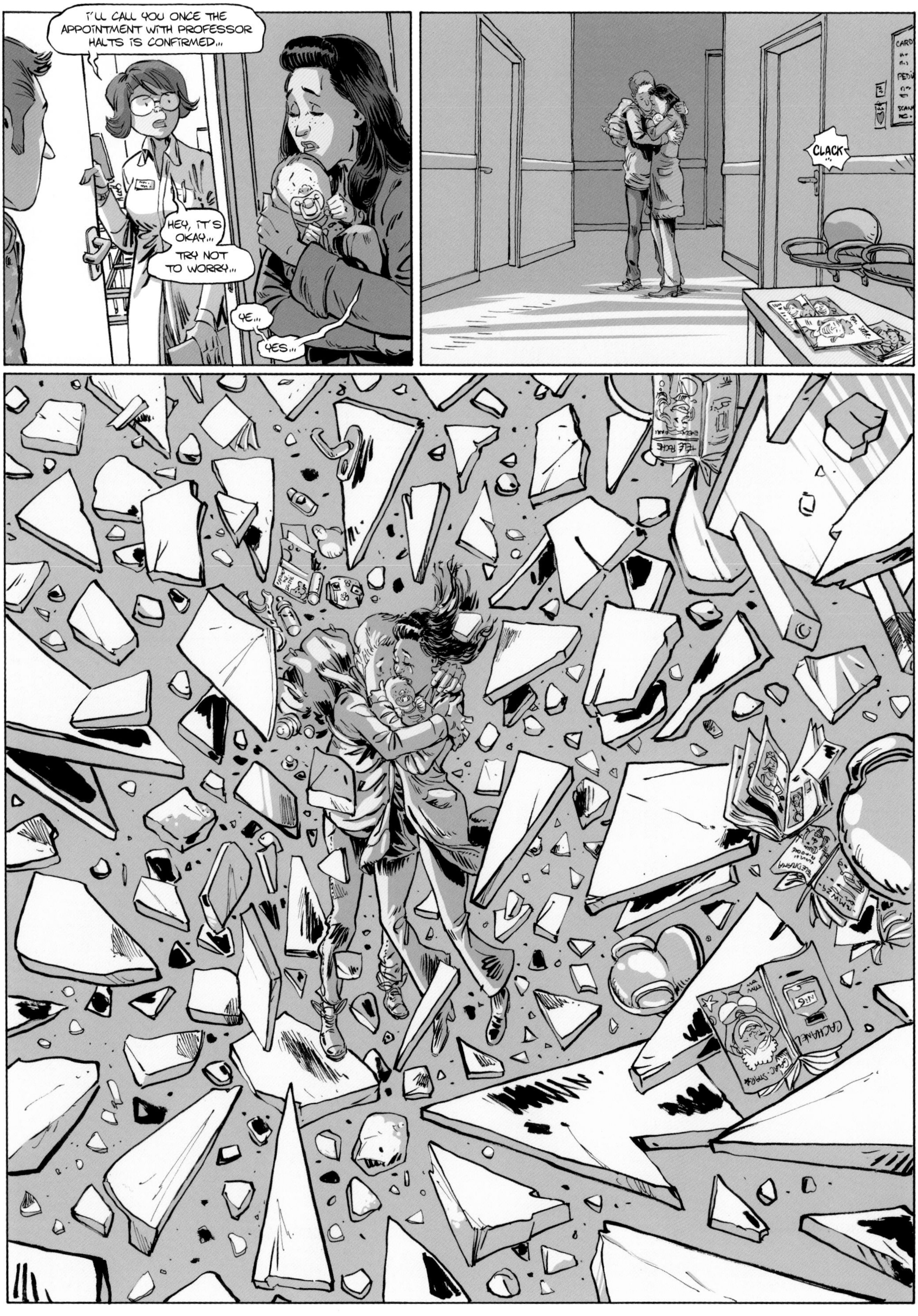

I'LL CALL YOU ONCE THE APPOINTMENT WITH PROFESSOR HALTS IS CONFIRMED...
HEY, IT'S OKAY... TRY NOT TO WORRY...
YE...
YES...
CLACK

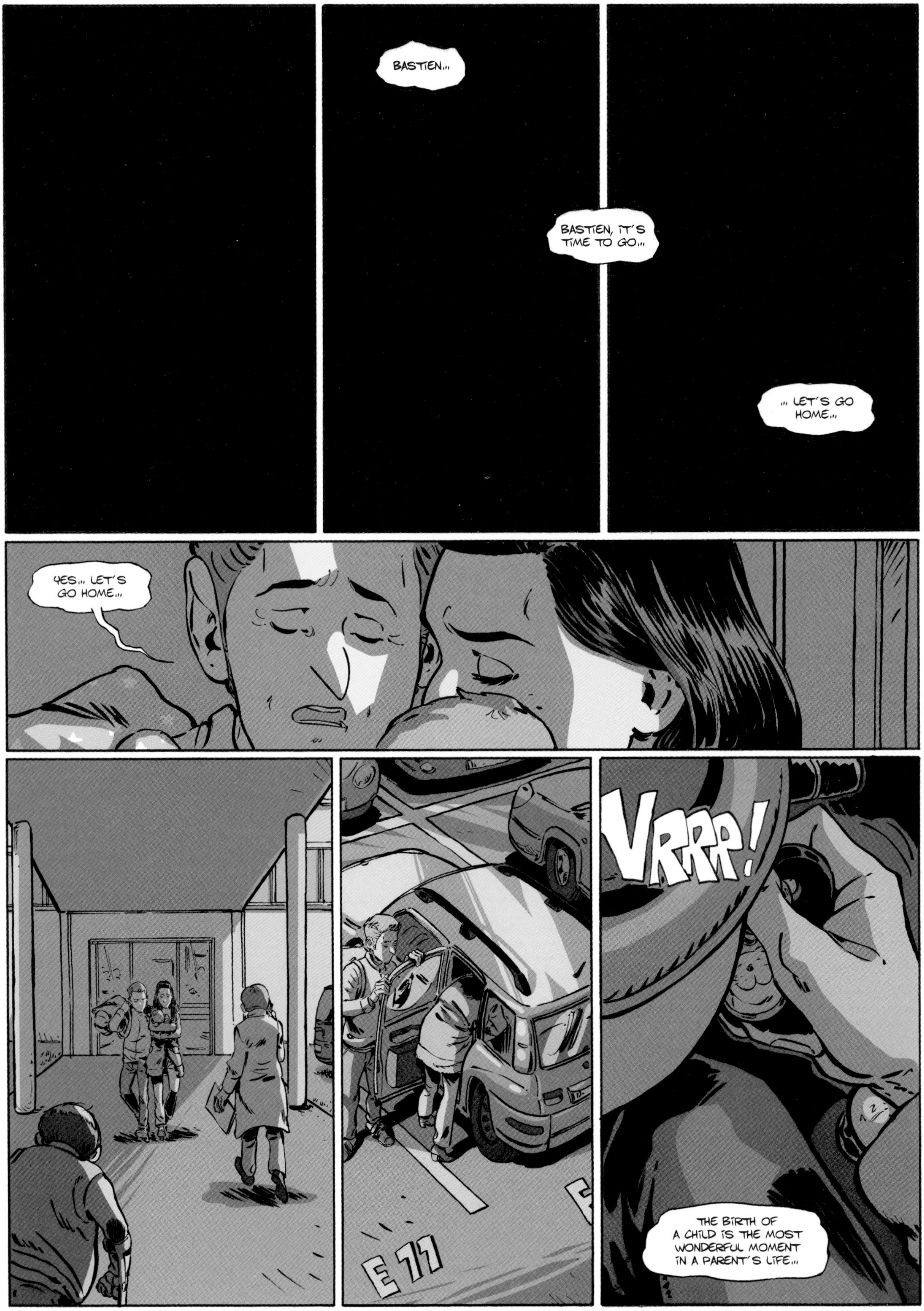
BASTIEN...
BASTIEN, IT'S TIME TO GO...
... LET'S GO HOME...
YES... LET'S GO HOME...
E 11
VRRP!
THE BIRTH OF A CHILD IS THE MOST WONDERFUL MOMENT IN A PARENT'S LIFE...

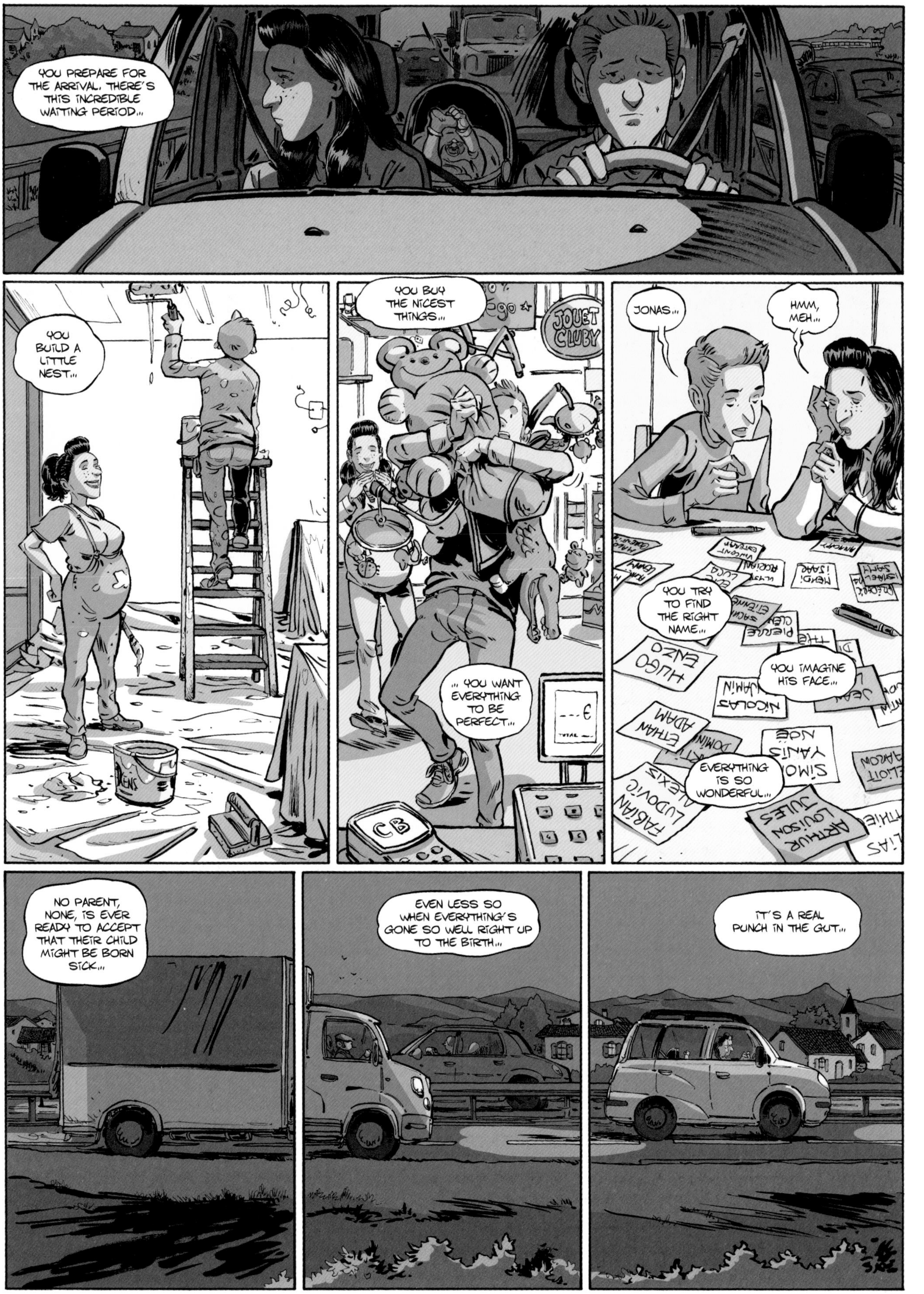
YOU PREPARE FOR THE ARRIVAL. THERE'S THIS INCREDIBLE WAITING PERIOD...
YOU BUILD A LITTLE NEST...
YOU BUY THE NICEST THINGS...
JOUET CLUBY
... YOU WANT EVERYTHING TO BE PERFECT...
CB
JONAS...
HMM, MEH...
YOU TRY TO FIND THE RIGHT NAME...
YOU IMAGINE HIS FACE...
EVERYTHING IS SO WONDERFUL...
NO PARENT, NONE, IS EVER READY TO ACCEPT THAT THEIR CHILD MIGHT BE BORN SICK...
EVEN LESS SO WHEN EVERYTHING'S GONE SO WELL RIGHT UP TO THE BIRTH...
IT'S A REAL PUNCH IN THE GUT...

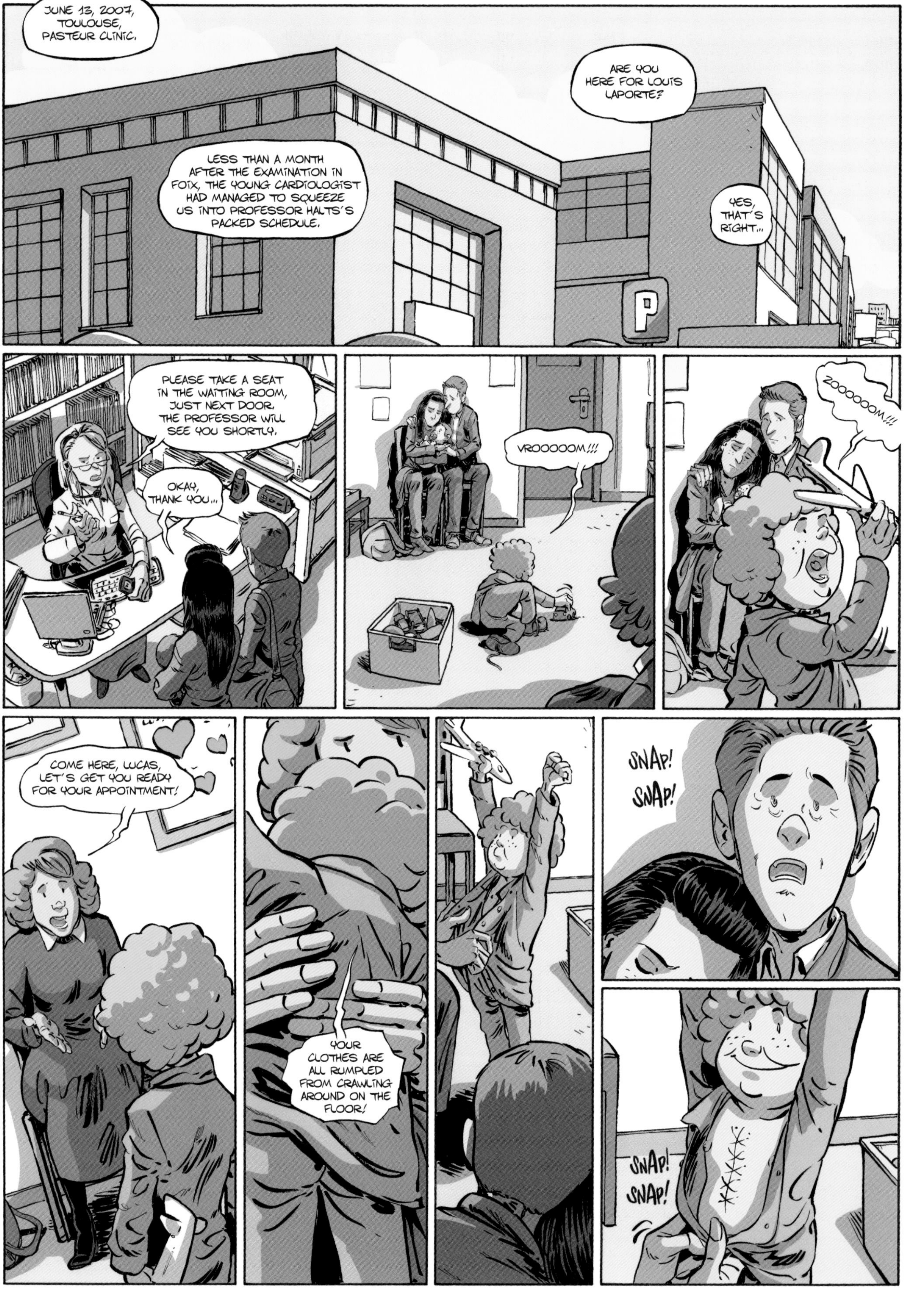

JUNE 13, 2007, TOULOUSE, PASTEUR CLINIC.
LESS THAN A MONTH AFTER THE EXAMINATION IN FOIX, THE YOUNG CARDIOLOGIST HAD MANAGED TO SQUEEZE US INTO PROFESSOR HALTS'S PACKED SCHEDULE.
ARE YOU HERE FOR LOUIS LAPORTE?
YES, THAT'S RIGHT...
P
PLEASE TAKE A SEAT IN THE WAITING ROOM, JUST NEXT DOOR. THE PROFESSOR WILL SEE YOU SHORTLY.
OKAY, THANK YOU...
VROOOOOM!!!
ZOOOOOOM!!!
COME HERE, LUCAS, LET'S GET YOU READY FOR YOUR APPOINTMENT!
YOUR CLOTHES ARE ALL RUMPLED FROM CRAWLING AROUND ON THE FLOOR!
SNAP! SNAP!
SNAP! SNAP!

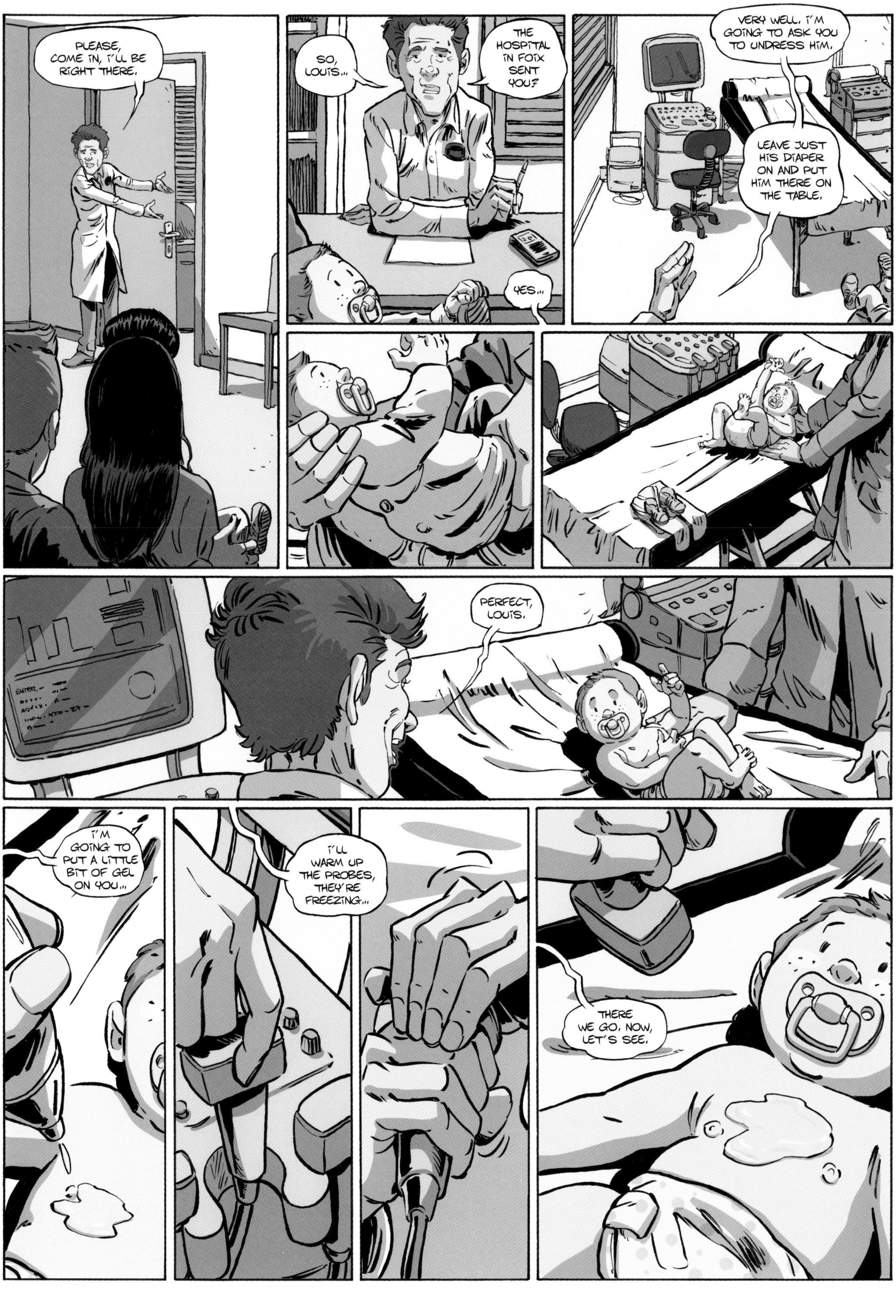
PLEASE, COME IN, I'LL BE RIGHT THERE.
SO, LOUIS...
THE HOSPITAL IN FOIX SENT YOU?
YES...
VERY WELL. I'M GOING TO ASK YOU TO UNDRESS HIM.
LEAVE JUST HIS DIAPER ON AND PUT HIM THERE ON THE TABLE.
PERFECT, LOUIS.
I'M GOING TO PUT A LITTLE BIT OF GEL ON YOU...
I'LL WARM UP THE PROBES, THEY'RE FREEZING...
THERE WE GO. NOW, LET'S SEE.

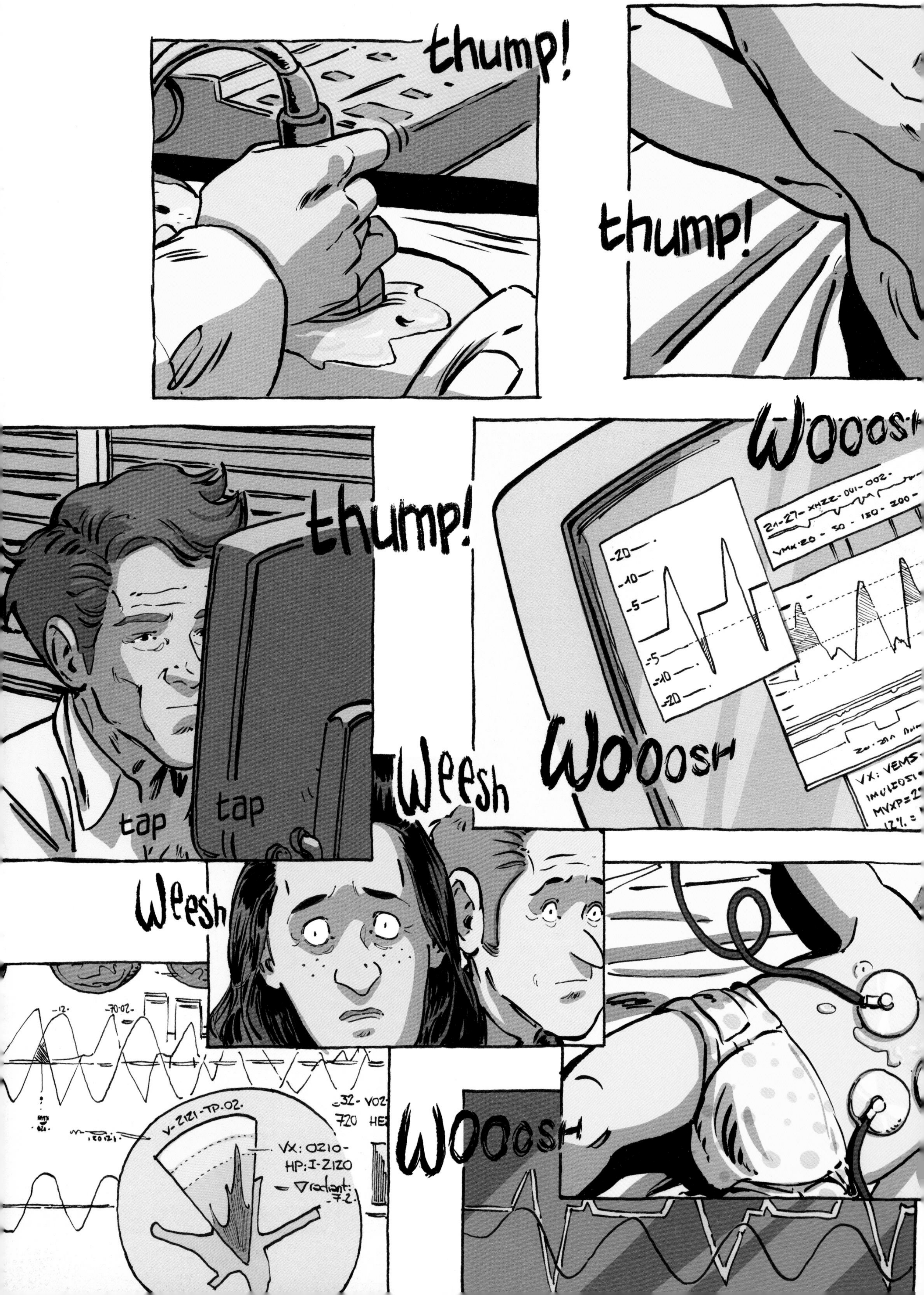

thump!
thump!
thump!
tap
tap
Wooosh
Wooosh
Weesh
Weesh
Wooosh

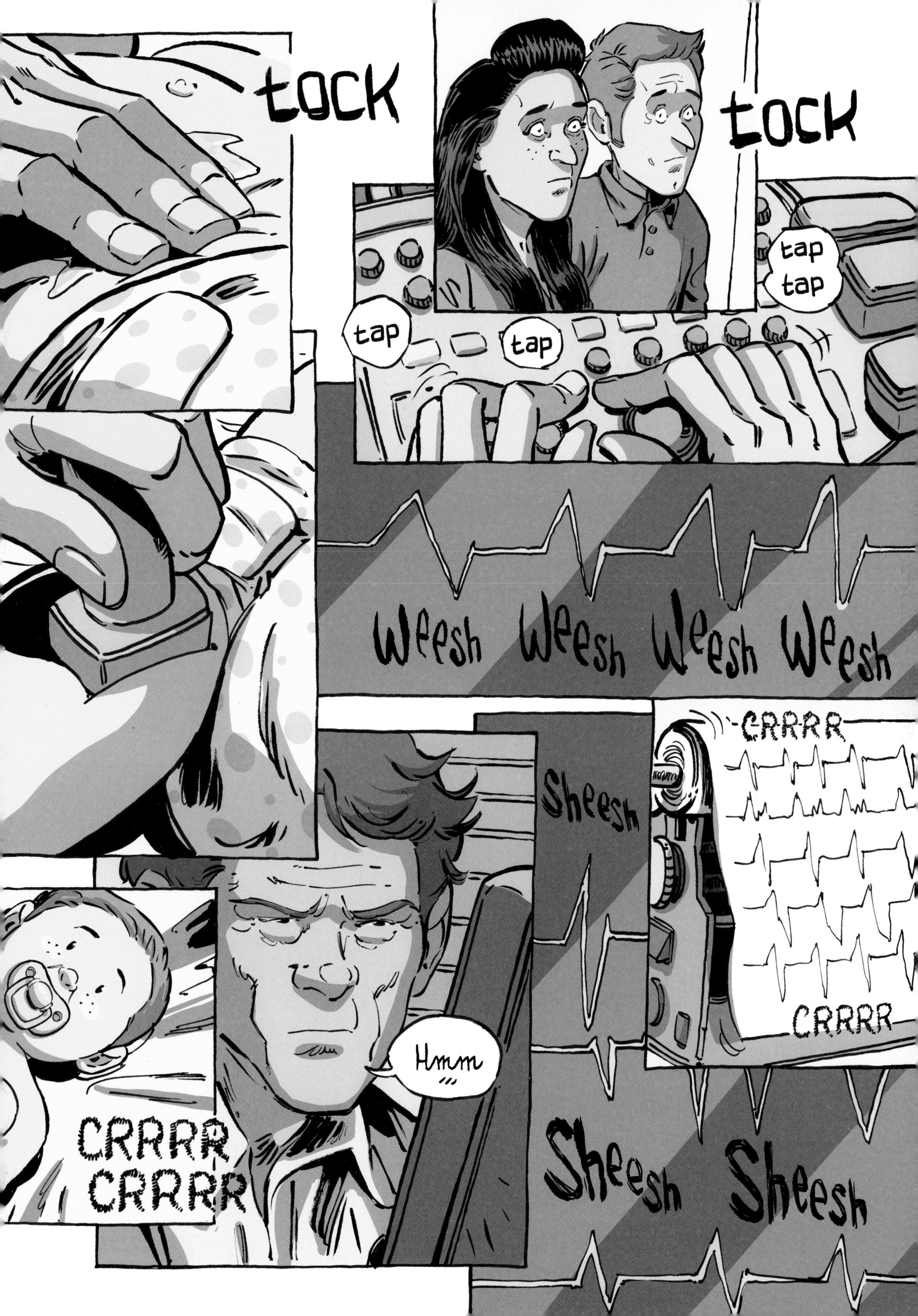
tock
tock
tap
tap
tap
tap
Weesh Weesh Weesh Weesh
Sheesh
CRRRR
CRRRR
Hmm
CRRRR
CRRRR
Sheesh Sheesh

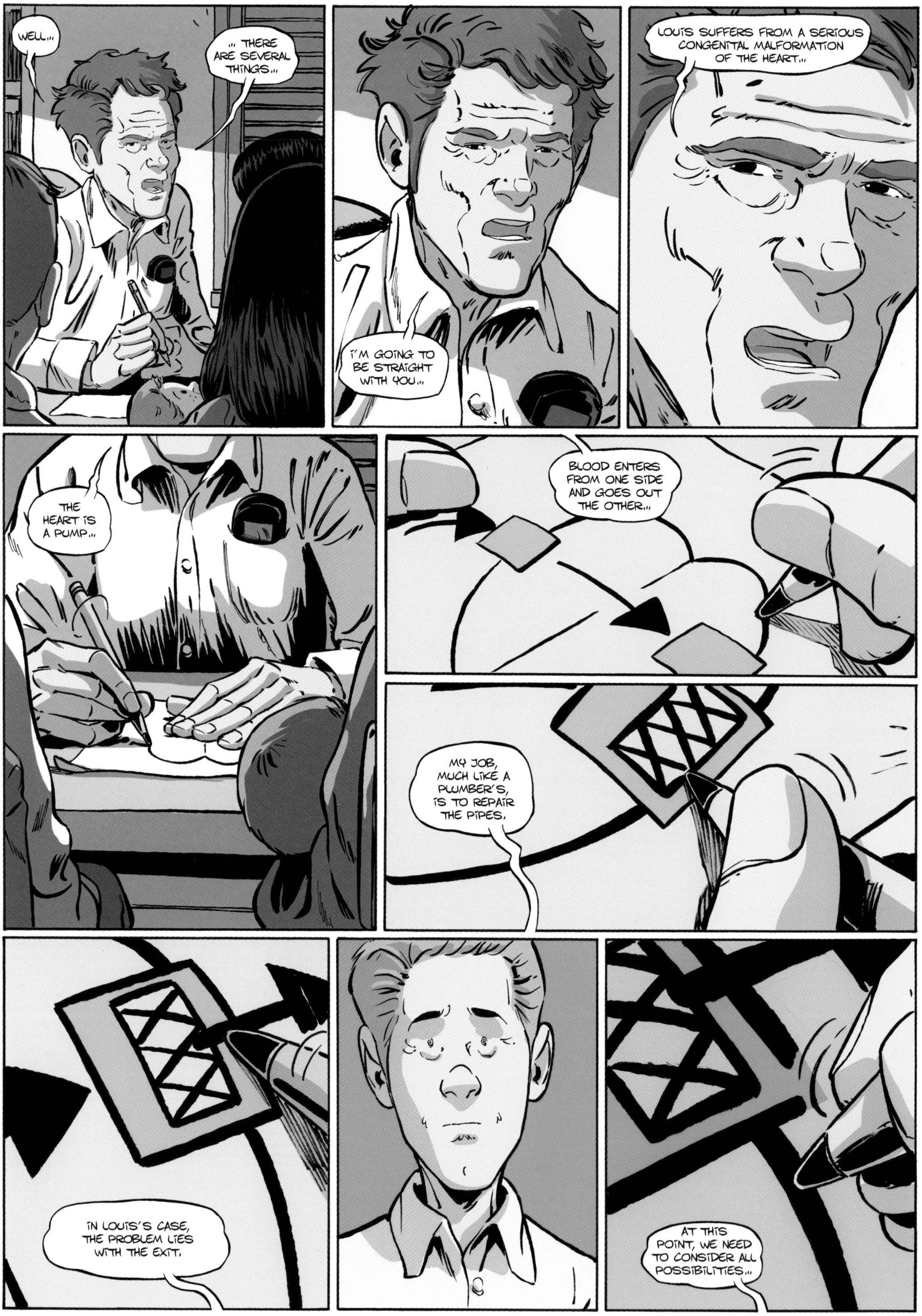
WELL...
... THERE ARE SEVERAL THINGS...
I'M GOING TO BE STRAIGHT WITH YOU...
LOUIS SUFFERS FROM A SERIOUS CONGENITAL MALFORMATION OF THE HEART...
THE HEART IS A PUMP...
BLOOD ENTERS FROM ONE SIDE AND GOES OUT THE OTHER...
MY JOB, MUCH LIKE A PLUMBER'S, IS TO REPAIR THE PIPES.
IN LOUIS'S CASE, THE PROBLEM LIES WITH THE EXIT.
AT THIS POINT, WE NEED TO CONSIDER ALL POSSIBILITIES...

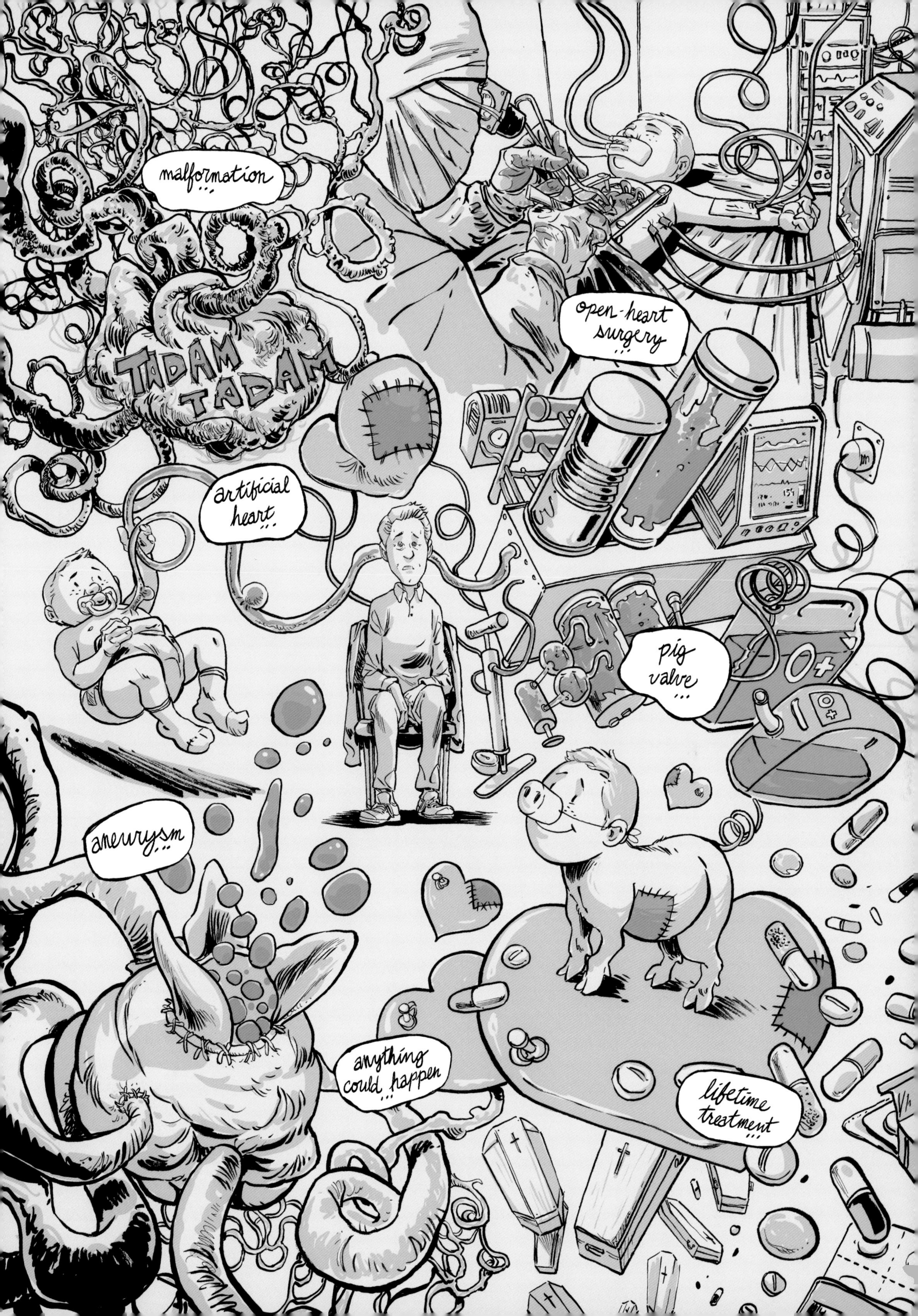
malformation...
TADAM TADAM
open-heart surgery...
artificial heart...
pig valve...
aneurysm...
anything could happen...
lifetime treatment...

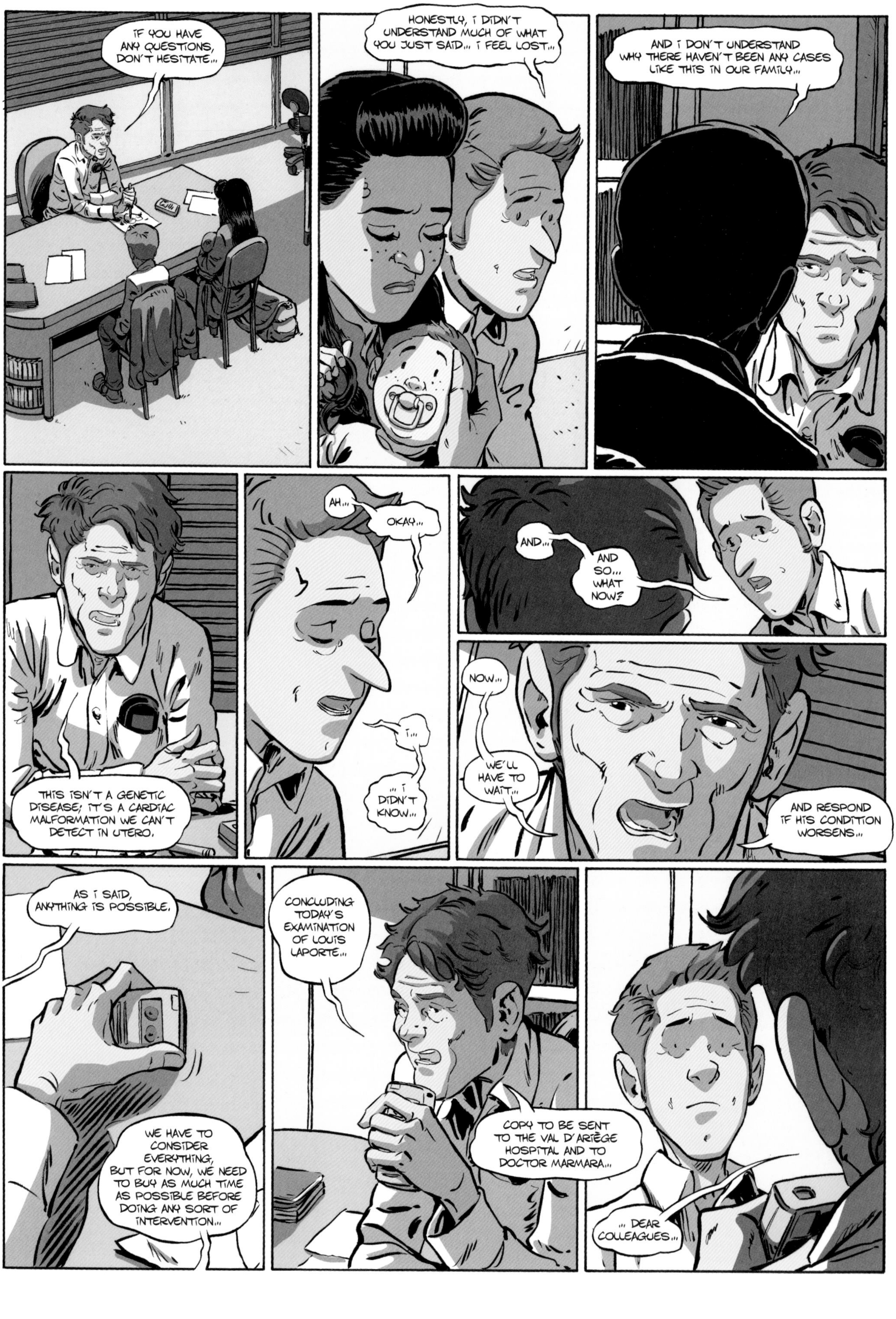
IF YOU HAVE ANY QUESTIONS, DON'T HESITATE...
HONESTLY, I DIDN'T UNDERSTAND MUCH OF WHAT YOU JUST SAID... I FEEL LOST...
AND I DON'T UNDERSTAND WHY THERE HAVEN'T BEEN ANY CASES LIKE THIS IN OUR FAMILY...
THIS ISN'T A GENETIC DISEASE; IT'S A CARDIAC MALFORMATION WE CAN'T DETECT IN UTERO.
AH...
OKAY...
I...
... I DIDN'T KNOW...
AND...
AND SO... WHAT NOW?
NOW...
WE'LL HAVE TO WAIT...
AND RESPOND IF HIS CONDITION WORSENS...
AS I SAID, ANYTHING IS POSSIBLE.
WE HAVE TO CONSIDER EVERYTHING, BUT FOR NOW, WE NEED TO BUY AS MUCH TIME AS POSSIBLE BEFORE DOING ANY SORT OF INTERVENTION...
CONCLUDING TODAY'S EXAMINATION OF LOUIS LAPORTE...
COPY TO BE SENT TO THE VAL D'ARIÈGE HOSPITAL AND TO DOCTOR MARMARA...
... DEAR COLLEAGUES...

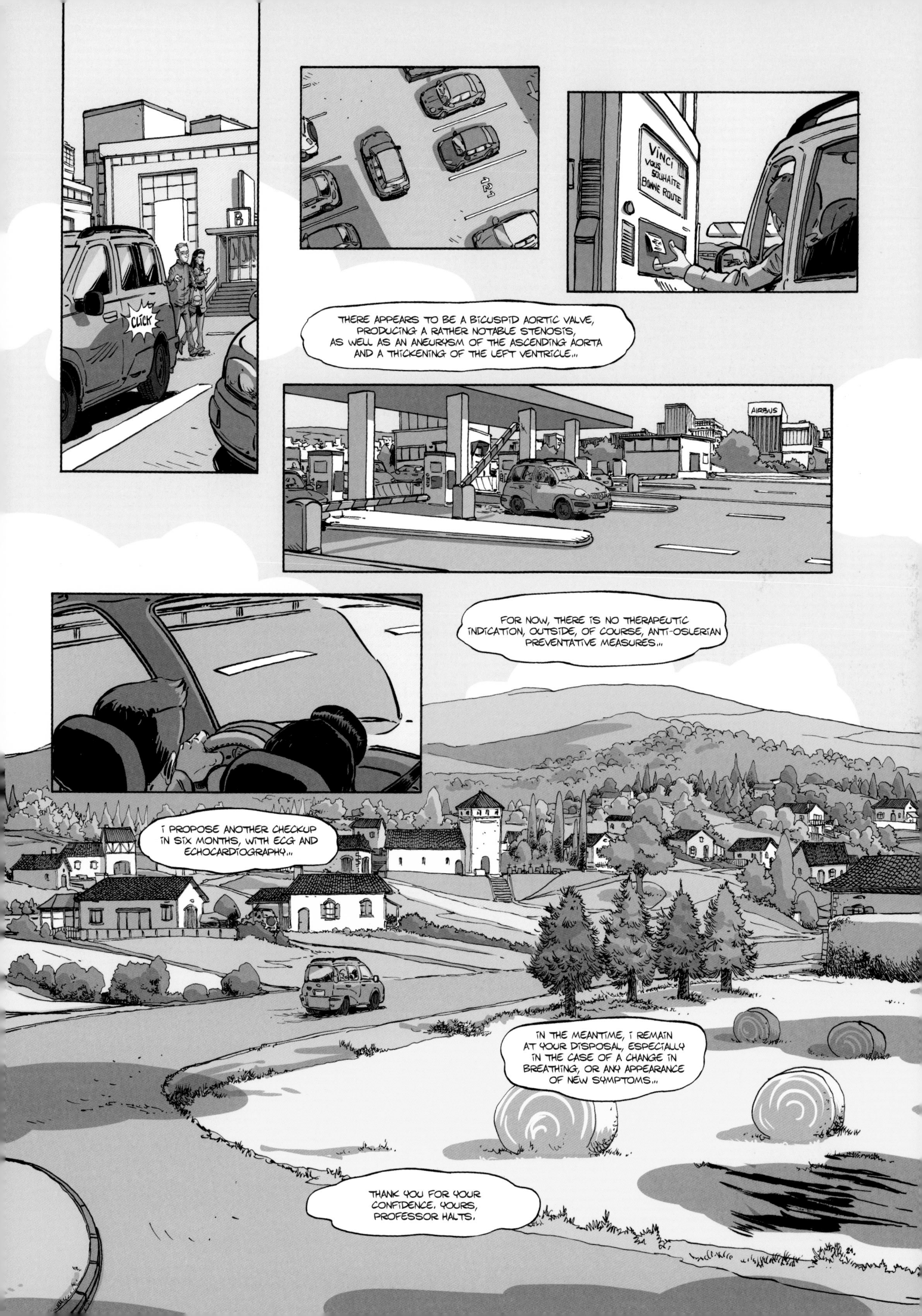

B
CLICK
121
VINCI VOUS SOUHAITE BONNE ROUTE
THERE APPEARS TO BE A BICUSPID AORTIC VALVE, PRODUCING A RATHER NOTABLE STENOSIS, AS WELL AS AN ANEURYSM OF THE ASCENDING AORTA AND A THICKENING OF THE LEFT VENTRICLE...
AIRBUS
FOR NOW, THERE IS NO THERAPEUTIC INDICATION, OUTSIDE, OF COURSE, ANTI-OSLERIAN PREVENTATIVE MEASURES...
I PROPOSE ANOTHER CHECKUP IN SIX MONTHS, WITH ECG AND ECHOCARDIOGRAPHY...
IN THE MEANTIME, I REMAIN AT YOUR DISPOSAL, ESPECIALLY IN THE CASE OF A CHANGE IN BREATHING, OR ANY APPEARANCE OF NEW SYMPTOMS...
THANK YOU FOR YOUR CONFIDENCE. YOURS, PROFESSOR HALTS.

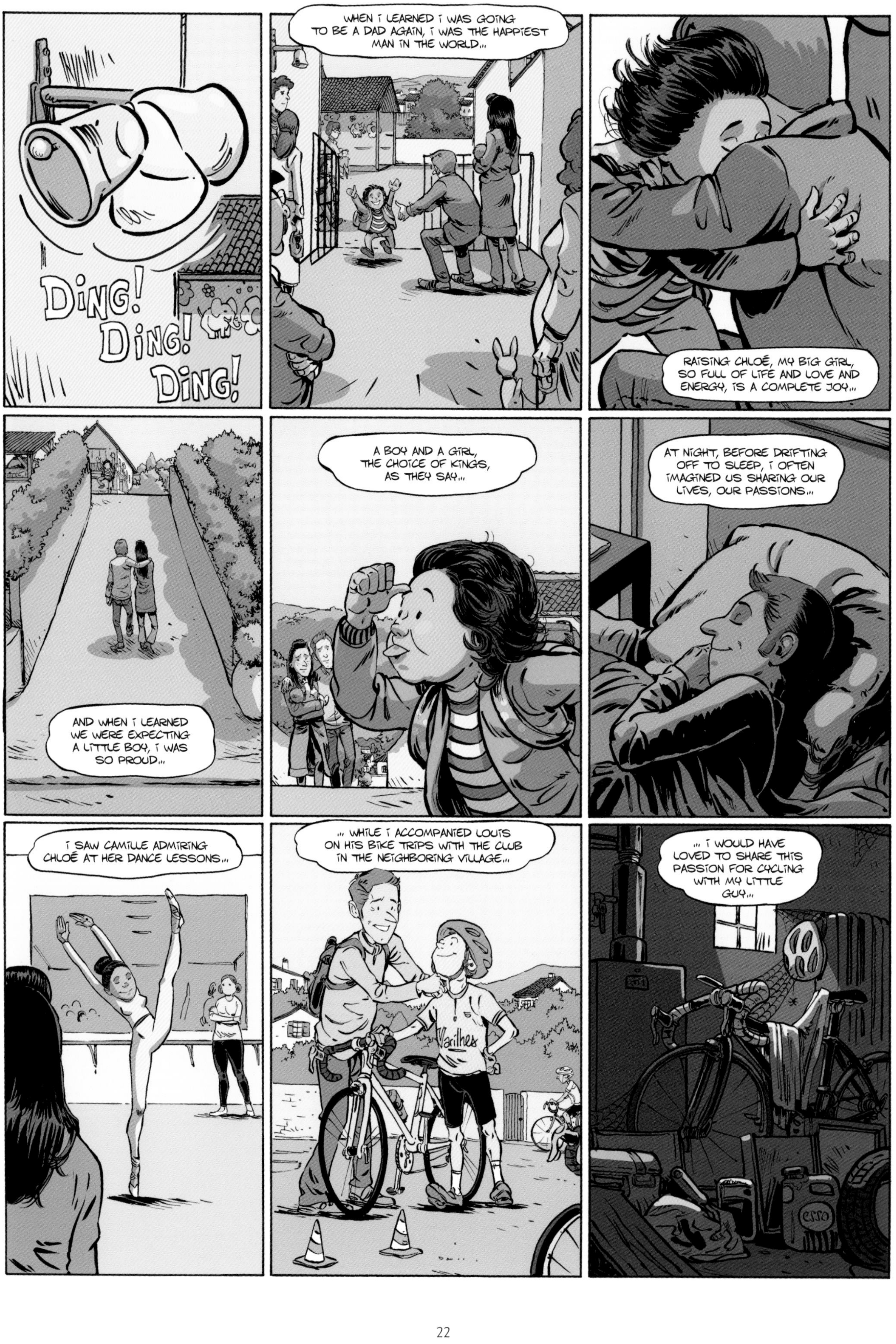
DING!
DING!
DING!
WHEN I LEARNED I WAS GOING TO BE A DAD AGAIN, I WAS THE HAPPIEST MAN IN THE WORLD...
RAISING CHLOÉ, MY BIG GIRL, SO FULL OF LIFE AND LOVE AND ENERGY, IS A COMPLETE JOY...
AND WHEN I LEARNED WE WERE EXPECTING A LITTLE BOY, I WAS SO PROUD...
A BOY AND A GIRL, THE CHOICE OF KINGS, AS THEY SAY...
AT NIGHT, BEFORE DRIFTING OFF TO SLEEP, I OFTEN IMAGINED US SHARING OUR LIVES, OUR PASSIONS...
I SAW CAMILLE ADMIRING CHLOÉ AT HER DANCE LESSONS...
... WHILE I ACCOMPANIED LOUIS ON HIS BIKE TRIPS WITH THE CLUB IN THE NEIGHBORING VILLAGE...
... I WOULD HAVE LOVED TO SHARE THIS PASSION FOR CYCLING WITH MY LITTLE GUY...

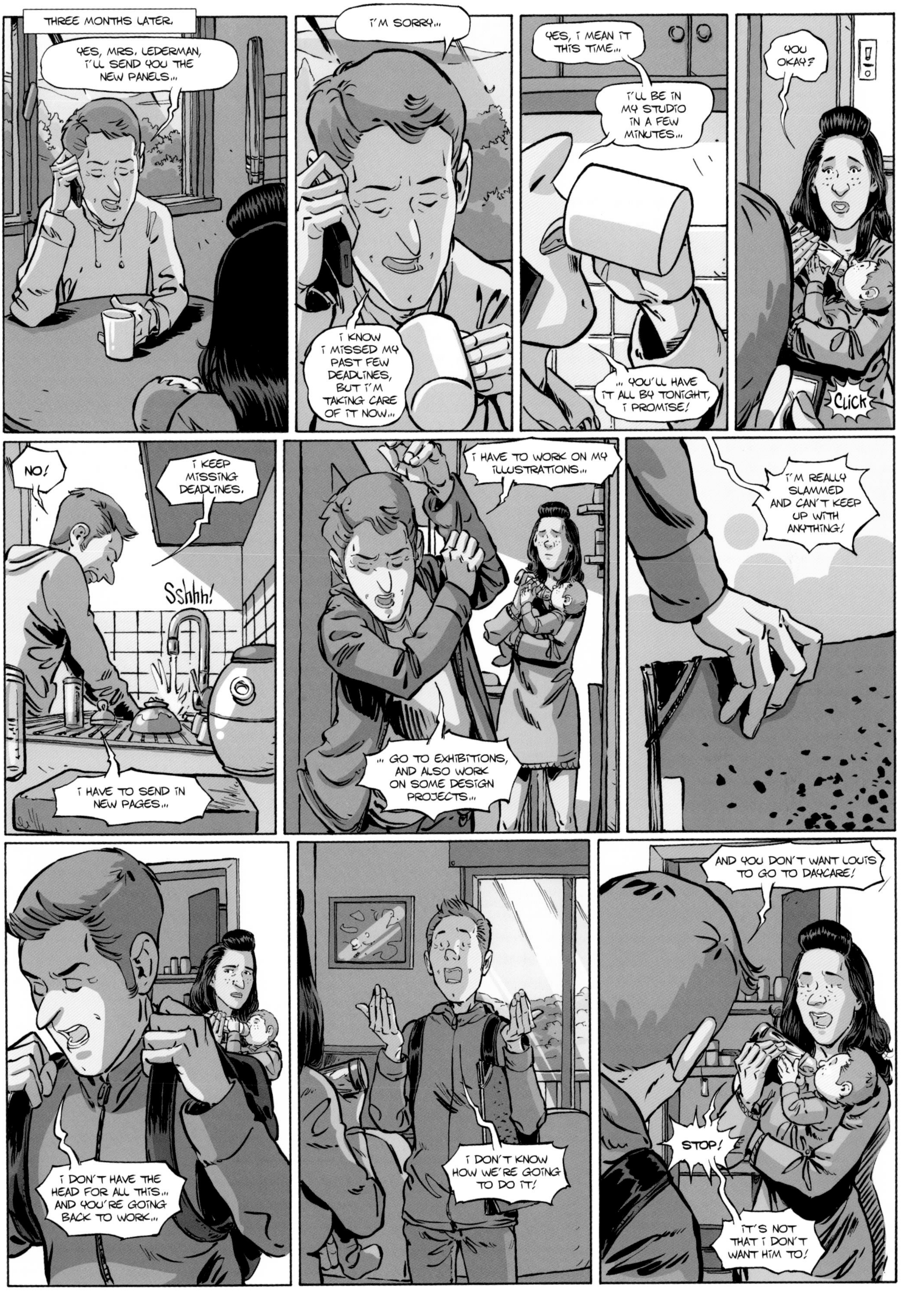

THREE MONTHS LATER.
YES, MRS. LEDERMAN, I'LL SEND YOU THE NEW PANELS...
I'M SORRY...
I KNOW I MISSED MY PAST FEW DEADLINES, BUT I'M TAKING CARE OF IT NOW...
YES, I MEAN IT THIS TIME...
I'LL BE IN MY STUDIO IN A FEW MINUTES...
... YOU'LL HAVE IT ALL BY TONIGHT, I PROMISE!
YOU OKAY?
CLICK
NO!
I KEEP MISSING DEADLINES.
Sshhh!
I HAVE TO SEND IN NEW PAGES...
I HAVE TO WORK ON MY ILLUSTRATIONS...
... GO TO EXHIBITIONS, AND ALSO WORK ON SOME DESIGN PROJECTS...
I'M REALLY SLAMMED AND CAN'T KEEP UP WITH ANYTHING!
I DON'T HAVE THE HEAD FOR ALL THIS... AND YOU'RE GOING BACK TO WORK...
I DON'T KNOW HOW WE'RE GOING TO DO IT!
AND YOU DON'T WANT LOUIS TO GO TO DAYCARE!
STOP!
IT'S NOT THAT I DON'T WANT HIM TO!

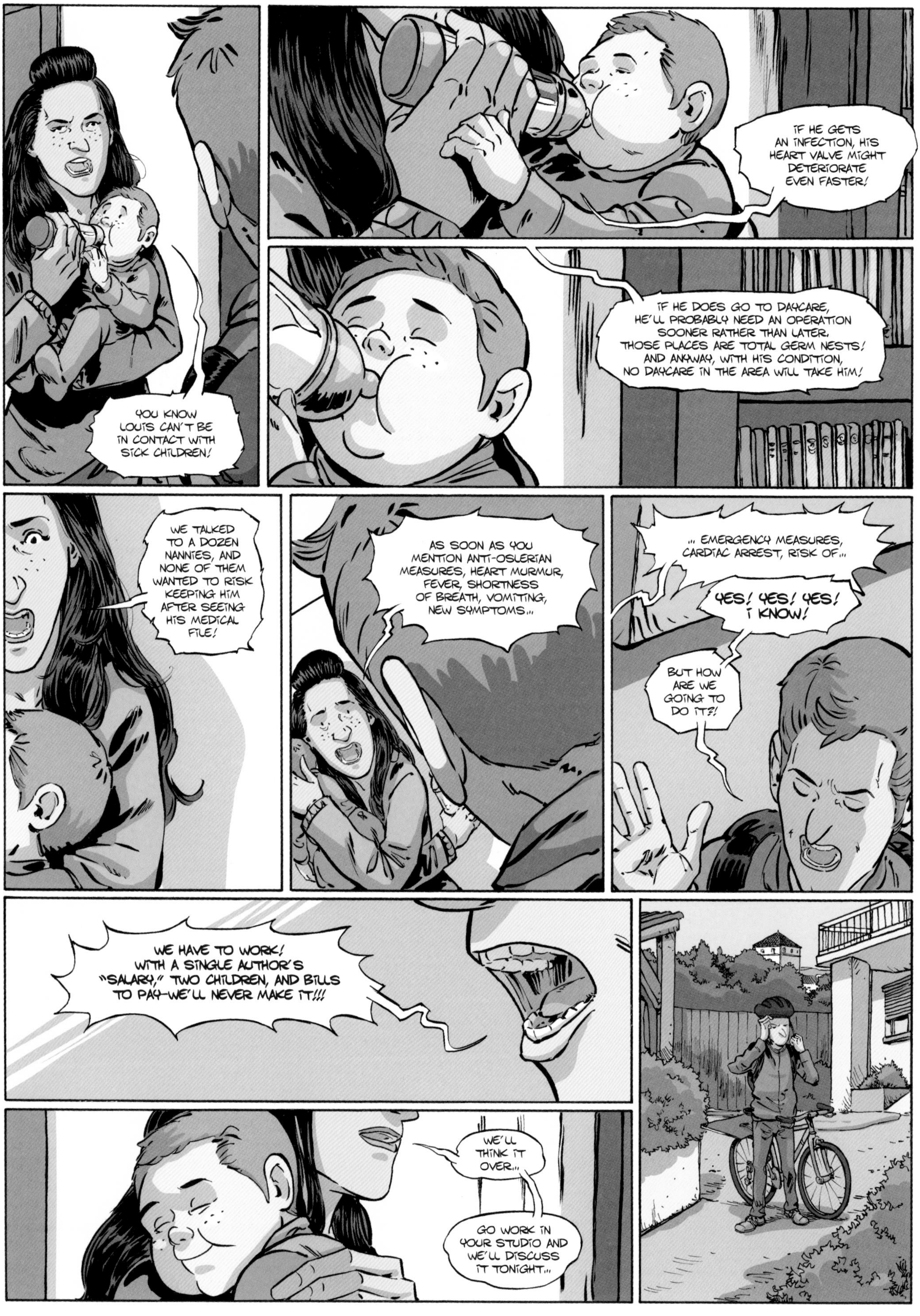
IF HE GETS AN INFECTION, HIS HEART VALVE MIGHT DETERIORATE EVEN FASTER!
YOU KNOW LOUIS CAN'T BE IN CONTACT WITH SICK CHILDREN!
IF HE DOES GO TO DAYCARE, HE'LL PROBABLY NEED AN OPERATION SOONER RATHER THAN LATER. THOSE PLACES ARE TOTAL GERM NESTS! AND ANYWAY, WITH HIS CONDITION, NO DAYCARE IN THE AREA WILL TAKE HIM!
WE TALKED TO A DOZEN NANNIES, AND NONE OF THEM WANTED TO RISK KEEPING HIM AFTER SEEING HIS MEDICAL FILE!
AS SOON AS YOU MENTION ANTI-OSLERIAN MEASURES, HEART MURMUR, FEVER, SHORTNESS OF BREATH, VOMITING, NEW SYMPTOMS...
... EMERGENCY MEASURES, CARDIAC ARREST, RISK OF...
YES! YES! YES! I KNOW!
BUT HOW ARE WE GOING TO DO IT?!
WE HAVE TO WORK! WITH A SINGLE AUTHOR'S "SALARY," TWO CHILDREN, AND BILLS TO PAY–WE'LL NEVER MAKE IT!!!
WE'LL THINK IT OVER...
GO WORK IN YOUR STUDIO AND WE'LL DISCUSS IT TONIGHT...

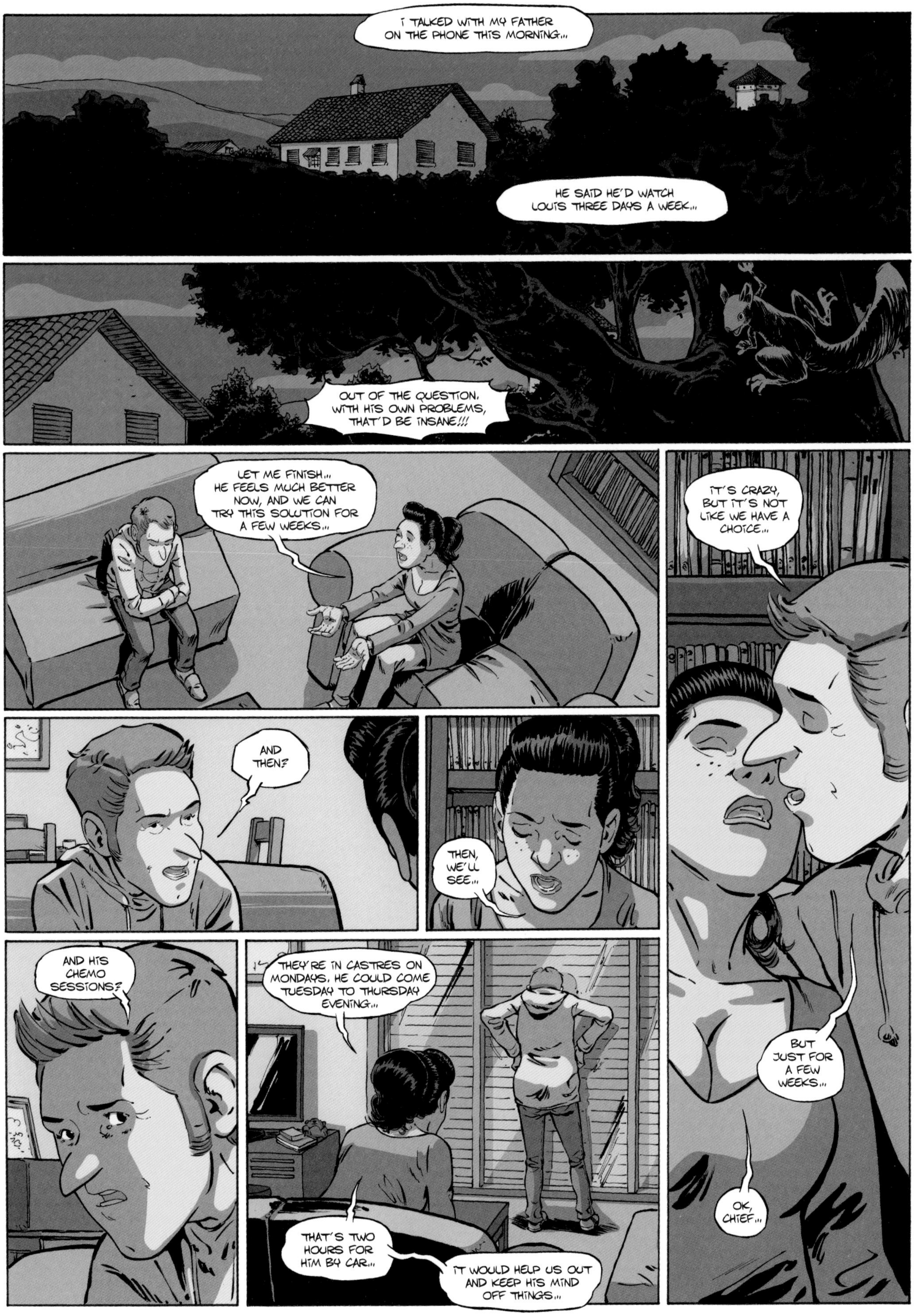

I TALKED WITH MY FATHER ON THE PHONE THIS MORNING...
HE SAID HE'D WATCH LOUIS THREE DAYS A WEEK...
OUT OF THE QUESTION, WITH HIS OWN PROBLEMS, THAT'D BE INSANE!!!
LET ME FINISH... HE FEELS MUCH BETTER NOW, AND WE CAN TRY THIS SOLUTION FOR A FEW WEEKS...
IT'S CRAZY, BUT IT'S NOT LIKE WE HAVE A CHOICE...
AND THEN?
THEN, WE'LL SEE...
AND HIS CHEMO SESSIONS?
THEY'RE IN CASTRES ON MONDAYS. HE COULD COME TUESDAY TO THURSDAY EVENING...
THAT'S TWO HOURS FOR HIM BY CAR...
IT WOULD HELP US OUT AND KEEP HIS MIND OFF THINGS...
BUT JUST FOR A FEW WEEKS...
OK, CHIEF...

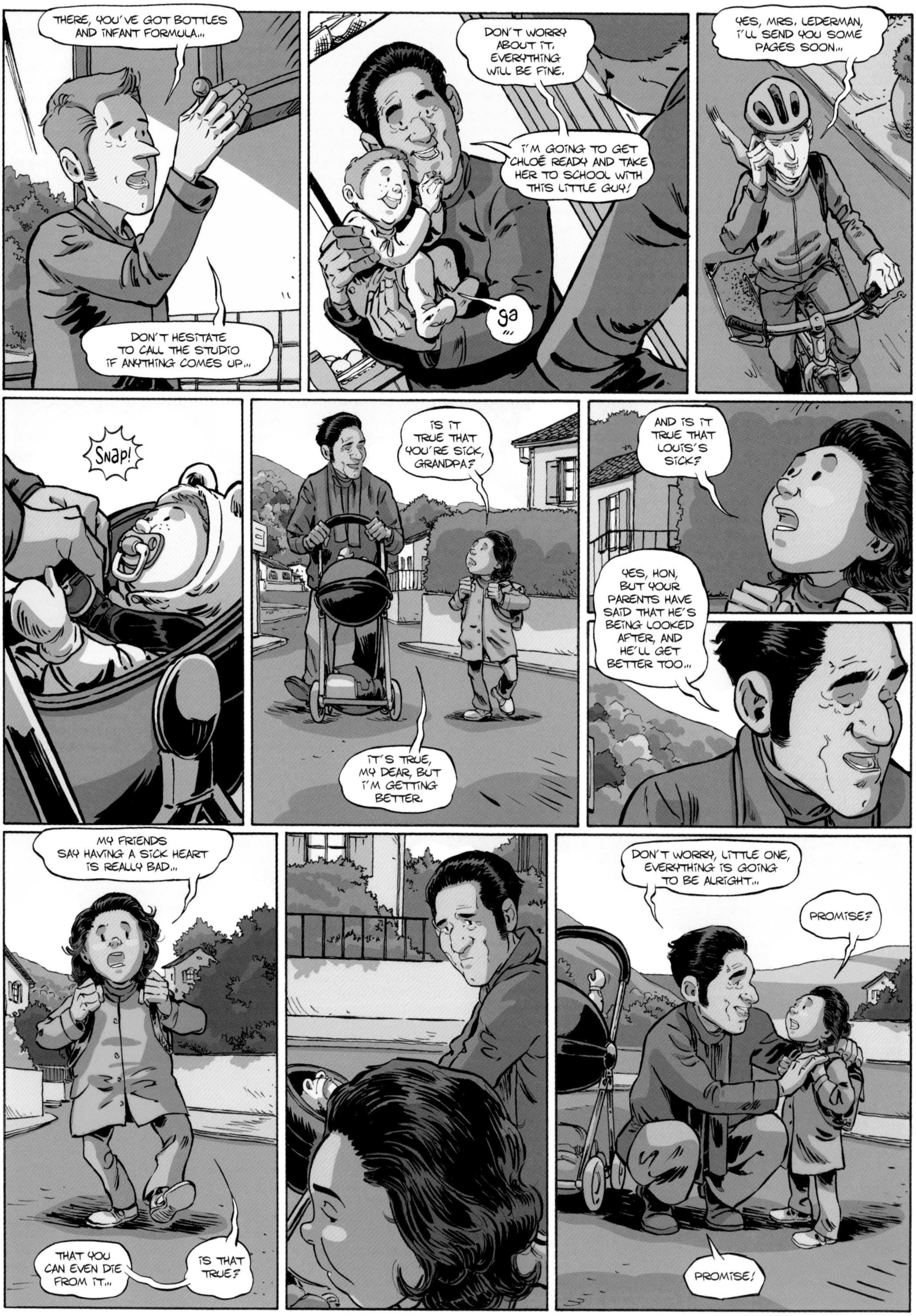
THERE, YOU'VE GOT BOTTLES AND INFANT FORMULA...
DON'T HESITATE TO CALL THE STUDIO IF ANYTHING COMES UP...
DON'T WORRY ABOUT IT. EVERYTHING WILL BE FINE.
I'M GOING TO GET CHLOÉ READY AND TAKE HER TO SCHOOL WITH THIS LITTLE GUY!
ga
YES, MRS. LEDERMAN, I'LL SEND YOU SOME PAGES SOON...
Snap!
IS IT TRUE THAT YOU'RE SICK, GRANDPA?
IT'S TRUE, MY DEAR, BUT I'M GETTING BETTER.
AND IS IT TRUE THAT LOUIS'S SICK?
YES, HON, BUT YOUR PARENTS HAVE SAID THAT HE'S BEING LOOKED AFTER, AND HE'LL GET BETTER TOO...
MY FRIENDS SAY HAVING A SICK HEART IS REALLY BAD...
THAT YOU CAN EVEN DIE FROM IT...
IS THAT TRUE?
DON'T WORRY, LITTLE ONE, EVERYTHING IS GOING TO BE ALRIGHT...
PROMISE?
PROMISE!

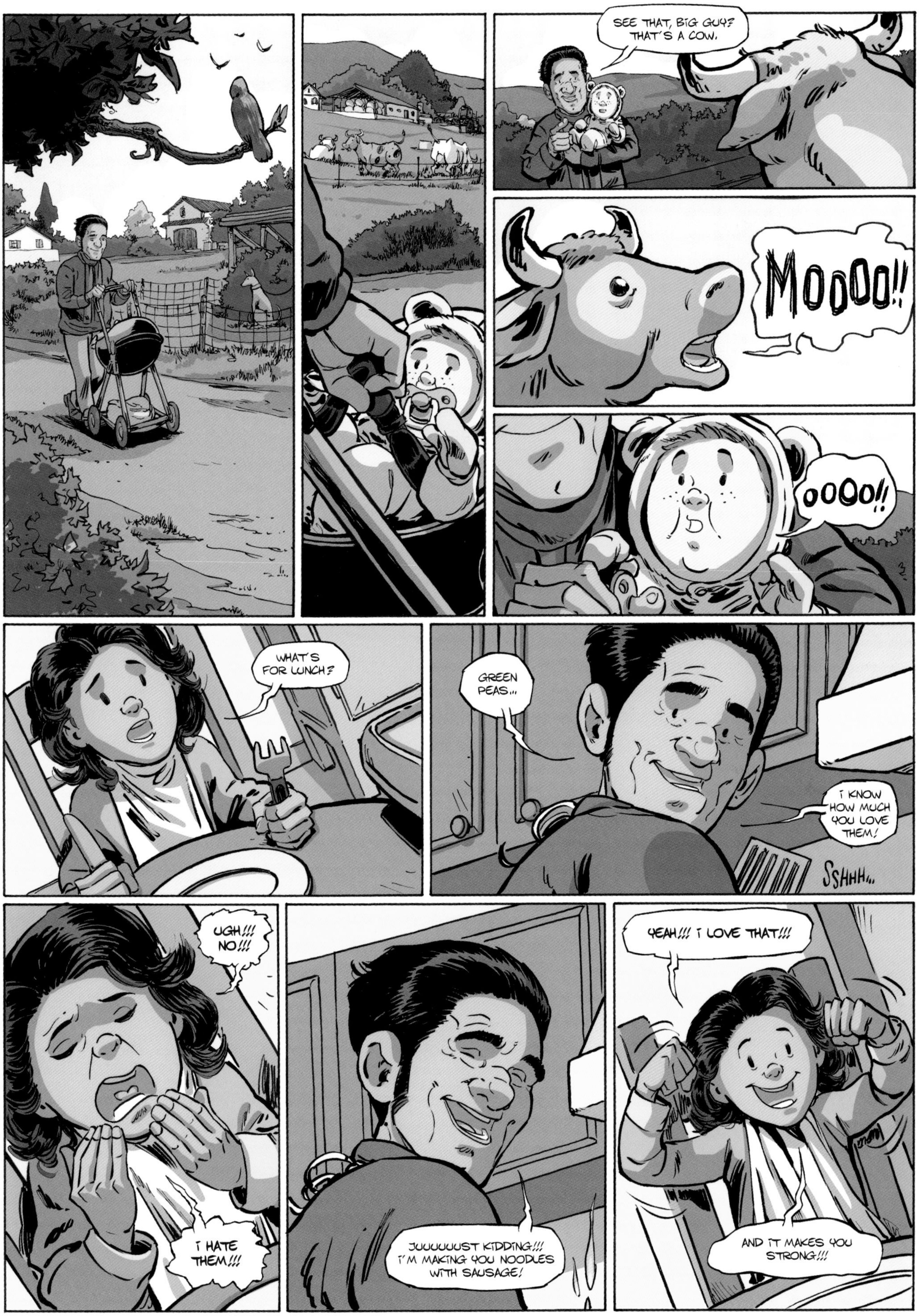
SEE THAT, BIG GUY? THAT'S A COW.
MOOOO!!
OOOO!!
WHAT'S FOR LUNCH?
GREEN PEAS...
I KNOW HOW MUCH YOU LOVE THEM!
SSHHH...
UGH!!! NO!!!
I HATE THEM!!!
JUUUUUUST KIDDING!!! I'M MAKING YOU NOODLES WITH SAUSAGE!
YEAH!!! I LOVE THAT!!!
AND IT MAKES YOU STRONG!!!

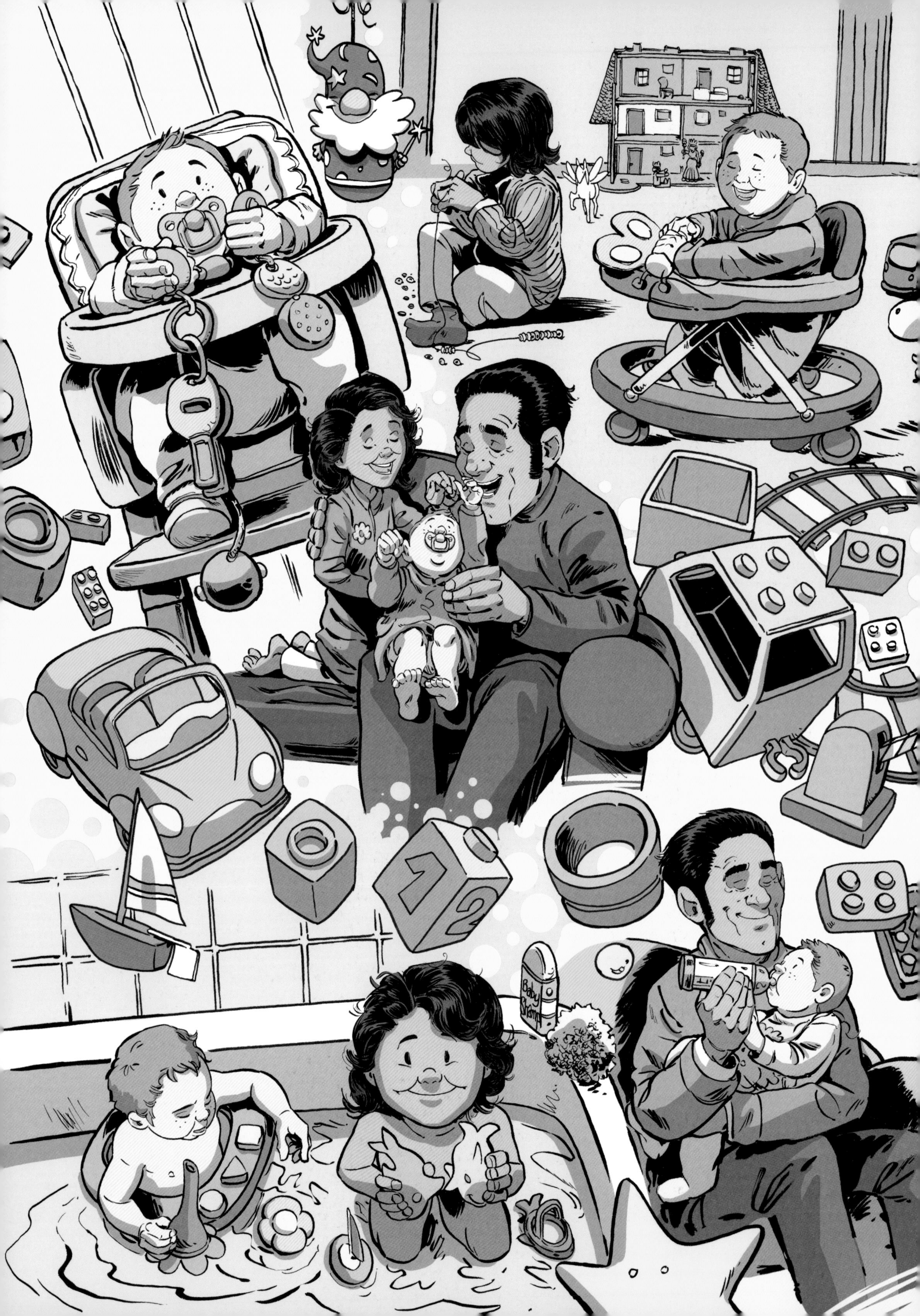
Baby
Shamp

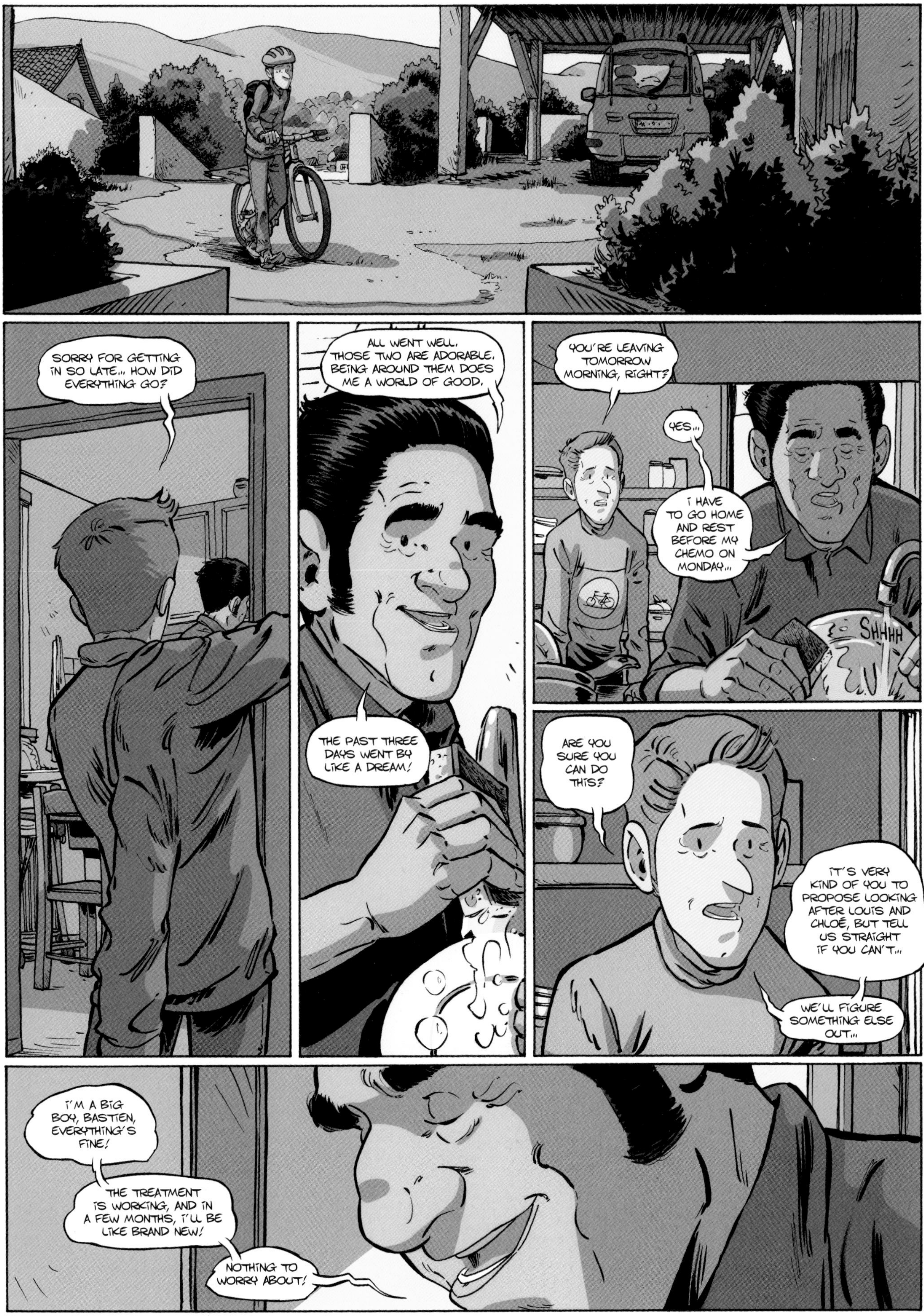
SORRY FOR GETTING IN SO LATE... HOW DID EVERYTHING GO?
ALL WENT WELL. THOSE TWO ARE ADORABLE. BEING AROUND THEM DOES ME A WORLD OF GOOD.
THE PAST THREE DAYS WENT BY LIKE A DREAM!
YOU'RE LEAVING TOMORROW MORNING, RIGHT?
YES...
I HAVE TO GO HOME AND REST BEFORE MY CHEMO ON MONDAY...
SHHHH
ARE YOU SURE YOU CAN DO THIS?
IT'S VERY KIND OF YOU TO PROPOSE LOOKING AFTER LOUIS AND CHLOÉ, BUT TELL US STRAIGHT IF YOU CAN'T...
WE'LL FIGURE SOMETHING ELSE OUT...
I'M A BIG BOY, BASTIEN, EVERYTHING'S FINE!
THE TREATMENT IS WORKING, AND IN A FEW MONTHS, I'LL BE LIKE BRAND NEW!
NOTHING TO WORRY ABOUT!

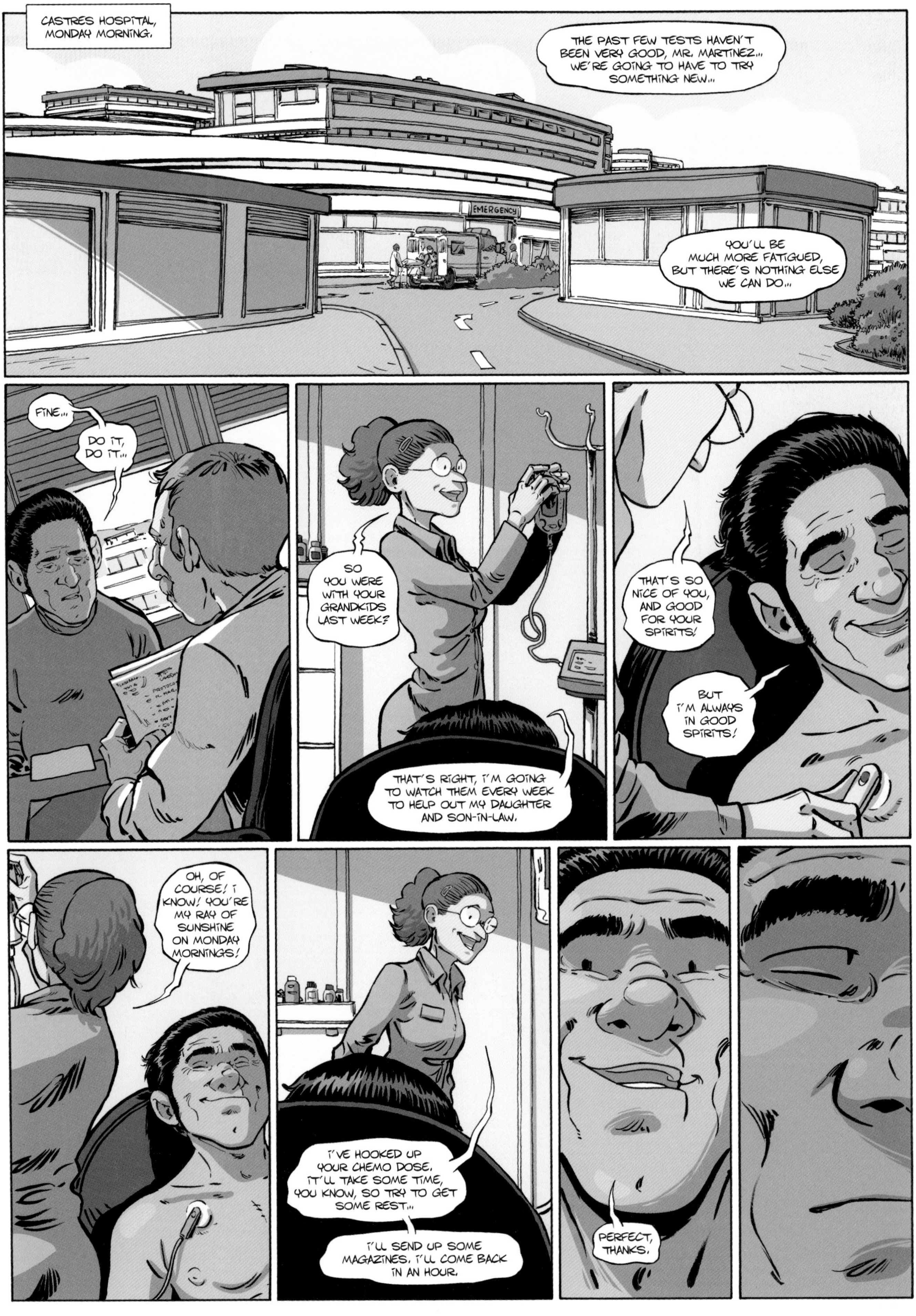
CASTRES HOSPITAL, MONDAY MORNING.
THE PAST FEW TESTS HAVEN'T BEEN VERY GOOD, MR. MARTINEZ... WE'RE GOING TO HAVE TO TRY SOMETHING NEW...
YOU'LL BE MUCH MORE FATIGUED, BUT THERE'S NOTHING ELSE WE CAN DO...
EMERGENCY
FINE...
DO IT, DO IT...
SO YOU WERE WITH YOUR GRANDKIDS LAST WEEK?
THAT'S RIGHT, I'M GOING TO WATCH THEM EVERY WEEK TO HELP OUT MY DAUGHTER AND SON-IN-LAW.
THAT'S SO NICE OF YOU, AND GOOD FOR YOUR SPIRITS!
BUT I'M ALWAYS IN GOOD SPIRITS!
OH, OF COURSE! I KNOW! YOU'RE MY RAY OF SUNSHINE ON MONDAY MORNINGS!
I'VE HOOKED UP YOUR CHEMO DOSE. IT'LL TAKE SOME TIME, YOU KNOW, SO TRY TO GET SOME REST...
I'LL SEND UP SOME MAGAZINES. I'LL COME BACK IN AN HOUR.
PERFECT, THANKS.

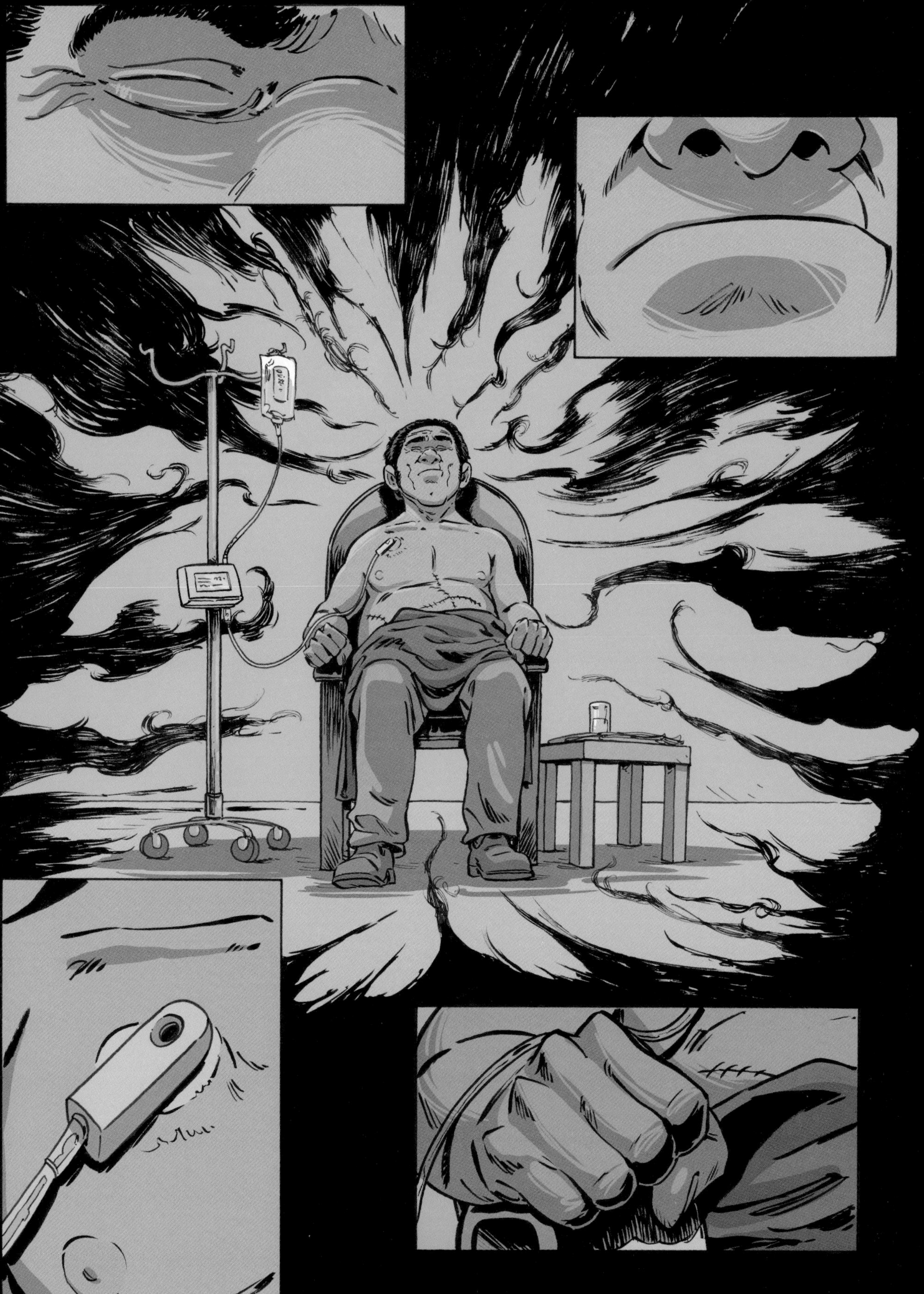

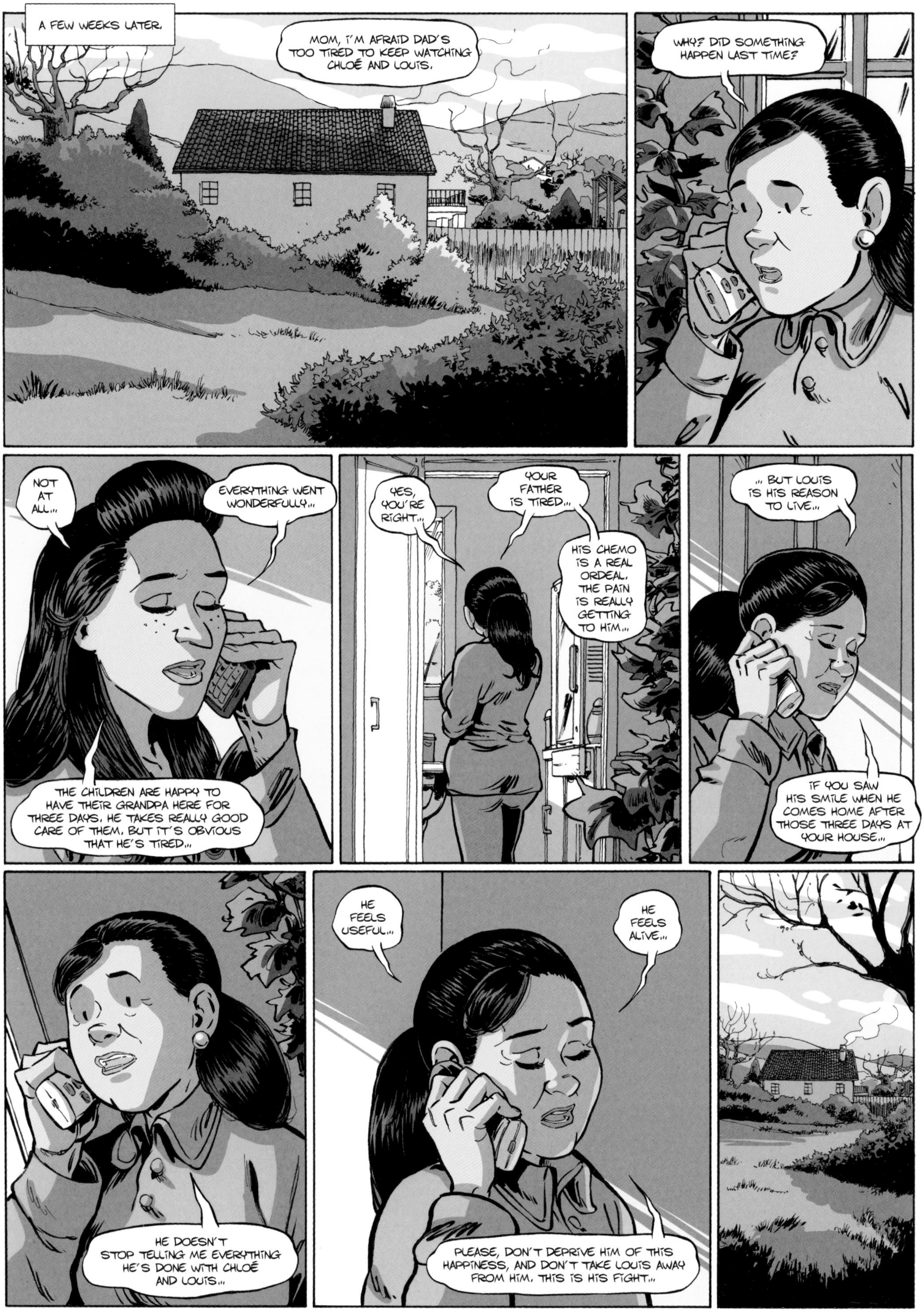
A FEW WEEKS LATER.
MOM, I'M AFRAID DAD'S TOO TIRED TO KEEP WATCHING CHLOÉ AND LOUIS.
WHY? DID SOMETHING HAPPEN LAST TIME?
NOT AT ALL...
EVERYTHING WENT WONDERFULLY...
THE CHILDREN ARE HAPPY TO HAVE THEIR GRANDPA HERE FOR THREE DAYS. HE TAKES REALLY GOOD CARE OF THEM. BUT IT'S OBVIOUS THAT HE'S TIRED...
YES, YOU'RE RIGHT...
YOUR FATHER IS TIRED...
HIS CHEMO IS A REAL ORDEAL. THE PAIN IS REALLY GETTING TO HIM...
... BUT LOUIS IS HIS REASON TO LIVE...
IF YOU SAW HIS SMILE WHEN HE COMES HOME AFTER THOSE THREE DAYS AT YOUR HOUSE...
HE DOESN'T STOP TELLING ME EVERYTHING HE'S DONE WITH CHLOÉ AND LOUIS...
HE FEELS USEFUL...
HE FEELS ALIVE...
PLEASE, DON'T DEPRIVE HIM OF THIS HAPPINESS, AND DON'T TAKE LOUIS AWAY FROM HIM. THIS IS HIS FIGHT...

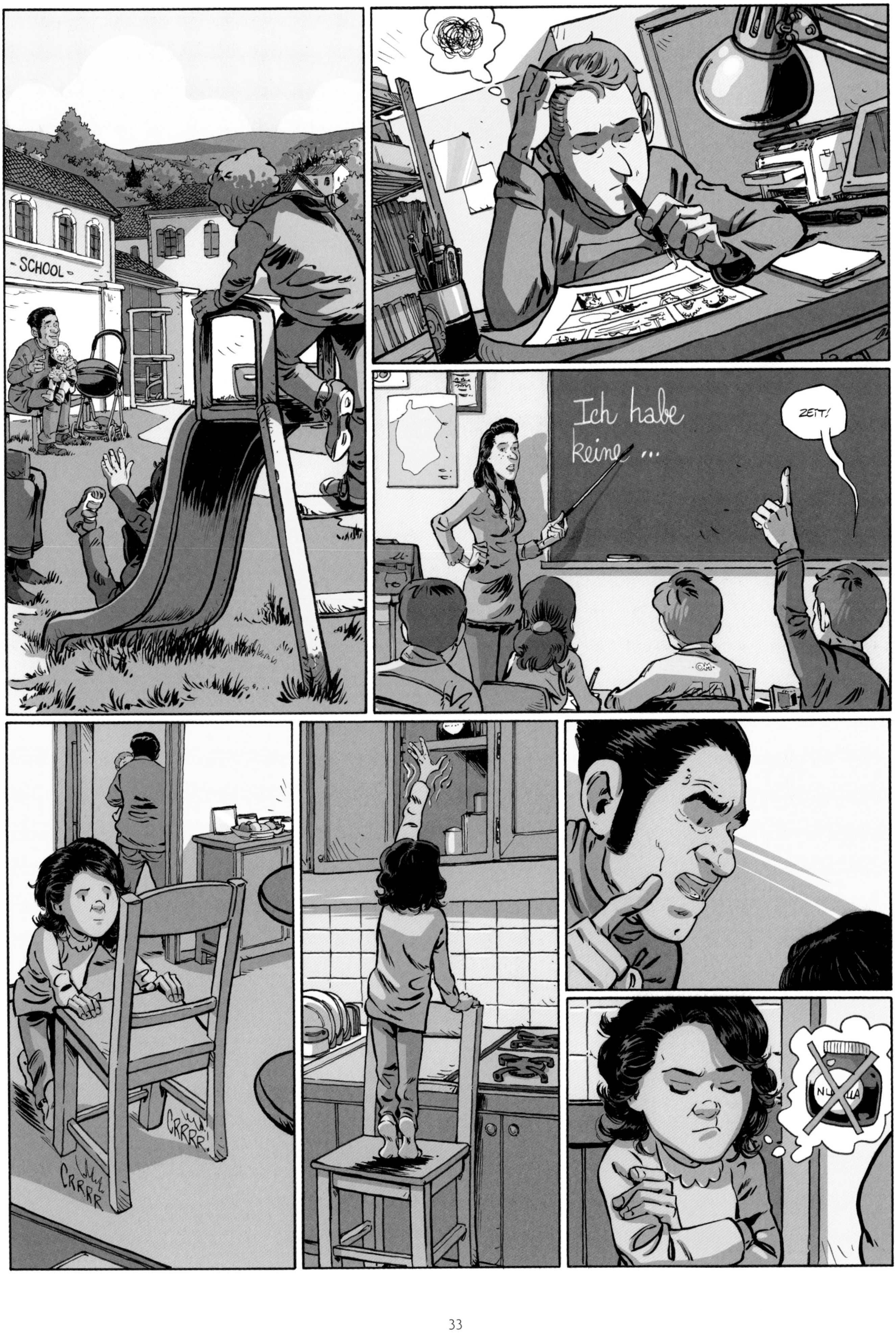
SCHOOL
Ich habe keine ...
ZEIT!
CRRRR!
CRRRR

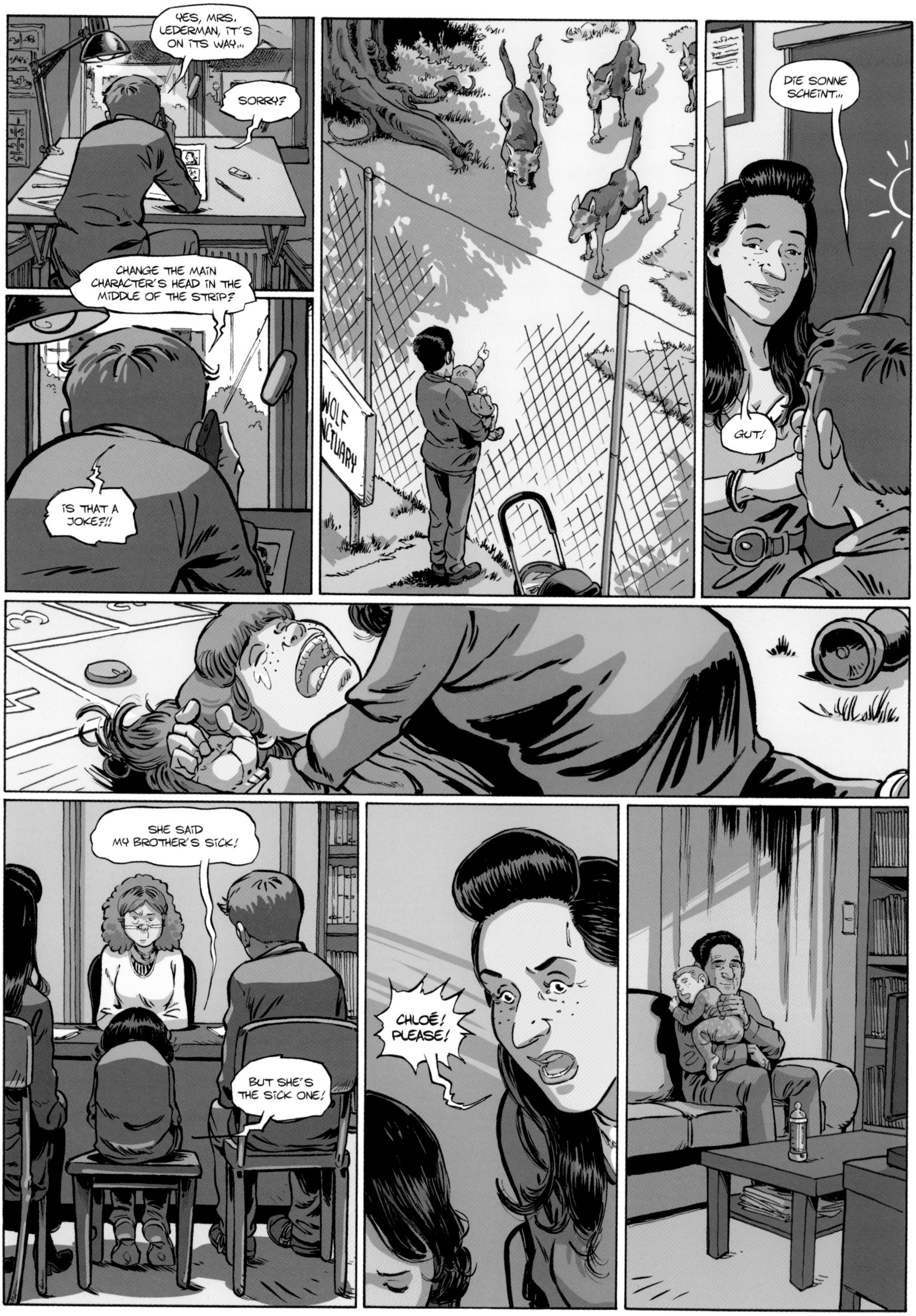

YES, MRS. LEDERMAN, IT'S ON ITS WAY...
SORRY?
CHANGE THE MAIN CHARACTER'S HEAD IN THE MIDDLE OF THE STRIP?
IS THAT A JOKE?!!
WOLF
NCTUARY
DIE SONNE SCHEINT...
GUT!
SHE SAID MY BROTHER'S SICK!
BUT SHE'S THE SICK ONE!
CHLOÉ! PLEASE!

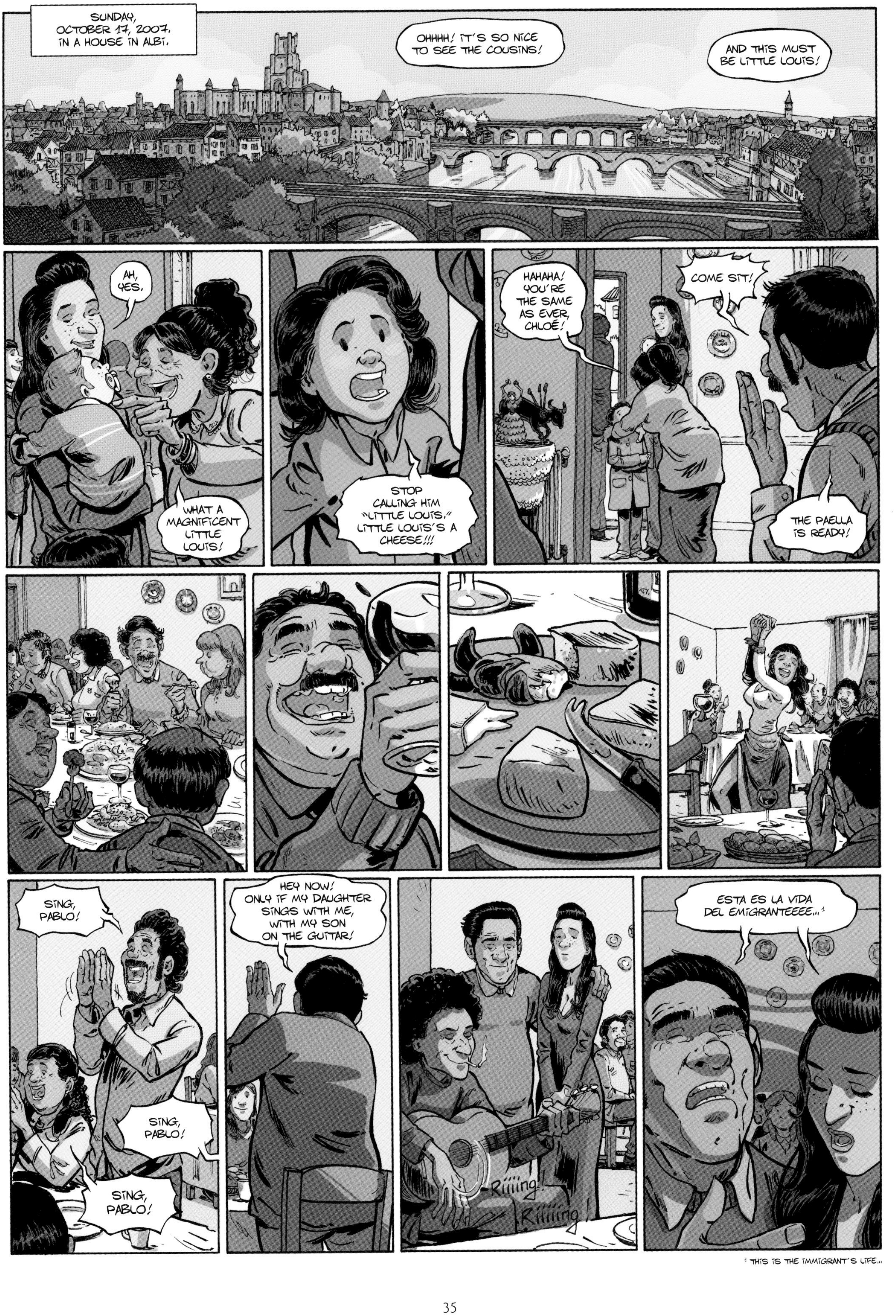
SUNDAY, OCTOBER 17, 2007. IN A HOUSE IN ALBI.
OHHHH! IT'S SO NICE TO SEE THE COUSINS!
AND THIS MUST BE LITTLE LOUIS!
AH, YES.
WHAT A MAGNIFICENT LITTLE LOUIS!
STOP CALLING HIM "LITTLE LOUIS." LITTLE LOUIS'S A CHEESE!!!
HAHAHA! YOU'RE THE SAME AS EVER, CHLOÉ!
COME SIT!
THE PAELLA IS READY!
SING, PABLO!
SING, PABLO!
SING, PABLO!
HEY NOW! ONLY IF MY DAUGHTER SINGS WITH ME, WITH MY SON ON THE GUITAR!
Riiing.
Riiiing.
ESTA ES LA VIDA DEL EMIGRANTEEEE...[1]

[1] THIS IS THE IMMIGRANT'S LIFE...

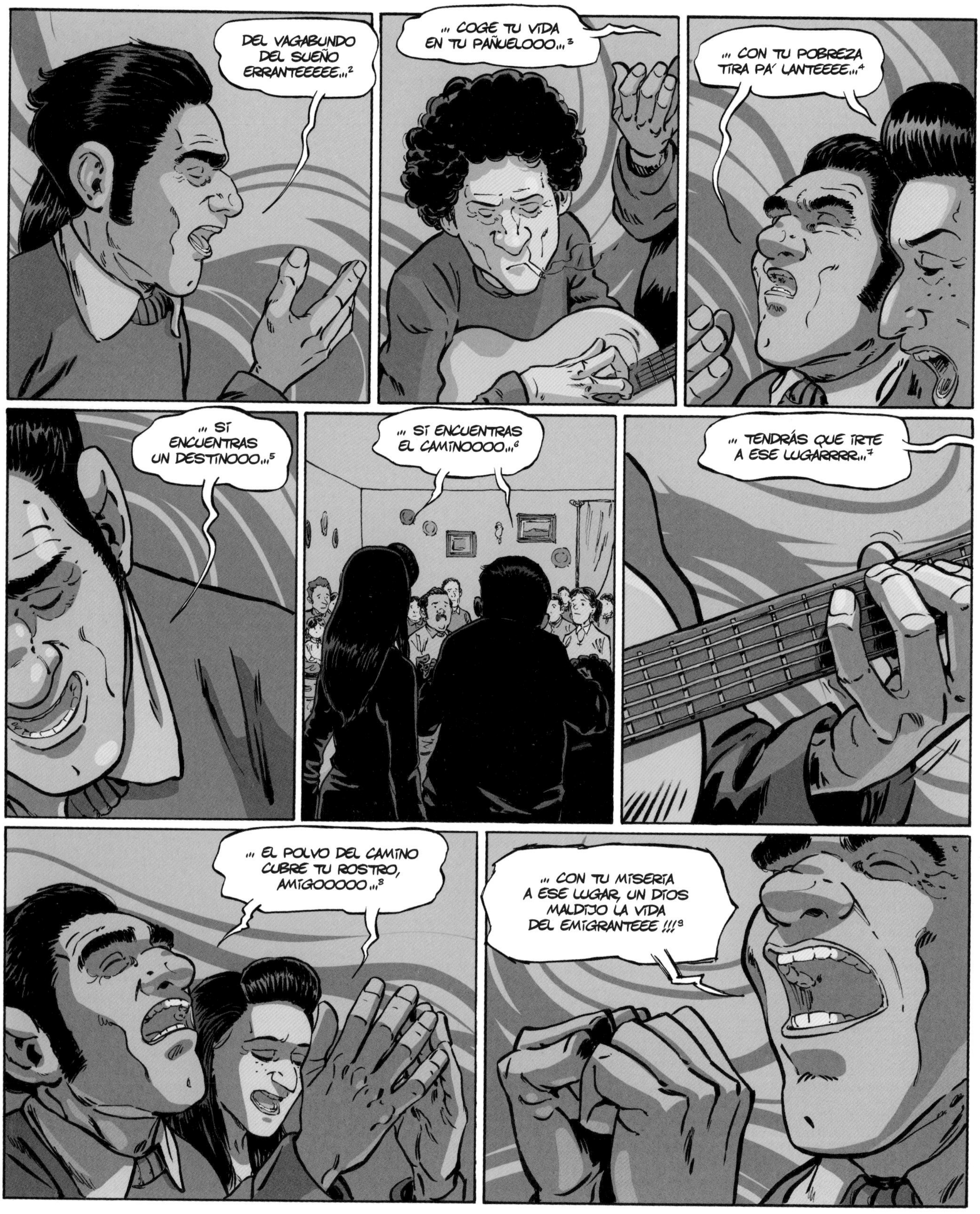
DEL VAGABUNDO DEL SUEÑO ERRANTEEEEE...[2]
... COGE TU VIDA EN TU PAÑUELOOO...[3]
... CON TU POBREZA TIRA PA' LANTEEEE...[4]
... SI ENCUENTRAS UN DESTINOOO...[5]
... SI ENCUENTRAS EL CAMINOOOO...[6]
... TENDRÁS QUE IRTE A ESE LUGARRRR...[7]
... EL POLVO DEL CAMINO CUBRE TU ROSTRO, AMIGOOOOO...[8]
... CON TU MISERIA A ESE LUGAR, UN DIOS MALDIJO LA VIDA DEL EMIGRANTEEE !!![9]

[2] OF THE VAGABOND AND HIS WANDERING DREAM...

[3] PACK YOUR LIFE IN YOUR BUNDLE...

[4] WITH YOUR POVERTY FORGE ONWARD...

[5] IF YOU FIND FORTUNE...

[6] IF YOU FIND THE PATH...

[7] YOU MUST GO TO THAT PLACE...

[8] THE DUST OF THE ROAD WILL COVER YOUR FACE, FRIEND...

[9] WHEN THAT PLACE FILLS YOU WITH WOE, A GOD CURSES THE IMMIGRANT'S LIFE!!!

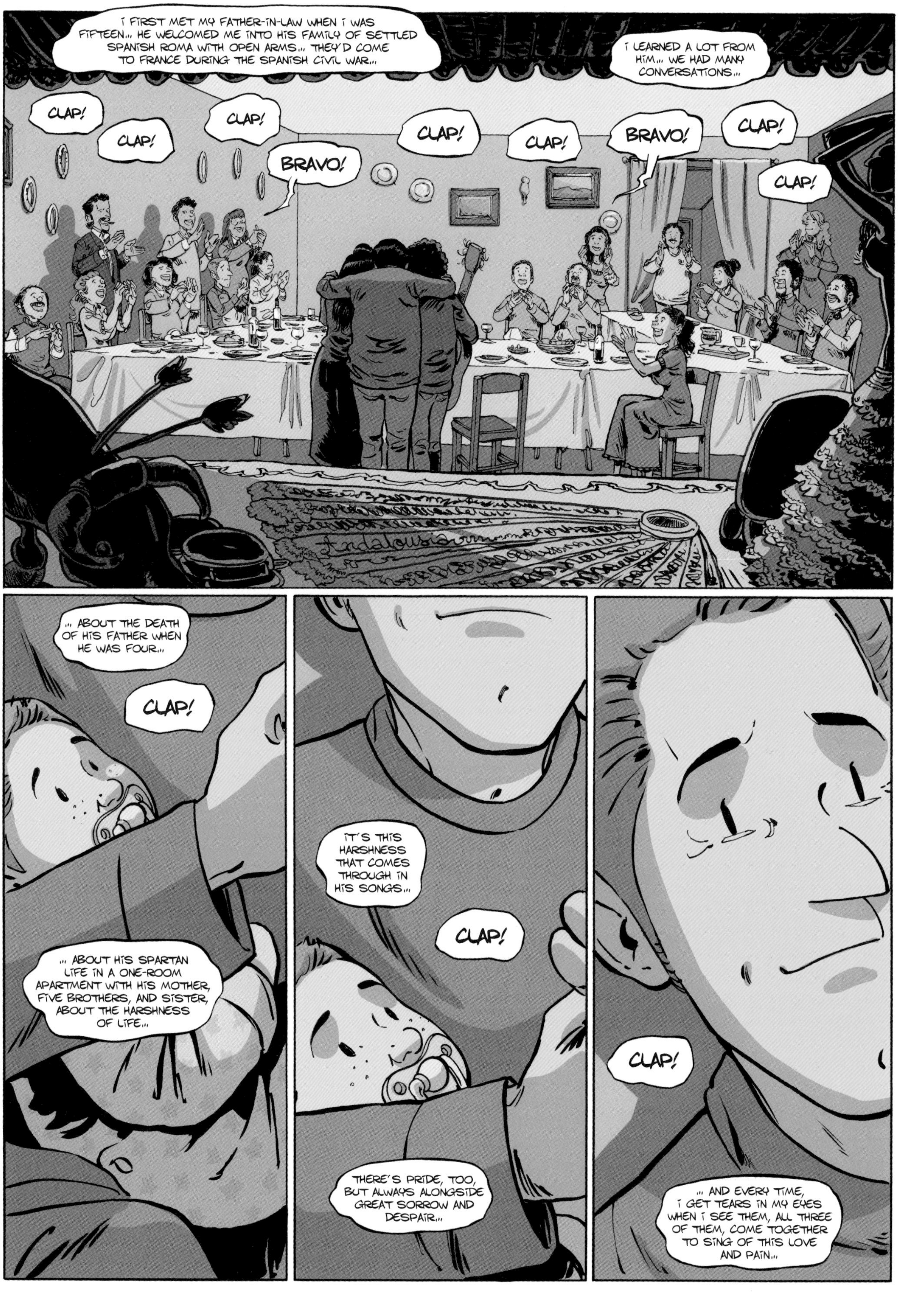
I FIRST MET MY FATHER-IN-LAW WHEN I WAS FIFTEEN... HE WELCOMED ME INTO HIS FAMILY OF SETTLED SPANISH ROMA WITH OPEN ARMS... THEY'D COME TO FRANCE DURING THE SPANISH CIVIL WAR...
I LEARNED A LOT FROM HIM... WE HAD MANY CONVERSATIONS...
CLAP!
CLAP!
CLAP!
BRAVO!
CLAP!
CLAP!
BRAVO!
CLAP!
CLAP!
... ABOUT THE DEATH OF HIS FATHER WHEN HE WAS FOUR...
CLAP!
... ABOUT HIS SPARTAN LIFE IN A ONE-ROOM APARTMENT WITH HIS MOTHER, FIVE BROTHERS, AND SISTER, ABOUT THE HARSHNESS OF LIFE...
IT'S THIS HARSHNESS THAT COMES THROUGH IN HIS SONGS...
CLAP!
THERE'S PRIDE, TOO, BUT ALWAYS ALONGSIDE GREAT SORROW AND DESPAIR...
CLAP!
... AND EVERY TIME, I GET TEARS IN MY EYES WHEN I SEE THEM, ALL THREE OF THEM, COME TOGETHER TO SING OF THIS LOVE AND PAIN...

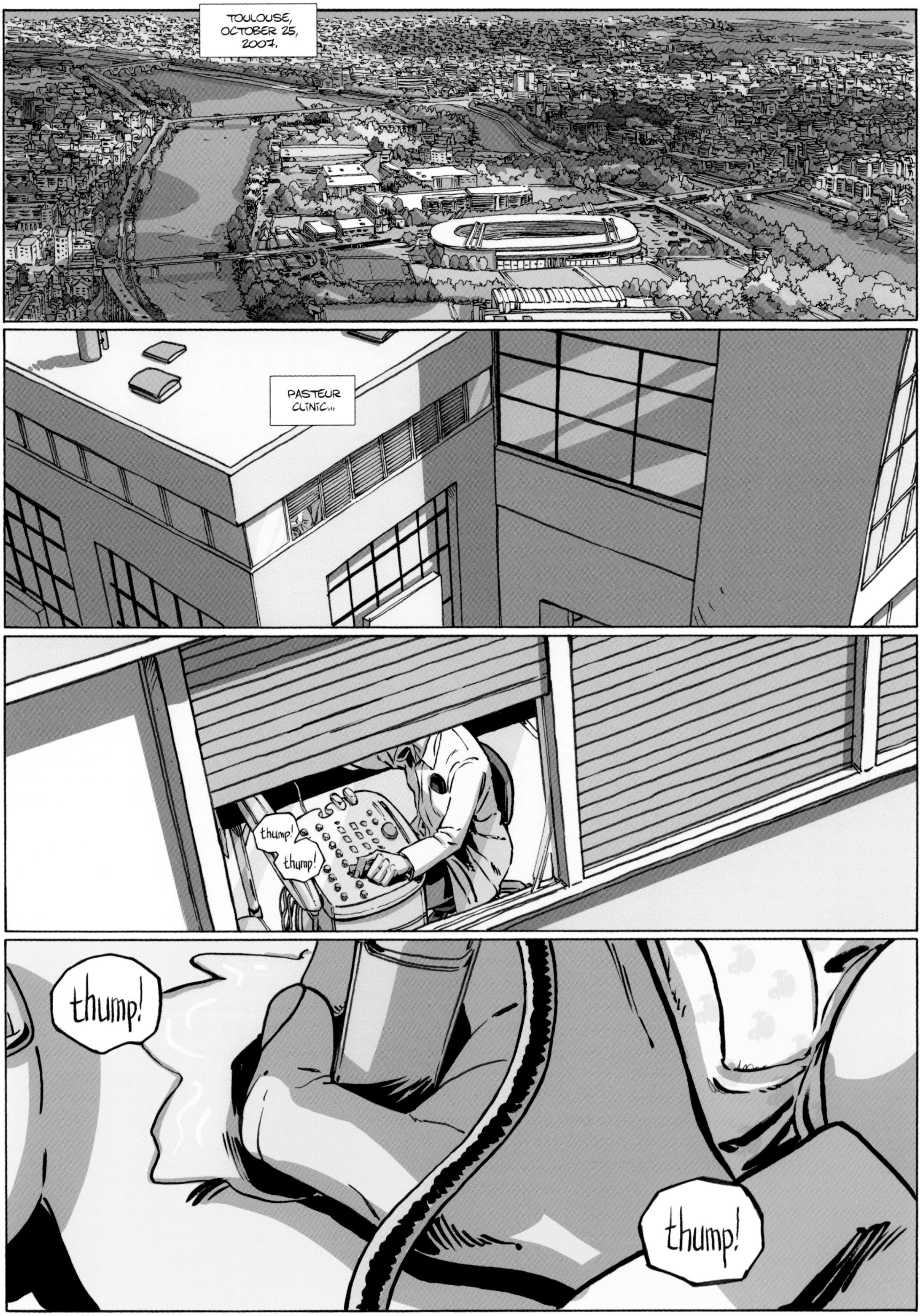
TOULOUSE, OCTOBER 25, 2007.
PASTEUR CLINIC...
thump!
thump!
thump!
thump!

HMM, I SEE...

WHAT IS IT, PROFESSOR?

LISTEN, I'M GOING TO BE FRANK WITH YOU, THESE NEW FINDINGS AREN'T GOOD...

THERE ARE QUITE A FEW PROBLEMS: THIS ASYMMETRICAL VALVE, THIS THICKENING OF THE LEFT VENTRICLE, AND THIS ANEURYSM OF THE ARTERY...

LOUIS'S CASE IS VERY PARTICULAR... WE HAVEN'T YET COME UP WITH AN EFFECTIVE TREATMENT FOR CASES LIKE THIS...

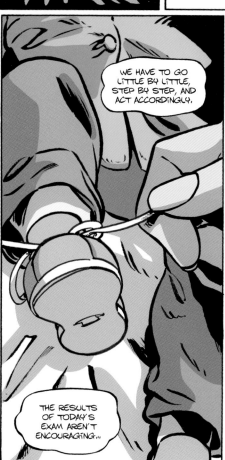

WE HAVE TO GO LITTLE BY LITTLE, STEP BY STEP, AND ACT ACCORDINGLY.

THE RESULTS OF TODAY'S EXAM AREN'T ENCOURAGING...

THE VALVE APPEARS TO BE TIGHTENING FURTHER...

WE'LL HAVE TO PREPARE FOR A SERIOUS OPERATION IF HIS CONDITION CONTINUES TO GET WORSE OVER THE NEXT FEW MONTHS...

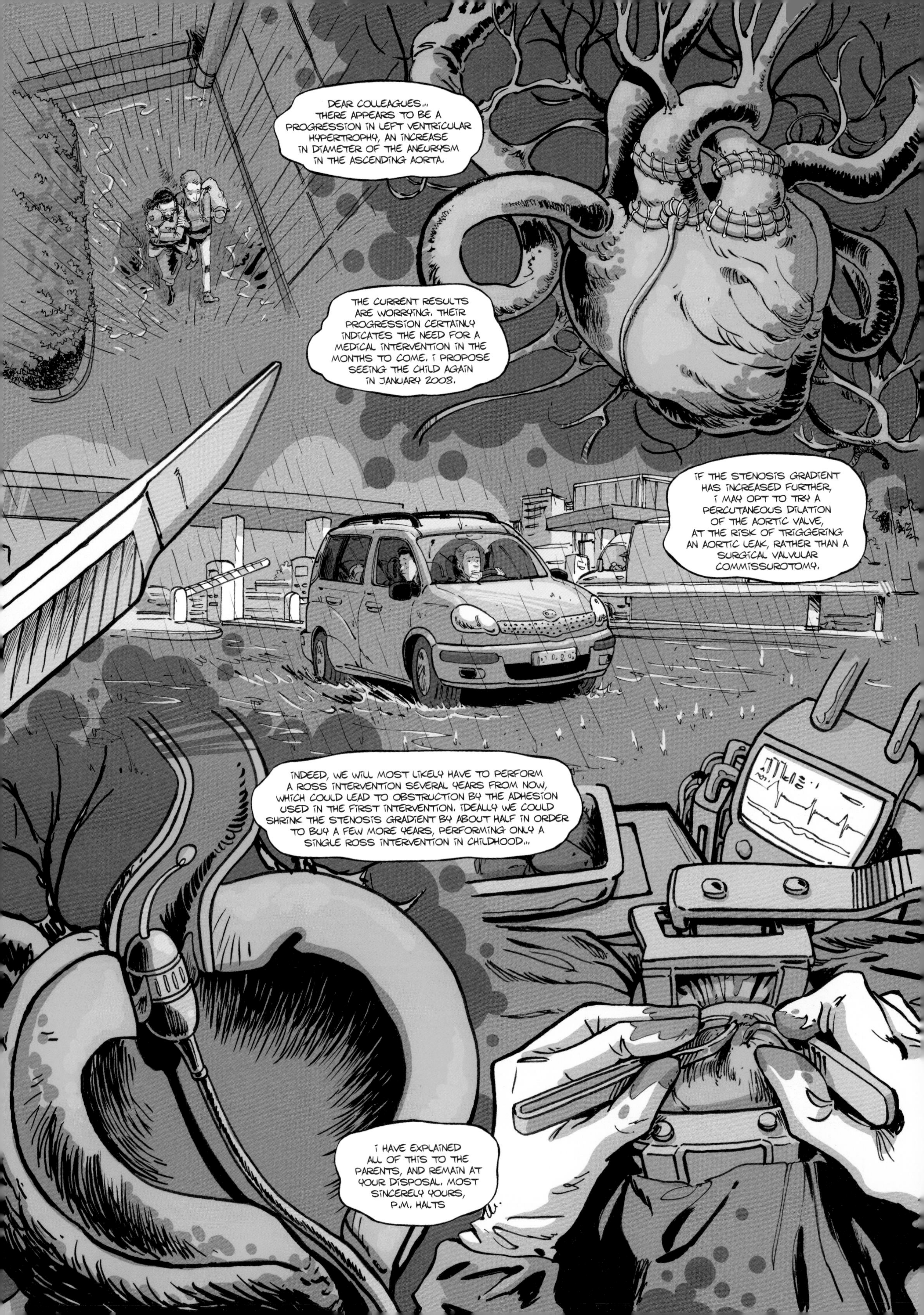
DEAR COLLEAGUES... THERE APPEARS TO BE A PROGRESSION IN LEFT VENTRICULAR HYPERTROPHY, AN INCREASE IN DIAMETER OF THE ANEURYSM IN THE ASCENDING AORTA.
THE CURRENT RESULTS ARE WORRYING. THEIR PROGRESSION CERTAINLY INDICATES THE NEED FOR A MEDICAL INTERVENTION IN THE MONTHS TO COME. I PROPOSE SEEING THE CHILD AGAIN IN JANUARY 2008.
IF THE STENOSIS GRADIENT HAS INCREASED FURTHER, I MAY OPT TO TRY A PERCUTANEOUS DILATION OF THE AORTIC VALVE, AT THE RISK OF TRIGGERING AN AORTIC LEAK, RATHER THAN A SURGICAL VALVULAR COMMISSUROTOMY.
INDEED, WE WILL MOST LIKELY HAVE TO PERFORM A ROSS INTERVENTION SEVERAL YEARS FROM NOW, WHICH COULD LEAD TO OBSTRUCTION BY THE ADHESION USED IN THE FIRST INTERVENTION. IDEALLY WE COULD SHRINK THE STENOSIS GRADIENT BY ABOUT HALF IN ORDER TO BUY A FEW MORE YEARS, PERFORMING ONLY A SINGLE ROSS INTERVENTION IN CHILDHOOD...
I HAVE EXPLAINED ALL OF THIS TO THE PARENTS, AND REMAIN AT YOUR DISPOSAL. MOST SINCERELY YOURS, P.M. HALTS

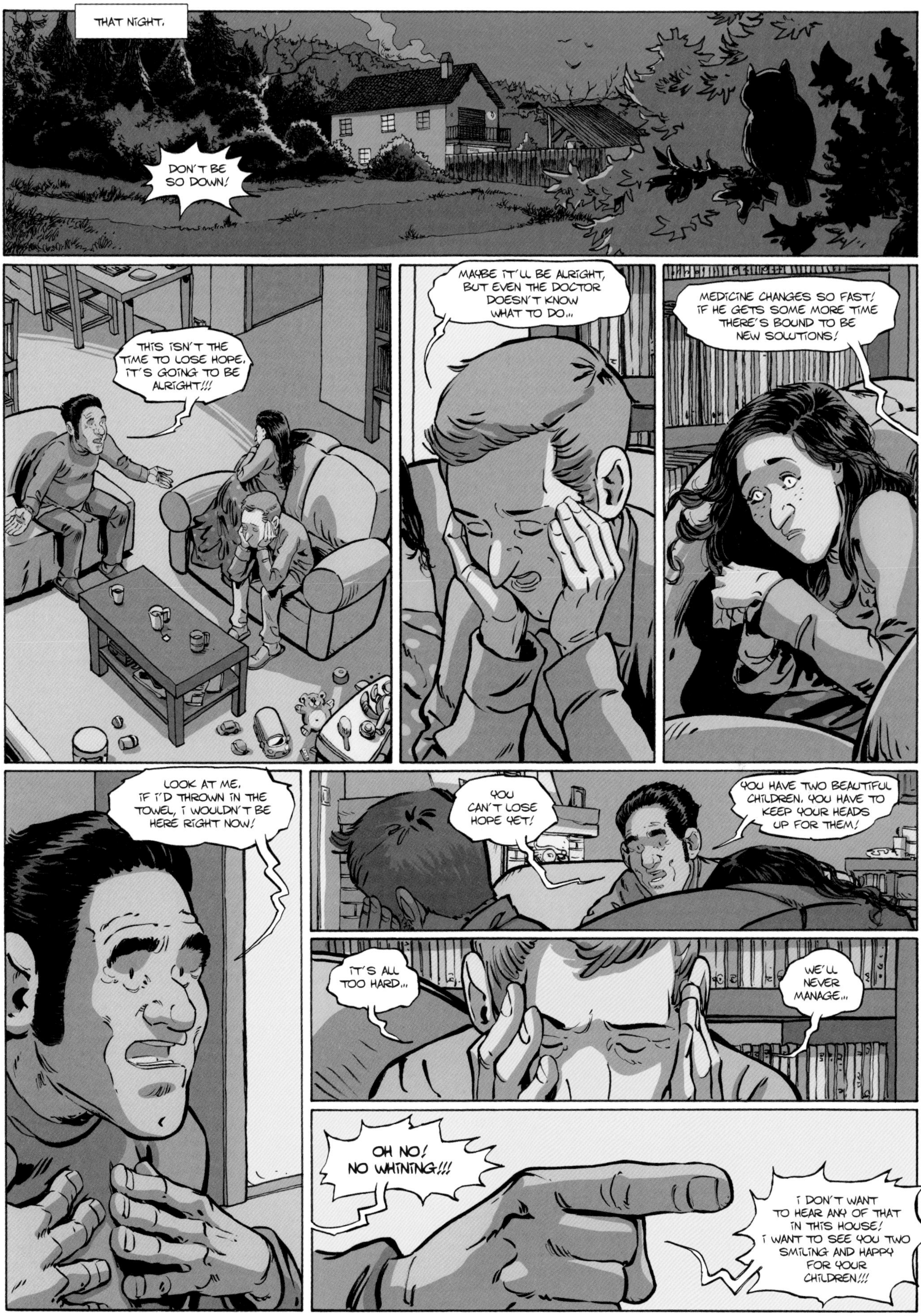
THAT NIGHT.
DON'T BE SO DOWN!
THIS ISN'T THE TIME TO LOSE HOPE, IT'S GOING TO BE ALRIGHT!!!
MAYBE IT'LL BE ALRIGHT, BUT EVEN THE DOCTOR DOESN'T KNOW WHAT TO DO...
MEDICINE CHANGES SO FAST! IF HE GETS SOME MORE TIME THERE'S BOUND TO BE NEW SOLUTIONS!
LOOK AT ME. IF I'D THROWN IN THE TOWEL, I WOULDN'T BE HERE RIGHT NOW!
YOU CAN'T LOSE HOPE YET!
YOU HAVE TWO BEAUTIFUL CHILDREN. YOU HAVE TO KEEP YOUR HEADS UP FOR THEM!
IT'S ALL TOO HARD...
WE'LL NEVER MANAGE...
OH NO! NO WHINING!!!
I DON'T WANT TO HEAR ANY OF THAT IN THIS HOUSE! I WANT TO SEE YOU TWO SMILING AND HAPPY FOR YOUR CHILDREN!!!

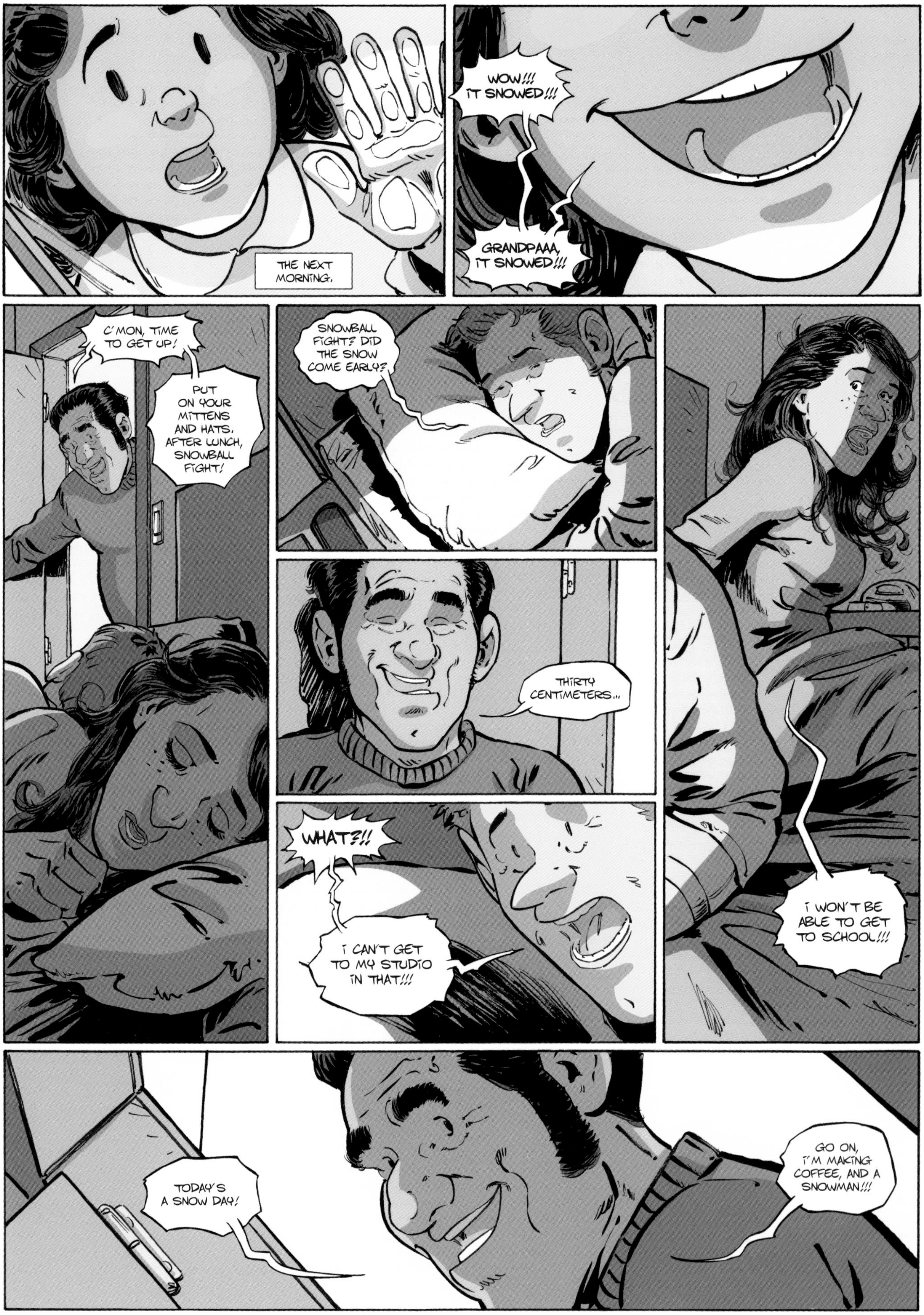
THE NEXT MORNING.
WOW!!! IT SNOWED!!!
GRANDPAAA, IT SNOWED!!!
C'MON, TIME TO GET UP!
PUT ON YOUR MITTENS AND HATS. AFTER LUNCH, SNOWBALL FIGHT!
SNOWBALL FIGHT? DID THE SNOW COME EARLY?
THIRTY CENTIMETERS...
WHAT?!!
I CAN'T GET TO MY STUDIO IN THAT!!!
I WON'T BE ABLE TO GET TO SCHOOL!!!
TODAY'S A SNOW DAY!
GO ON, I'M MAKING COFFEE, AND A SNOWMAN!!!

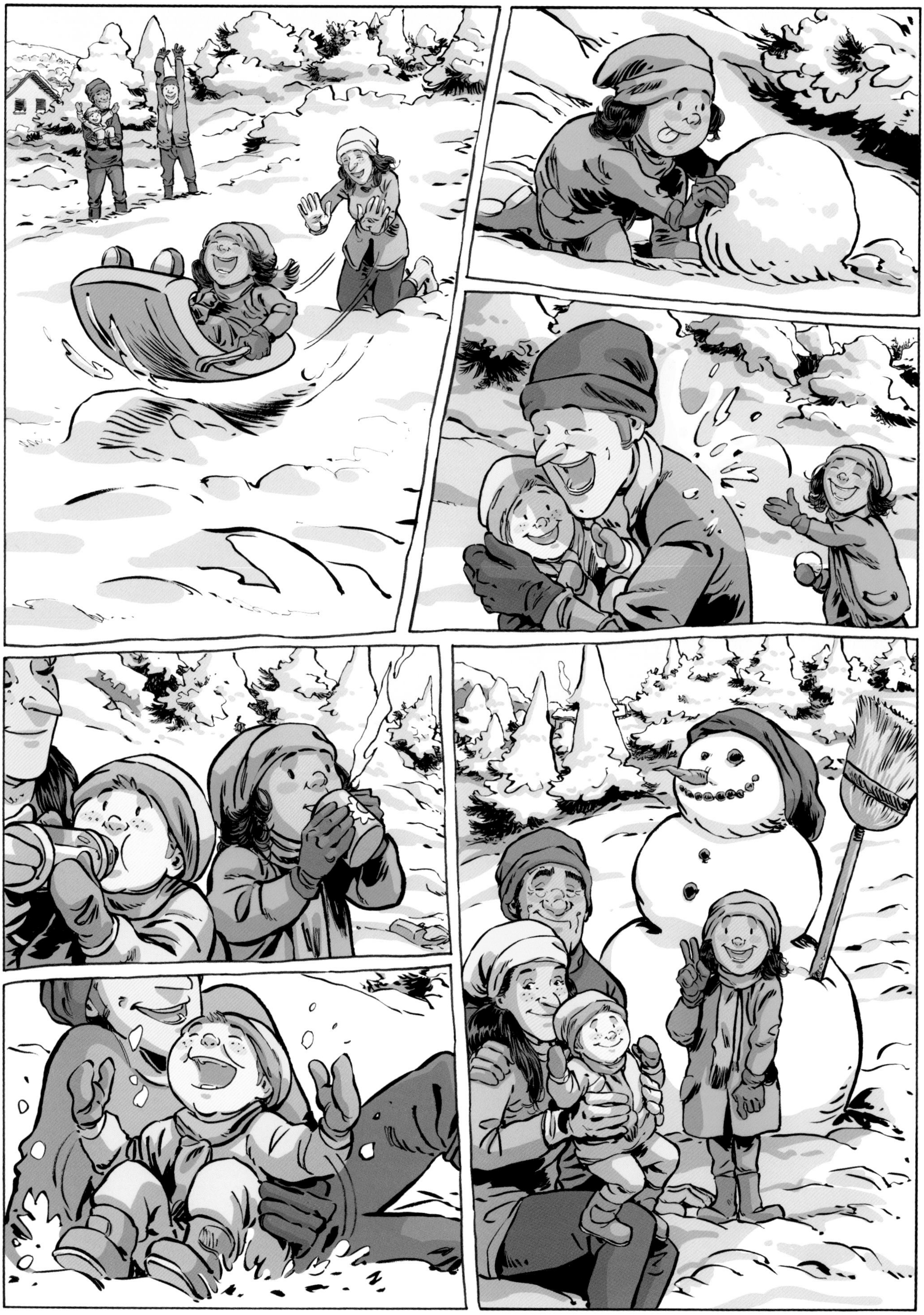

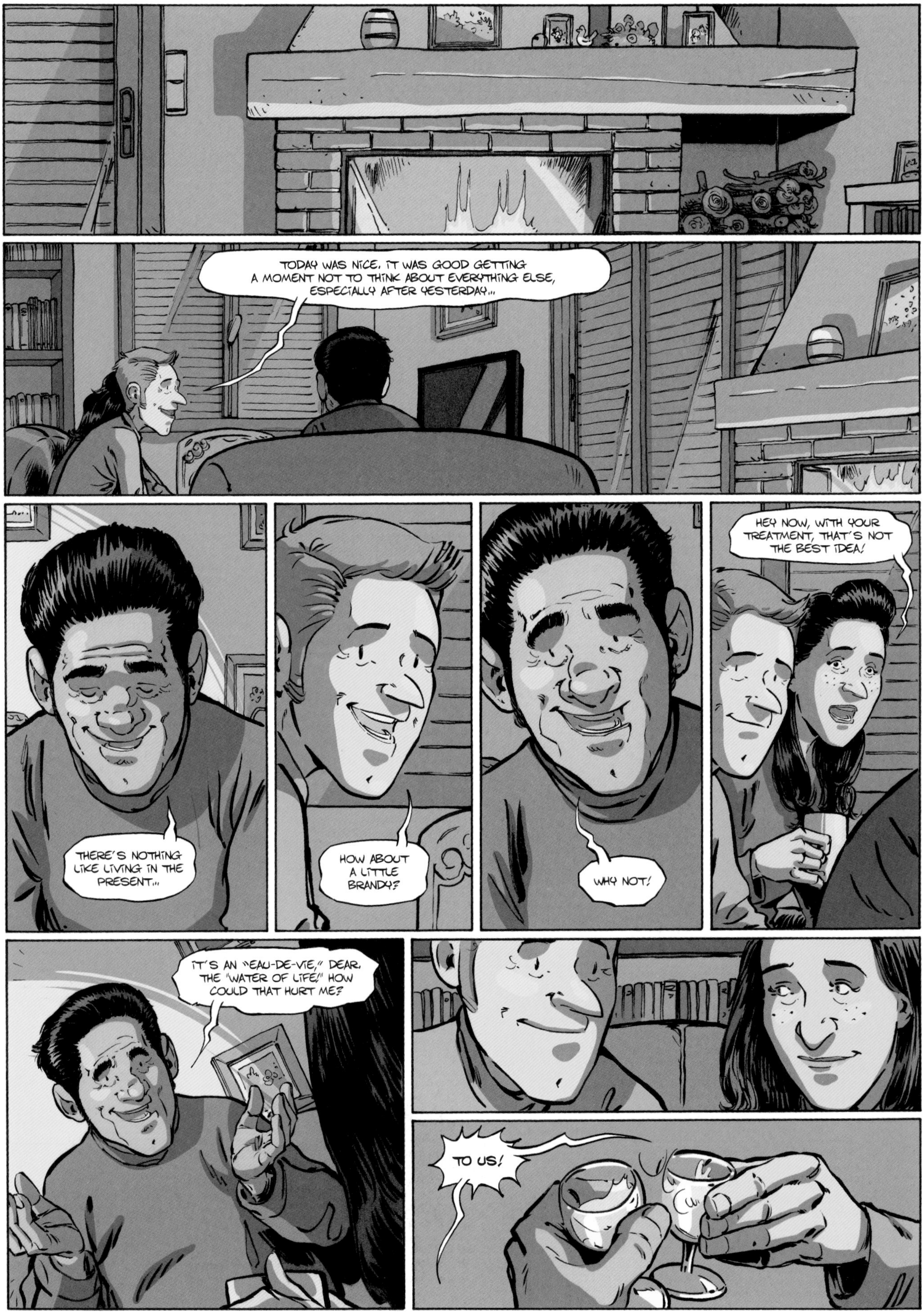
TODAY WAS NICE. IT WAS GOOD GETTING A MOMENT NOT TO THINK ABOUT EVERYTHING ELSE, ESPECIALLY AFTER YESTERDAY...
THERE'S NOTHING LIKE LIVING IN THE PRESENT...
HOW ABOUT A LITTLE BRANDY?
WHY NOT!
HEY NOW, WITH YOUR TREATMENT, THAT'S NOT THE BEST IDEA!
IT'S AN "EAU-DE-VIE," DEAR. THE "WATER OF LIFE!" HOW COULD THAT HURT ME?
TO US!

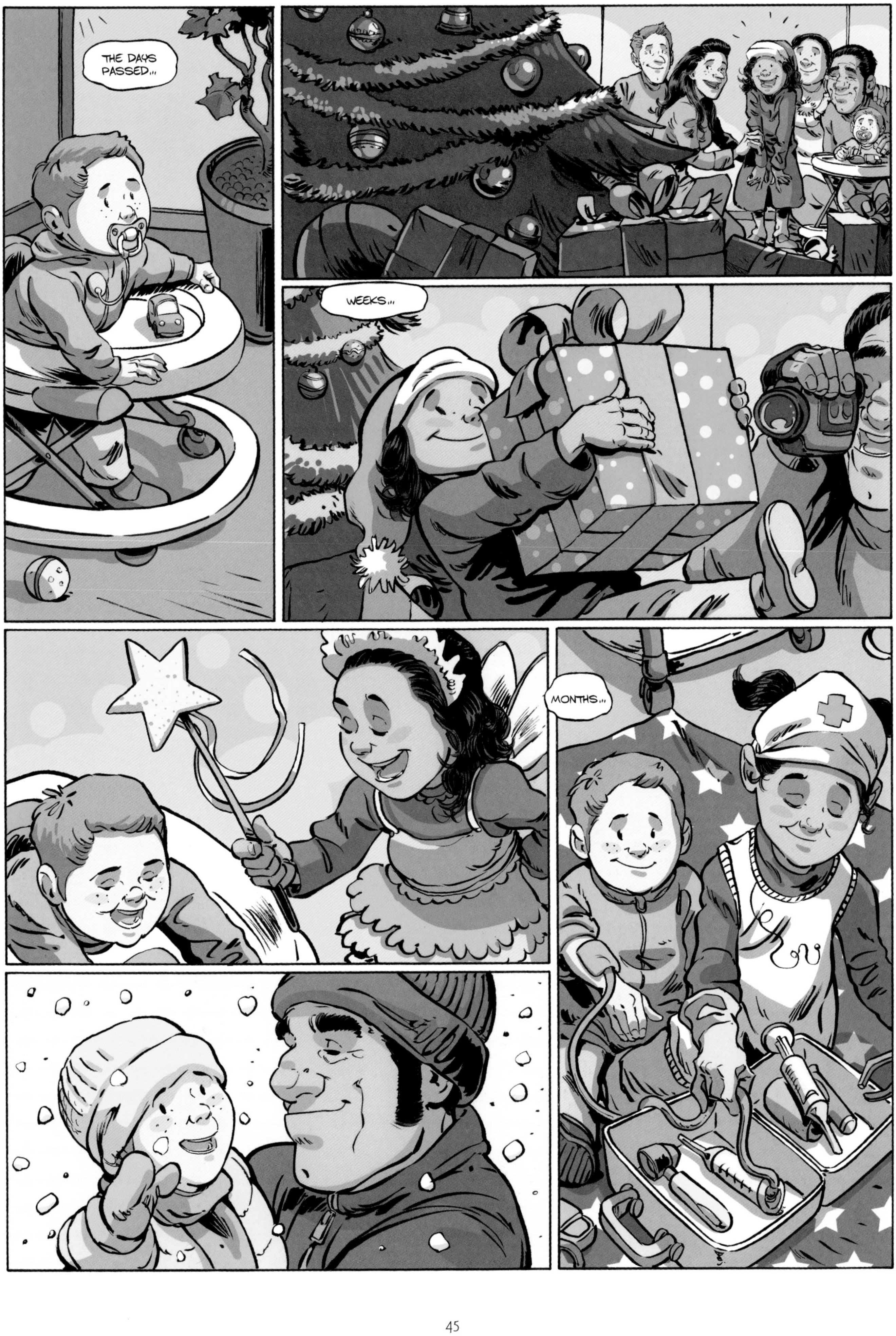
THE DAYS PASSED...
WEEKS...
MONTHS...

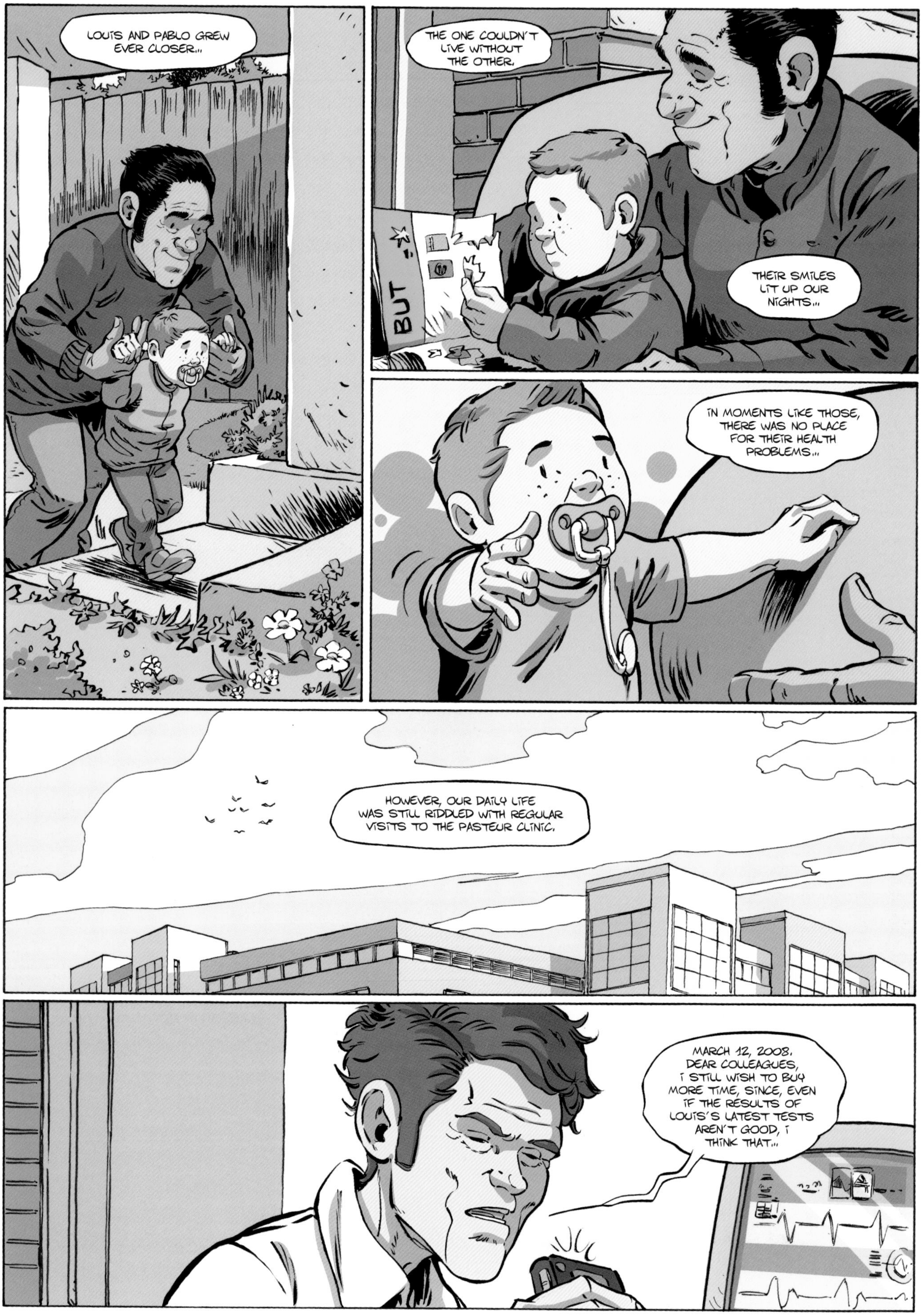
LOUIS AND PABLO GREW EVER CLOSER...
THE ONE COULDN'T LIVE WITHOUT THE OTHER.
BUT
THEIR SMILES LIT UP OUR NIGHTS...
IN MOMENTS LIKE THOSE, THERE WAS NO PLACE FOR THEIR HEALTH PROBLEMS...
HOWEVER, OUR DAILY LIFE WAS STILL RIDDLED WITH REGULAR VISITS TO THE PASTEUR CLINIC.
MARCH 12, 2008. DEAR COLLEAGUES, I STILL WISH TO BUY MORE TIME, SINCE, EVEN IF THE RESULTS OF LOUIS'S LATEST TESTS AREN'T GOOD, I THINK THAT...

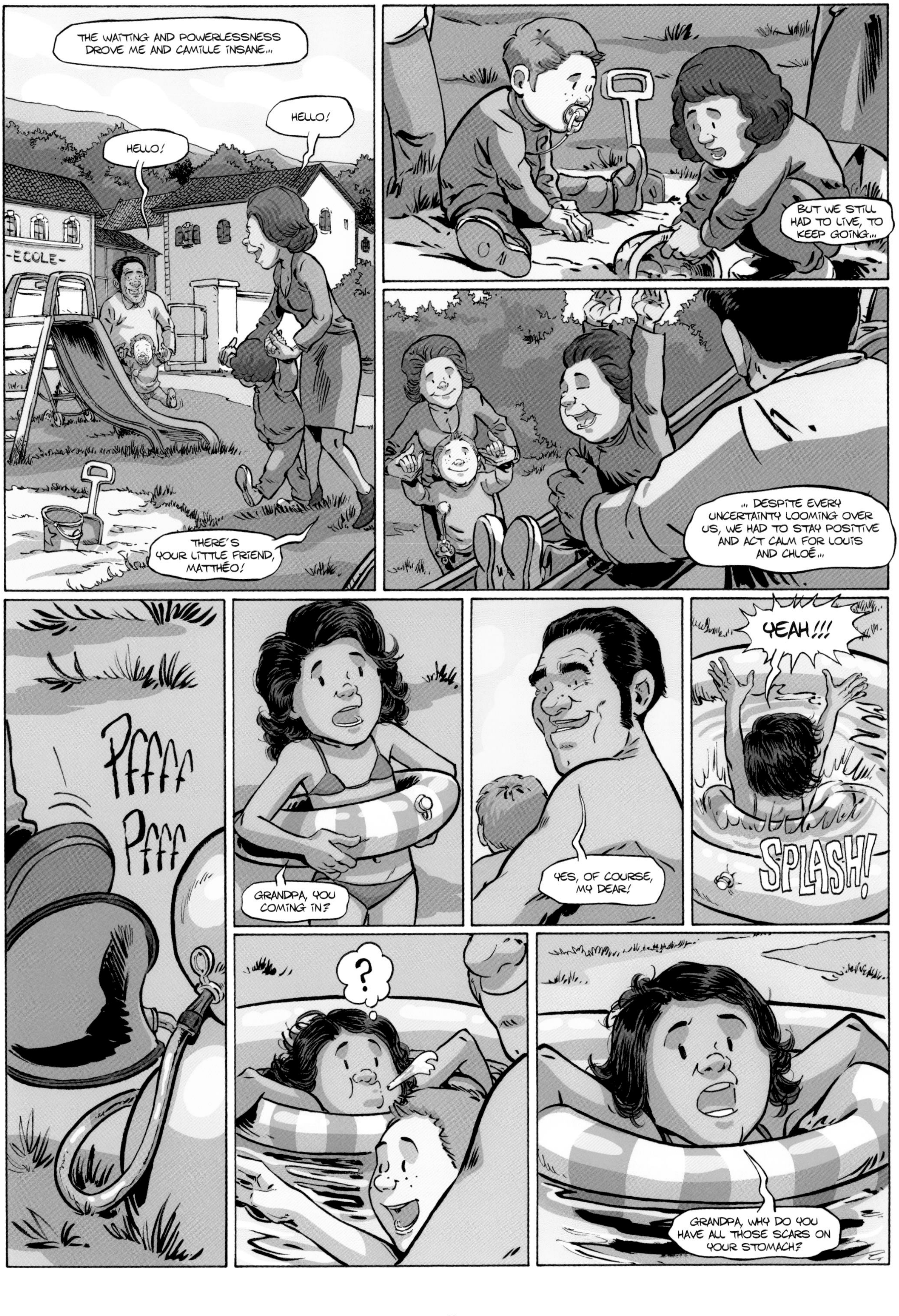

THE WAITING AND POWERLESSNESS DROVE ME AND CAMILLE INSANE...
HELLO!
HELLO!
-ECOLE-
THERE'S YOUR LITTLE FRIEND, MATTHÉO!
BUT WE STILL HAD TO LIVE, TO KEEP GOING...
... DESPITE EVERY UNCERTAINTY LOOMING OVER US, WE HAD TO STAY POSITIVE AND ACT CALM FOR LOUIS AND CHLOÉ...
Pffff
Pfff
GRANDPA, YOU COMING IN?
YES, OF COURSE, MY DEAR!
YEAH!!!
SPLASH!
?
GRANDPA, WHY DO YOU HAVE ALL THOSE SCARS ON YOUR STOMACH?

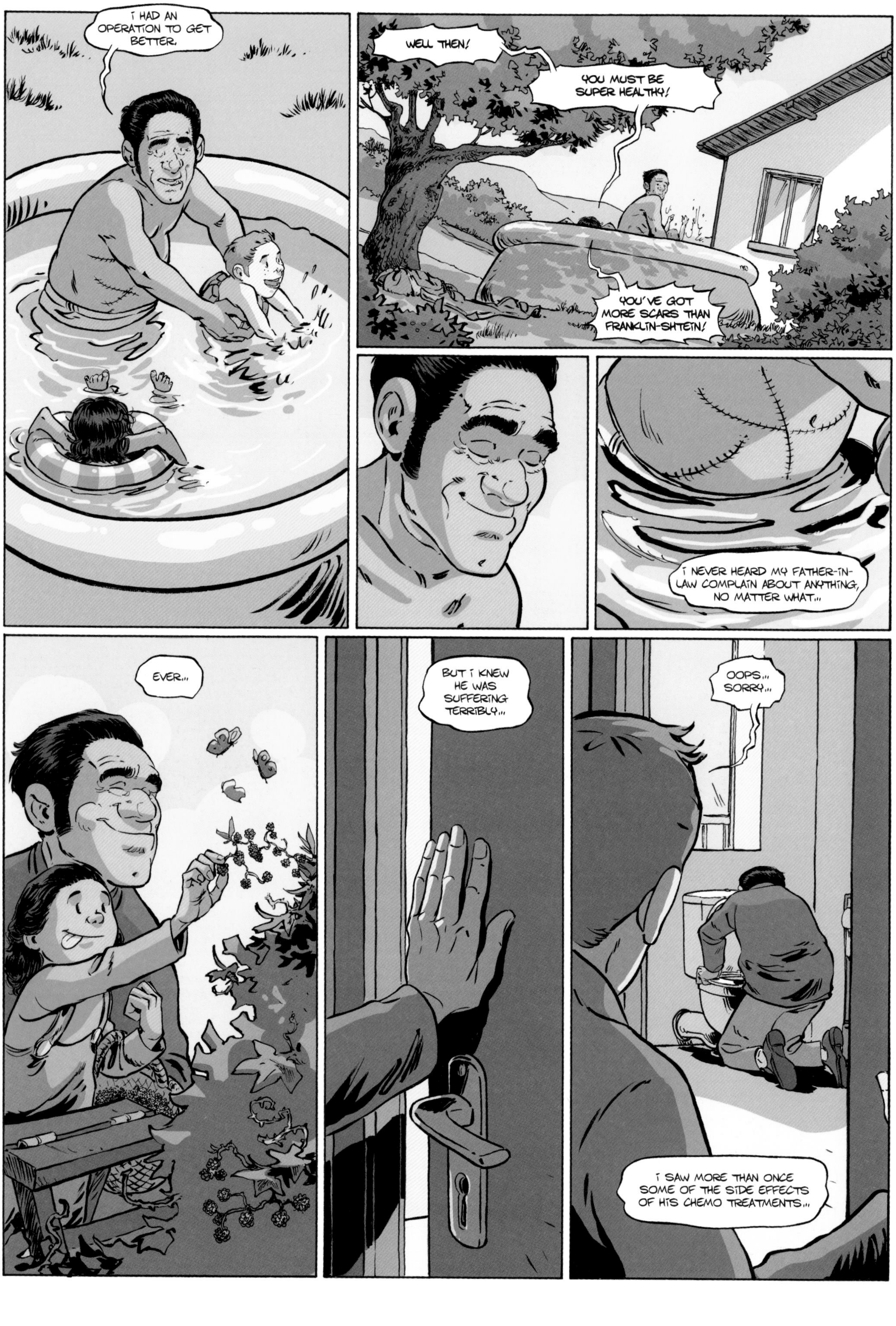
I HAD AN OPERATION TO GET BETTER.
WELL THEN!
YOU MUST BE SUPER HEALTHY!
YOU'VE GOT MORE SCARS THAN FRANKLIN-SHTEIN!
I NEVER HEARD MY FATHER-IN-LAW COMPLAIN ABOUT ANYTHING, NO MATTER WHAT...
EVER...
BUT I KNEW HE WAS SUFFERING TERRIBLY...
OOPS... SORRY...
I SAW MORE THAN ONCE SOME OF THE SIDE EFFECTS OF HIS CHEMO TREATMENTS...

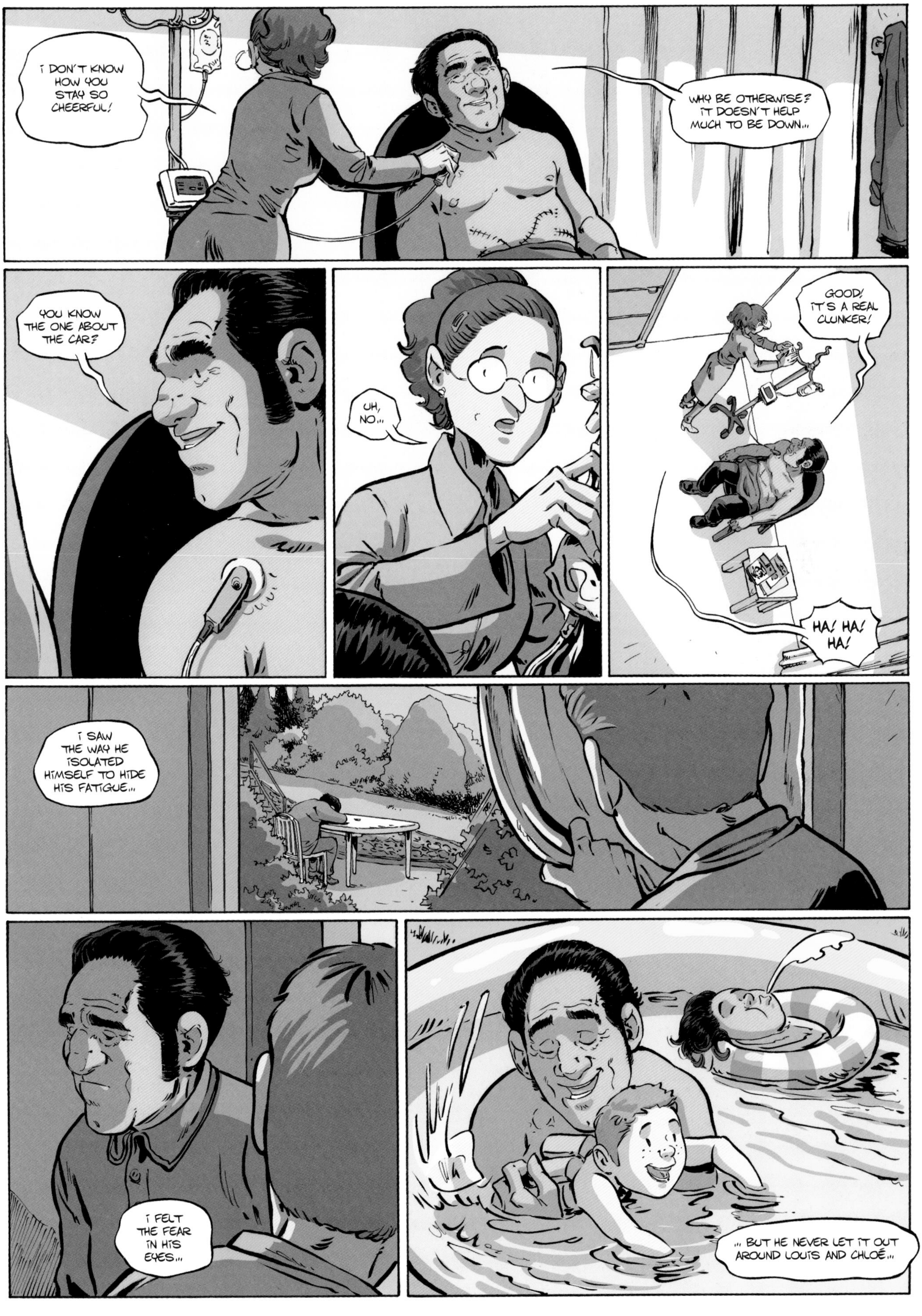

I DON'T KNOW HOW YOU STAY SO CHEERFUL!
WHY BE OTHERWISE? IT DOESN'T HELP MUCH TO BE DOWN...
YOU KNOW THE ONE ABOUT THE CAR?
UH, NO...
GOOD! IT'S A REAL CLUNKER!
HA! HA! HA!
I SAW THE WAY HE ISOLATED HIMSELF TO HIDE HIS FATIGUE...
I FELT THE FEAR IN HIS EYES...
... BUT HE NEVER LET IT OUT AROUND LOUIS AND CHLOÉ...

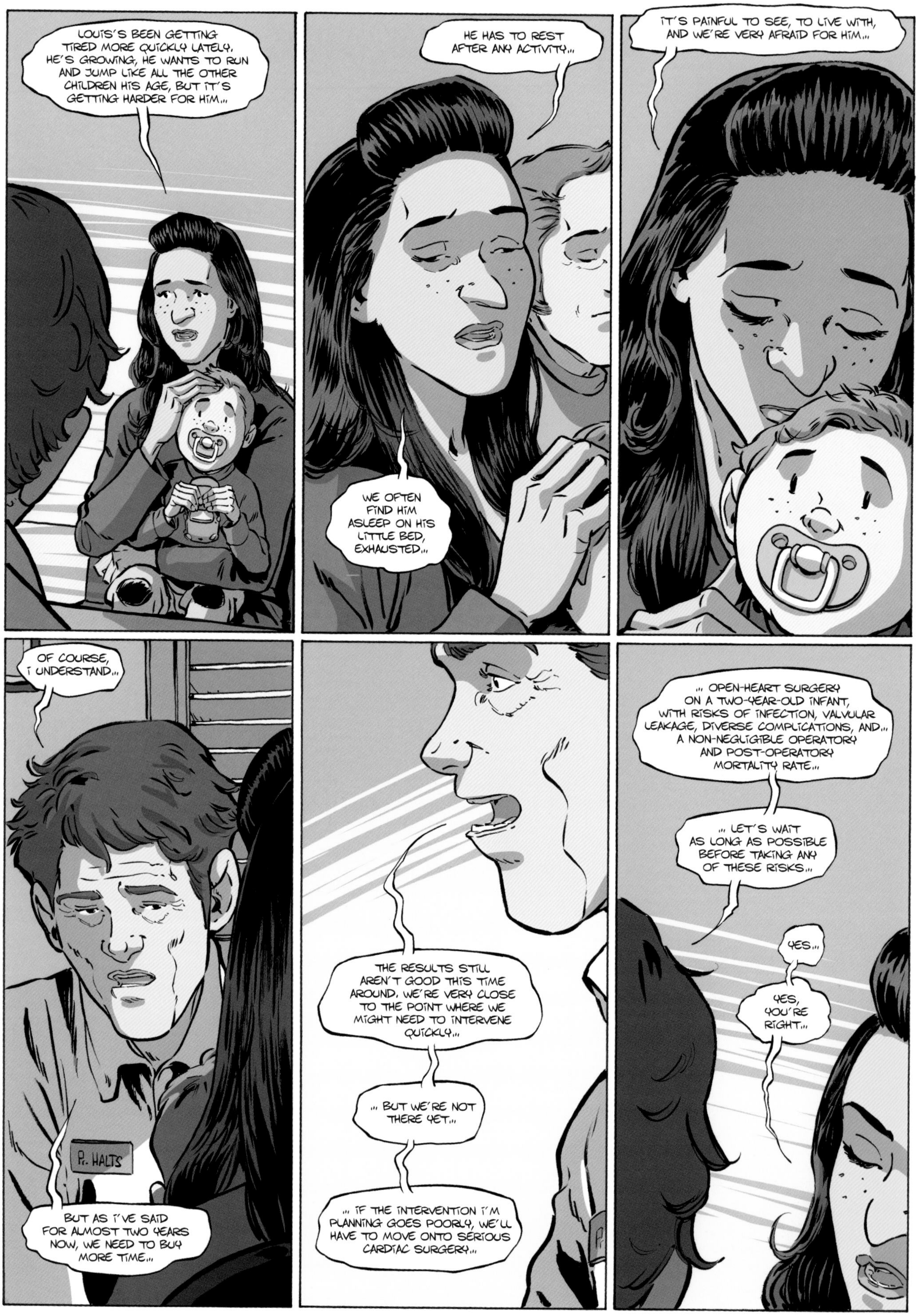
LOUIS'S BEEN GETTING TIRED MORE QUICKLY LATELY. HE'S GROWING, HE WANTS TO RUN AND JUMP LIKE ALL THE OTHER CHILDREN HIS AGE, BUT IT'S GETTING HARDER FOR HIM...
HE HAS TO REST AFTER ANY ACTIVITY...
WE OFTEN FIND HIM ASLEEP ON HIS LITTLE BED, EXHAUSTED...
IT'S PAINFUL TO SEE, TO LIVE WITH, AND WE'RE VERY AFRAID FOR HIM...
OF COURSE, I UNDERSTAND...
Pr. HALTS
BUT AS I'VE SAID FOR ALMOST TWO YEARS NOW, WE NEED TO BUY MORE TIME...
THE RESULTS STILL AREN'T GOOD THIS TIME AROUND. WE'RE VERY CLOSE TO THE POINT WHERE WE MIGHT NEED TO INTERVENE QUICKLY...
... BUT WE'RE NOT THERE YET...
... IF THE INTERVENTION I'M PLANNING GOES POORLY, WE'LL HAVE TO MOVE ONTO SERIOUS CARDIAC SURGERY...
... OPEN-HEART SURGERY ON A TWO-YEAR-OLD INFANT, WITH RISKS OF INFECTION, VALVULAR LEAKAGE, DIVERSE COMPLICATIONS, AND... A NON-NEGLIGIBLE OPERATORY AND POST-OPERATORY MORTALITY RATE...
... LET'S WAIT AS LONG AS POSSIBLE BEFORE TAKING ANY OF THESE RISKS...
YES...
YES, YOU'RE RIGHT...

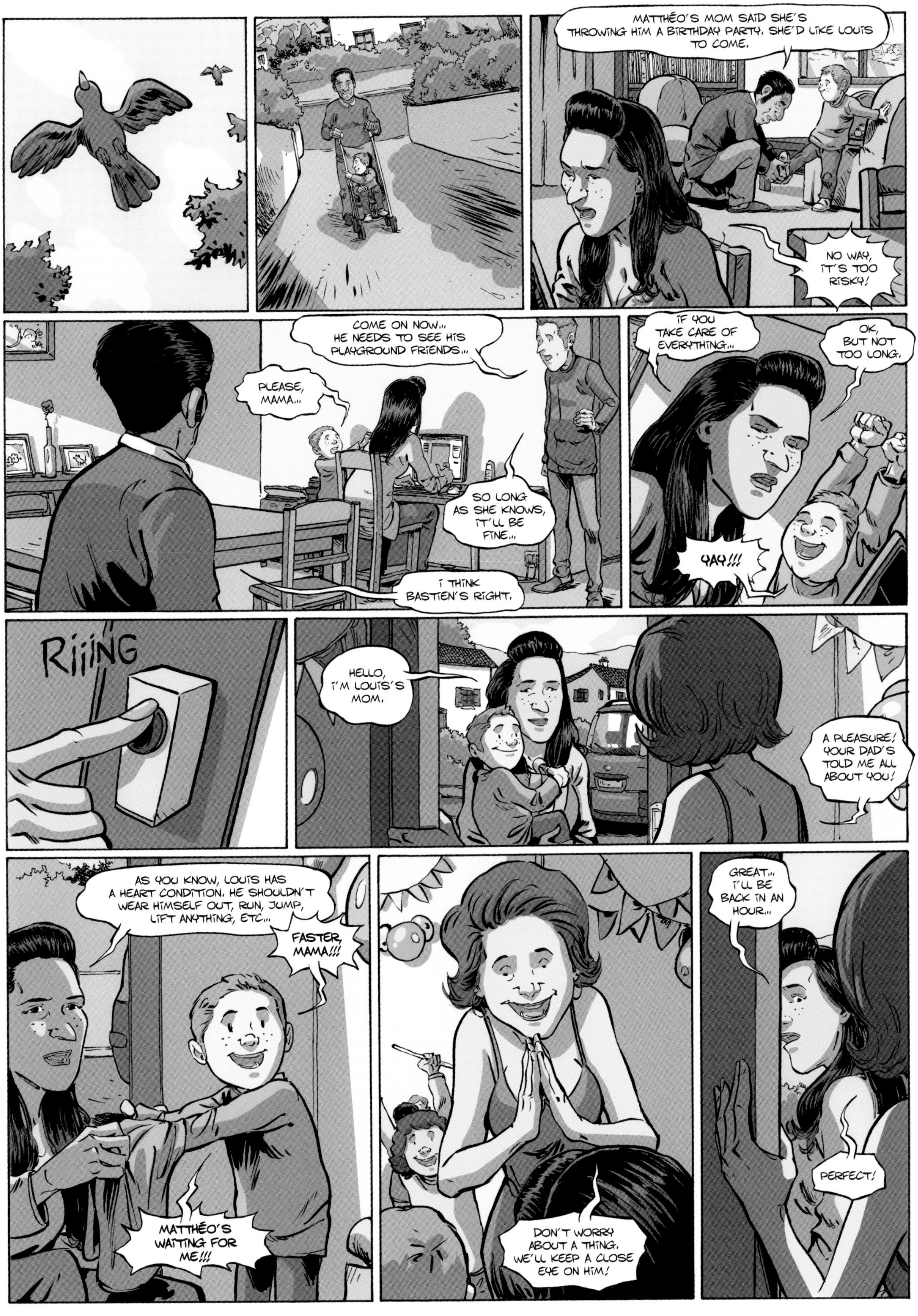
MATTHÉO'S MOM SAID SHE'S THROWING HIM A BIRTHDAY PARTY. SHE'D LIKE LOUIS TO COME.
NO WAY, IT'S TOO RISKY!
COME ON NOW... HE NEEDS TO SEE HIS PLAYGROUND FRIENDS...
PLEASE, MAMA...
SO LONG AS SHE KNOWS, IT'LL BE FINE...
I THINK BASTIEN'S RIGHT.
IF YOU TAKE CARE OF EVERYTHING...
OK, BUT NOT TOO LONG.
YAY!!!
RIIING
HELLO, I'M LOUIS'S MOM.
A PLEASURE! YOUR DAD'S TOLD ME ALL ABOUT YOU!
AS YOU KNOW, LOUIS HAS A HEART CONDITION. HE SHOULDN'T WEAR HIMSELF OUT, RUN, JUMP, LIFT ANYTHING, ETC...
FASTER, MAMA!!!
MATTHÉO'S WAITING FOR ME!!!
DON'T WORRY ABOUT A THING. WE'LL KEEP A CLOSE EYE ON HIM!
GREAT... I'LL BE BACK IN AN HOUR...
PERFECT!

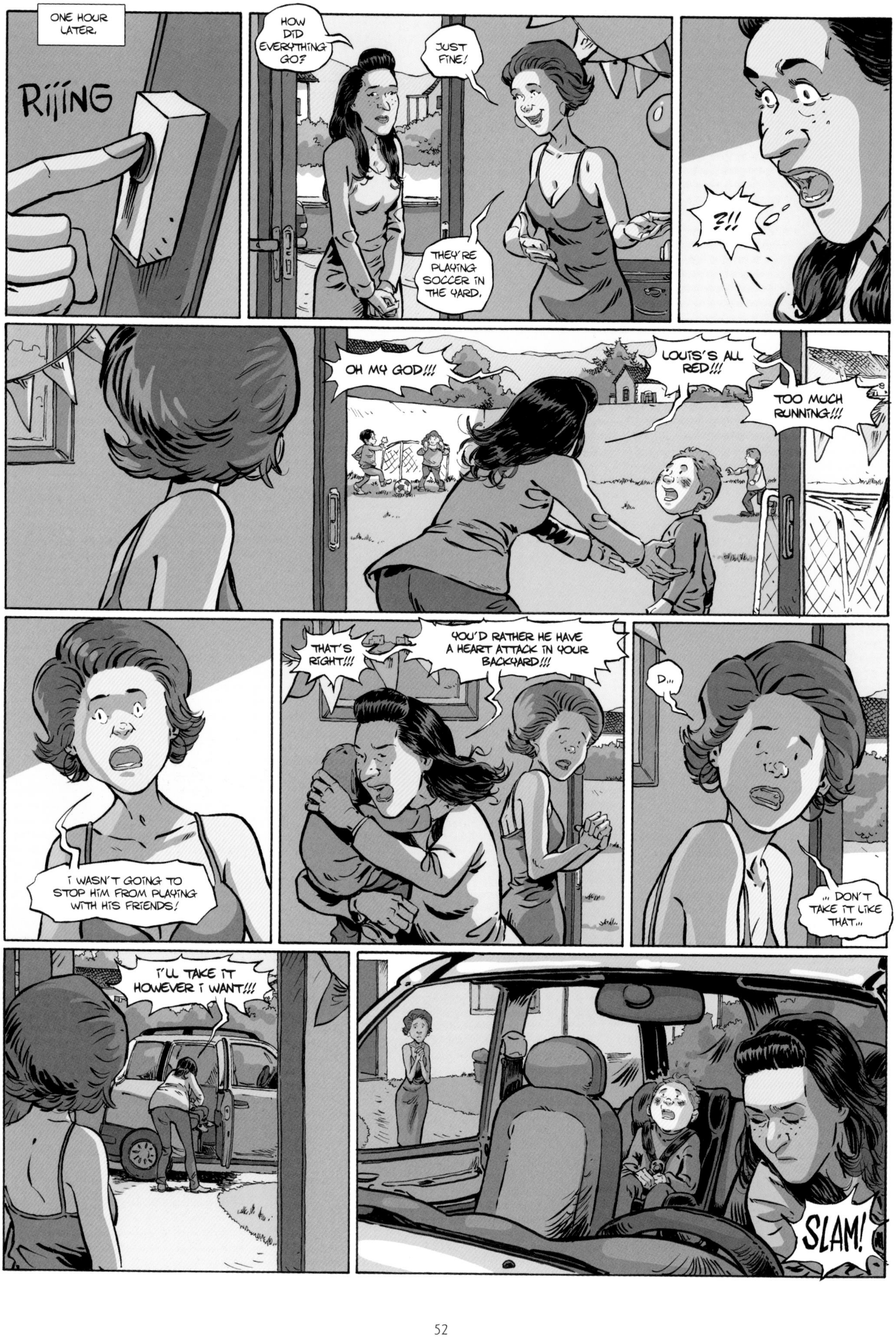
ONE HOUR LATER.
RIIING
HOW DID EVERYTHING GO?
JUST FINE!
THEY'RE PLAYING SOCCER IN THE YARD.
?!!
OH MY GOD!!!
LOUIS'S ALL RED!!!
TOO MUCH RUNNING!!!
I WASN'T GOING TO STOP HIM FROM PLAYING WITH HIS FRIENDS!
THAT'S RIGHT!!!
YOU'D RATHER HE HAVE A HEART ATTACK IN YOUR BACKYARD!!!
D...
... DON'T TAKE IT LIKE THAT...
I'LL TAKE IT HOWEVER I WANT!!!
SLAM!

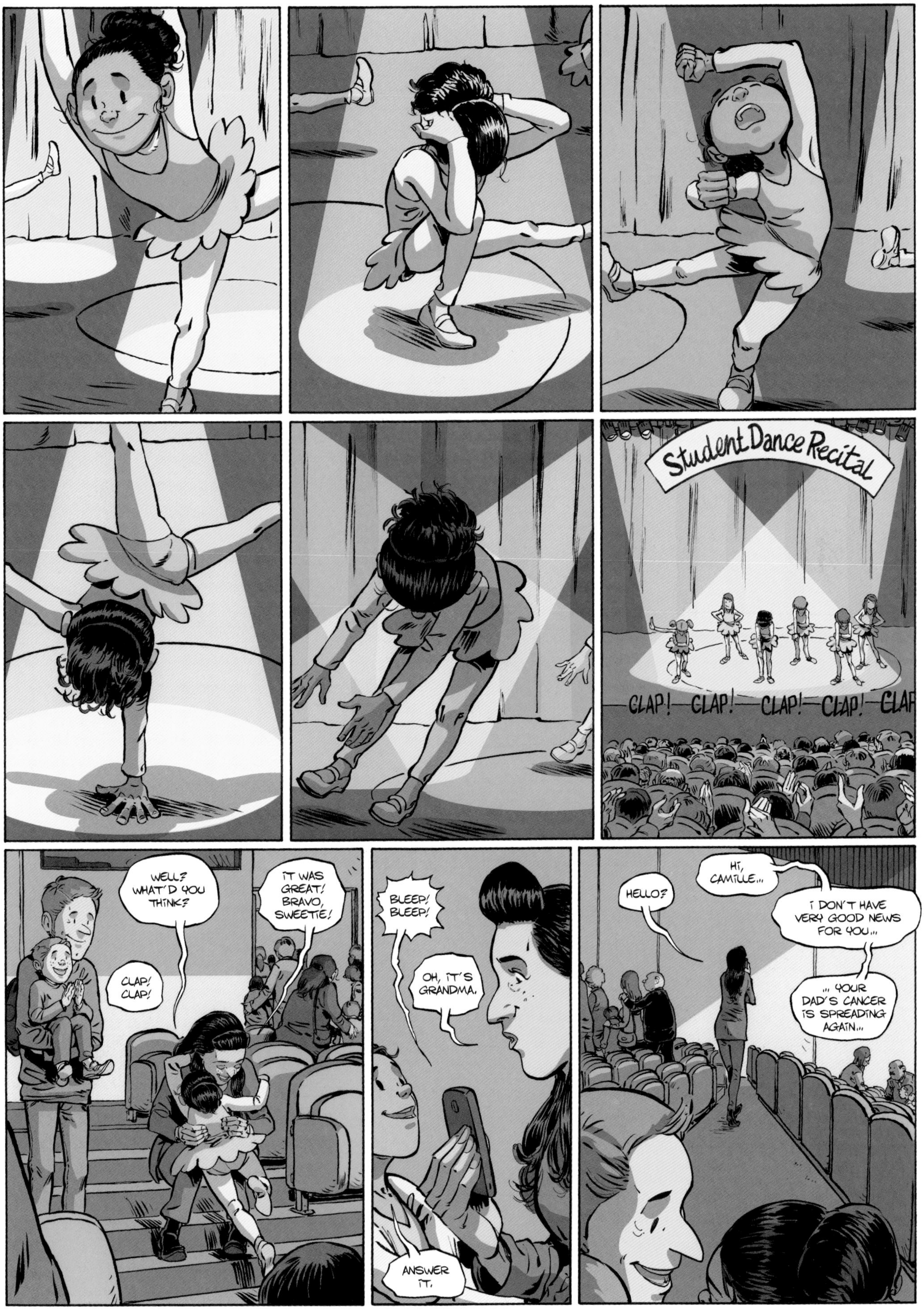
Student Dance Recital
CLAP! CLAP! CLAP! CLAP! CLAP
WELL? WHAT'D YOU THINK?
CLAP! CLAP!
IT WAS GREAT! BRAVO, SWEETIE!
BLEEP! BLEEP!
OH, IT'S GRANDMA.
ANSWER IT.
HELLO?
HI, CAMILLE...
I DON'T HAVE VERY GOOD NEWS FOR YOU...
...YOUR DAD'S CANCER IS SPREADING AGAIN...

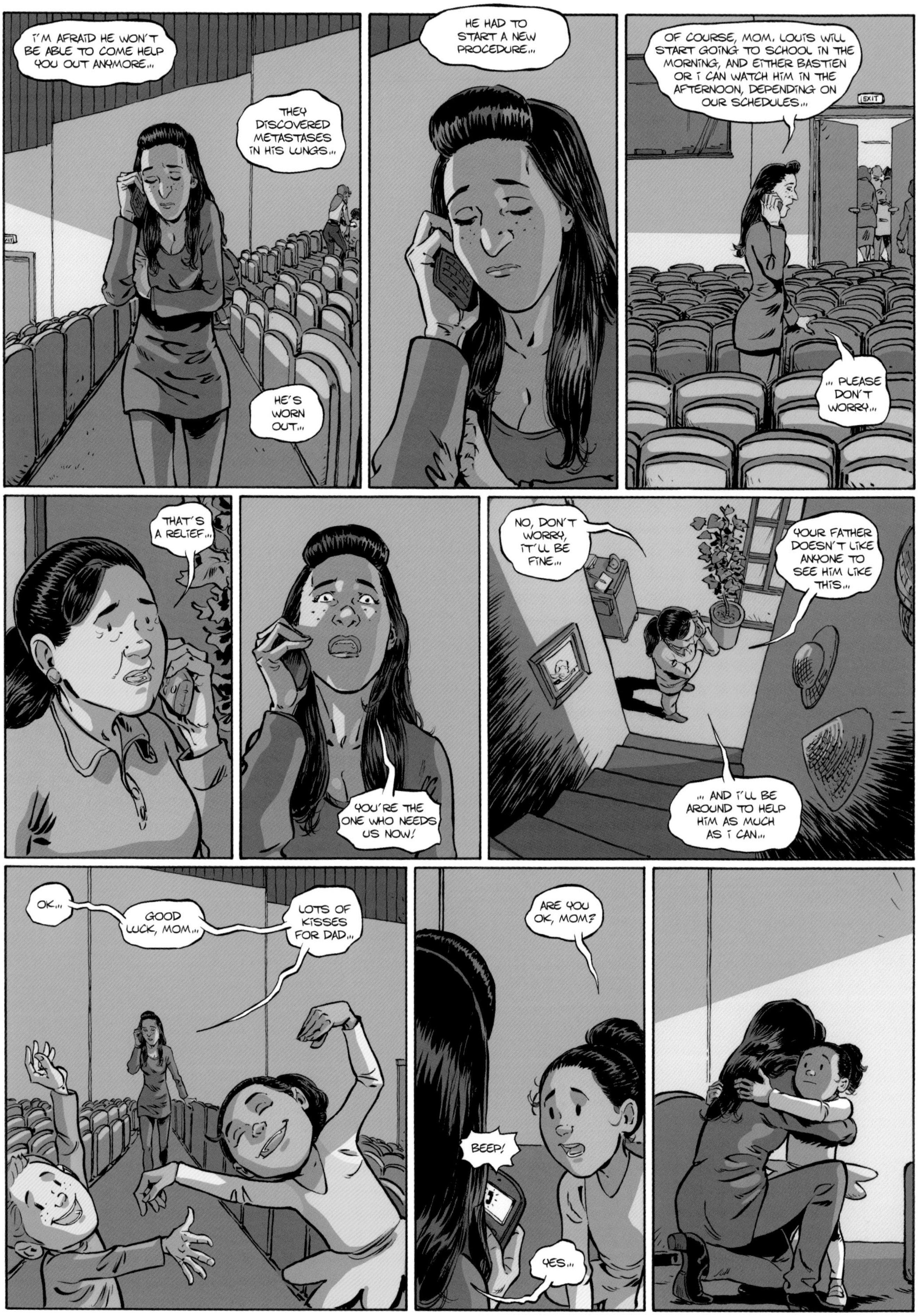
I'M AFRAID HE WON'T BE ABLE TO COME HELP YOU OUT ANYMORE...
THEY DISCOVERED METASTASES IN HIS LUNGS...
HE'S WORN OUT...
HE HAD TO START A NEW PROCEDURE...
OF COURSE, MOM. LOUIS WILL START GOING TO SCHOOL IN THE MORNING, AND EITHER BASTIEN OR I CAN WATCH HIM IN THE AFTERNOON, DEPENDING ON OUR SCHEDULES...
EXIT
... PLEASE DON'T WORRY...
THAT'S A RELIEF...
YOU'RE THE ONE WHO NEEDS US NOW!
NO, DON'T WORRY, IT'LL BE FINE...
YOUR FATHER DOESN'T LIKE ANYONE TO SEE HIM LIKE THIS...
... AND I'LL BE AROUND TO HELP HIM AS MUCH AS I CAN...
OK...
GOOD LUCK, MOM...
LOTS OF KISSES FOR DAD...
ARE YOU OK, MOM?
BEEP!
YES...

THE NEXT DAY.

WHOA, YOU'RE BREAKING OUT THE OLD STUFF!

YES...

I WANT TO TRY GOING ON A RIDE WITH SOME FRIENDS THIS AFTERNOON IN VARILHES.

EXCELLENT IDEA! I'M GOING TO SEE A CARTOON AT THE THEATER IN PAMIERS WITH LOUIS AND CHLOÉ.

YOU WON'T HAVE TO BE ALL ALONE NOW SINCE YOU HATE MOVIES SO MUCH...

BLAH BLAH BLAH...

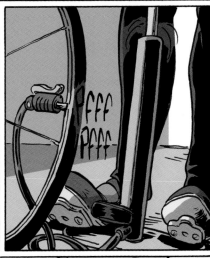

PFFF PFFF

WILL YOU TAKE ME ON A BIKE RIDE ONE DAY, DAD?

OF COURSE, LOUIS, WE'LL GO RIDING TOGETHER WHEN YOU'RE OLDER!

BUT SLOWLY, RIGHT?

... WITH MY HEART PROBLEMS, I CAN'T GO FAST...

I KNOW, MY TREASURE...

I KNOW...

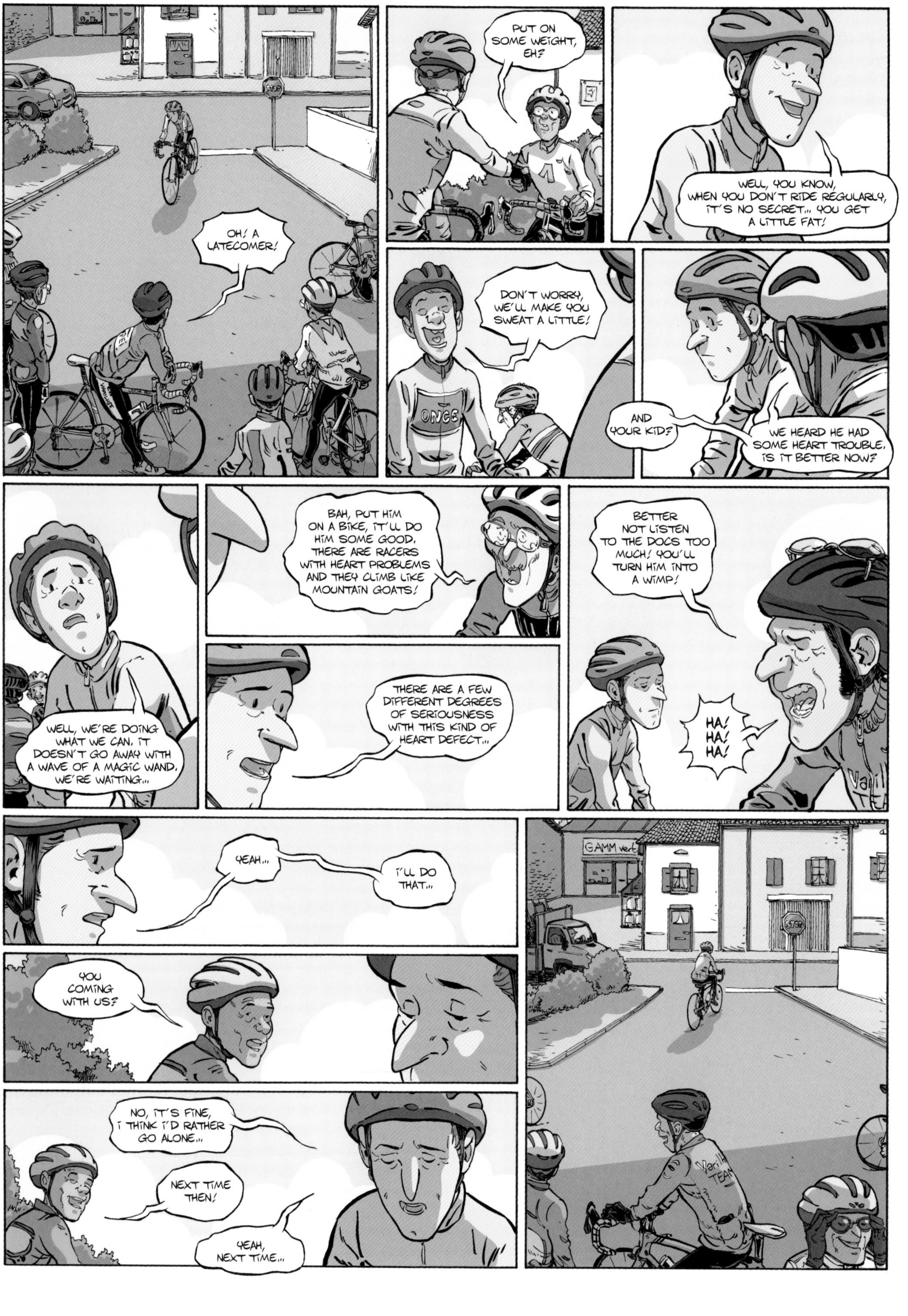
OH! A LATECOMER!
PUT ON SOME WEIGHT, EH?
WELL, YOU KNOW, WHEN YOU DON'T RIDE REGULARLY, IT'S NO SECRET... YOU GET A LITTLE FAT!
DON'T WORRY, WE'LL MAKE YOU SWEAT A LITTLE!
ONCE
WE HEARD HE HAD SOME HEART TROUBLE, IS IT BETTER NOW?
AND YOUR KID?
WELL, WE'RE DOING WHAT WE CAN. IT DOESN'T GO AWAY WITH A WAVE OF A MAGIC WAND. WE'RE WAITING...
BAH, PUT HIM ON A BIKE, IT'LL DO HIM SOME GOOD. THERE ARE RACERS WITH HEART PROBLEMS AND THEY CLIMB LIKE MOUNTAIN GOATS!
THERE ARE A FEW DIFFERENT DEGREES OF SERIOUSNESS WITH THIS KIND OF HEART DEFECT...
BETTER NOT LISTEN TO THE DOCS TOO MUCH! YOU'LL TURN HIM INTO A WIMP!
HA! HA! HA!
YEAH...
I'LL DO THAT...
GAMM vert
STOP
YOU COMING WITH US?
NO, IT'S FINE, I THINK I'D RATHER GO ALONE...
NEXT TIME THEN!
YEAH, NEXT TIME...

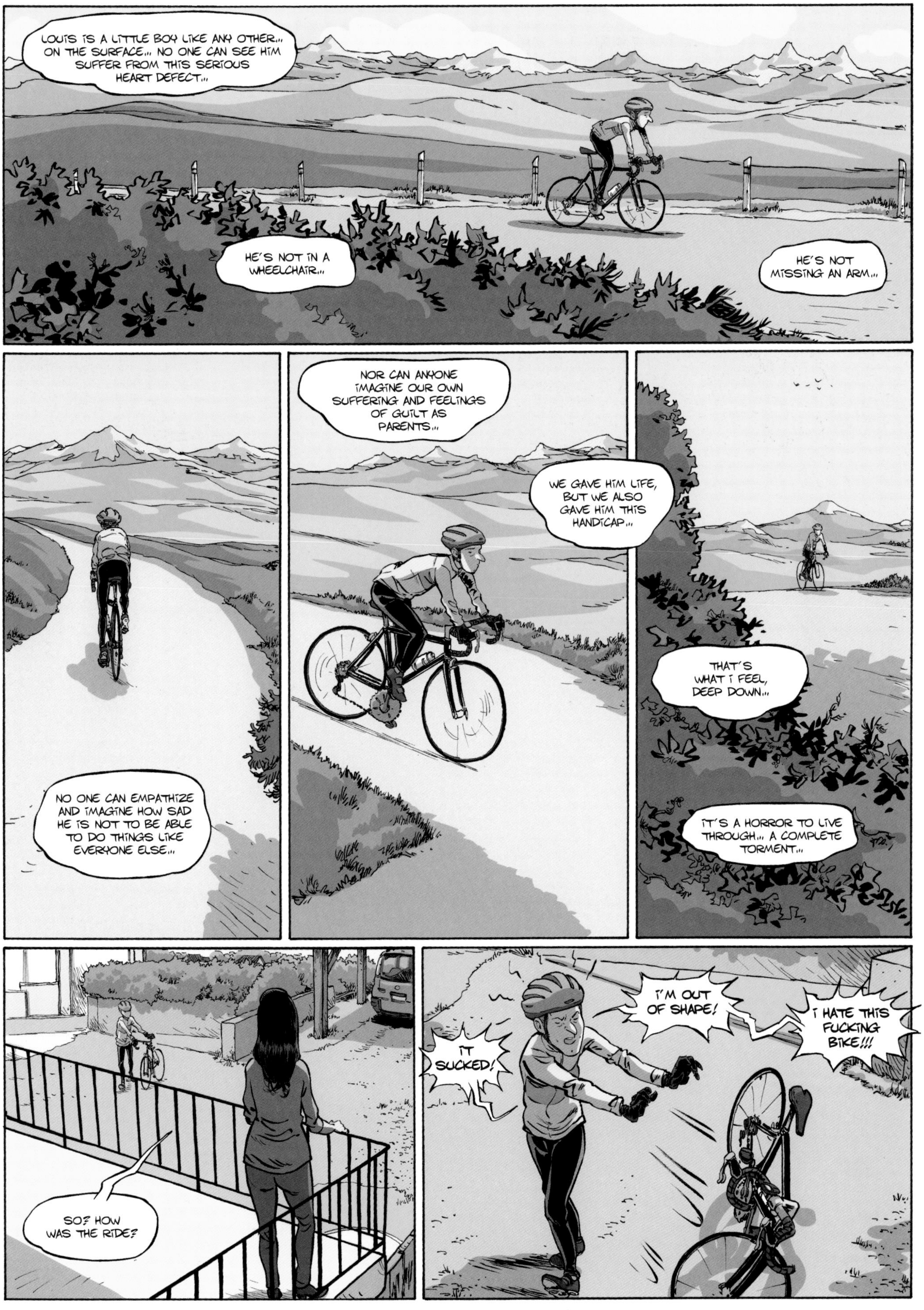
LOUIS IS A LITTLE BOY LIKE ANY OTHER... ON THE SURFACE... NO ONE CAN SEE HIM SUFFER FROM THIS SERIOUS HEART DEFECT...
HE'S NOT IN A WHEELCHAIR...
HE'S NOT MISSING AN ARM...
NO ONE CAN EMPATHIZE AND IMAGINE HOW SAD HE IS NOT TO BE ABLE TO DO THINGS LIKE EVERYONE ELSE...
NOR CAN ANYONE IMAGINE OUR OWN SUFFERING AND FEELINGS OF GUILT AS PARENTS...
WE GAVE HIM LIFE, BUT WE ALSO GAVE HIM THIS HANDICAP...
THAT'S WHAT I FEEL, DEEP DOWN...
IT'S A HORROR TO LIVE THROUGH... A COMPLETE TORMENT...
SO? HOW WAS THE RIDE?
IT SUCKED!
I'M OUT OF SHAPE!
I HATE THIS FUCKING BIKE!!!

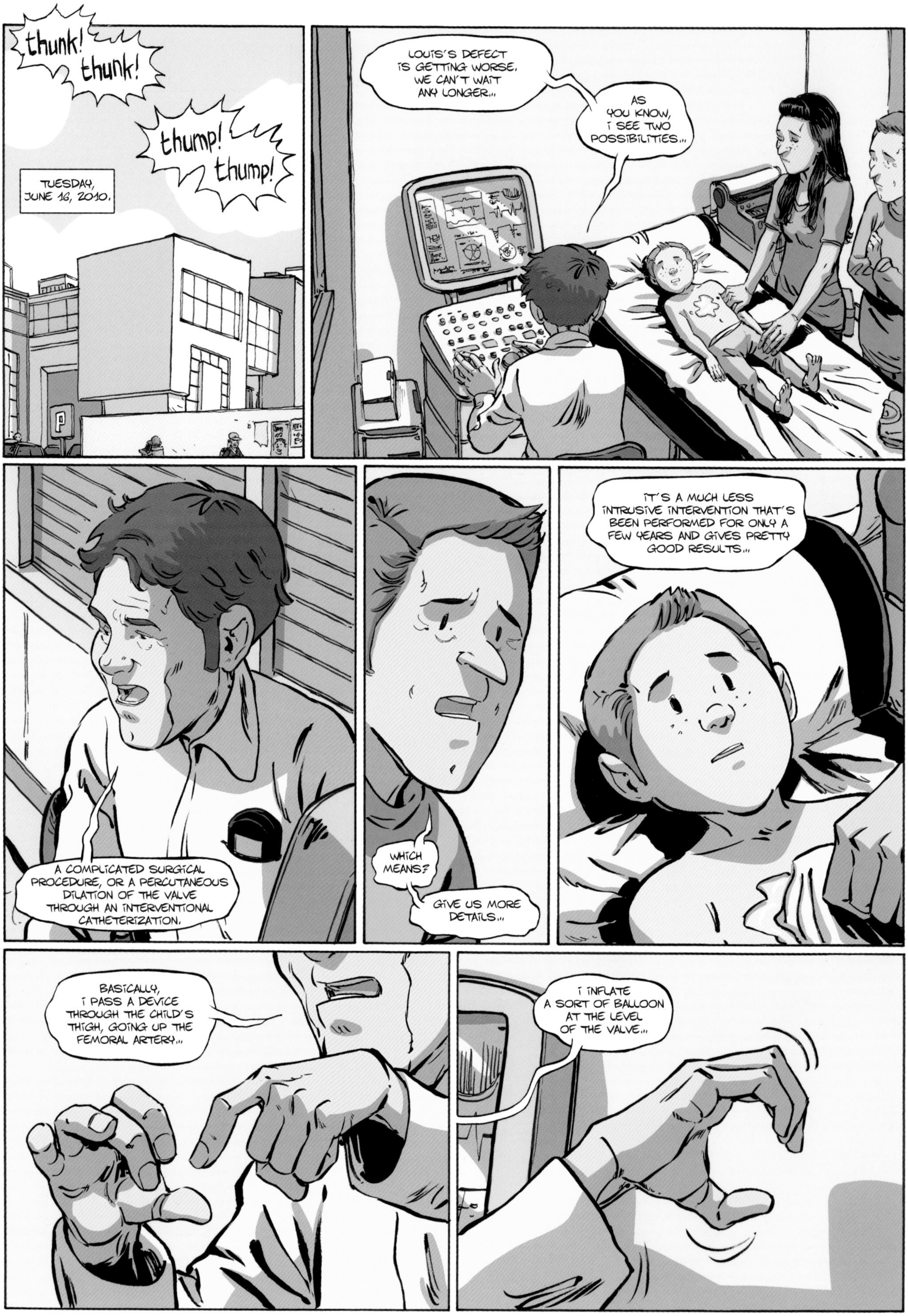
thunk! thunk!
thump! thump!
TUESDAY, JUNE 16, 2010.
LOUIS'S DEFECT IS GETTING WORSE, WE CAN'T WAIT ANY LONGER...
AS YOU KNOW, I SEE TWO POSSIBILITIES...
A COMPLICATED SURGICAL PROCEDURE, OR A PERCUTANEOUS DILATION OF THE VALVE THROUGH AN INTERVENTIONAL CATHETERIZATION.
WHICH MEANS?
GIVE US MORE DETAILS...
IT'S A MUCH LESS INTRUSIVE INTERVENTION THAT'S BEEN PERFORMED FOR ONLY A FEW YEARS AND GIVES PRETTY GOOD RESULTS...
BASICALLY, I PASS A DEVICE THROUGH THE CHILD'S THIGH, GOING UP THE FEMORAL ARTERY...
I INFLATE A SORT OF BALLOON AT THE LEVEL OF THE VALVE...

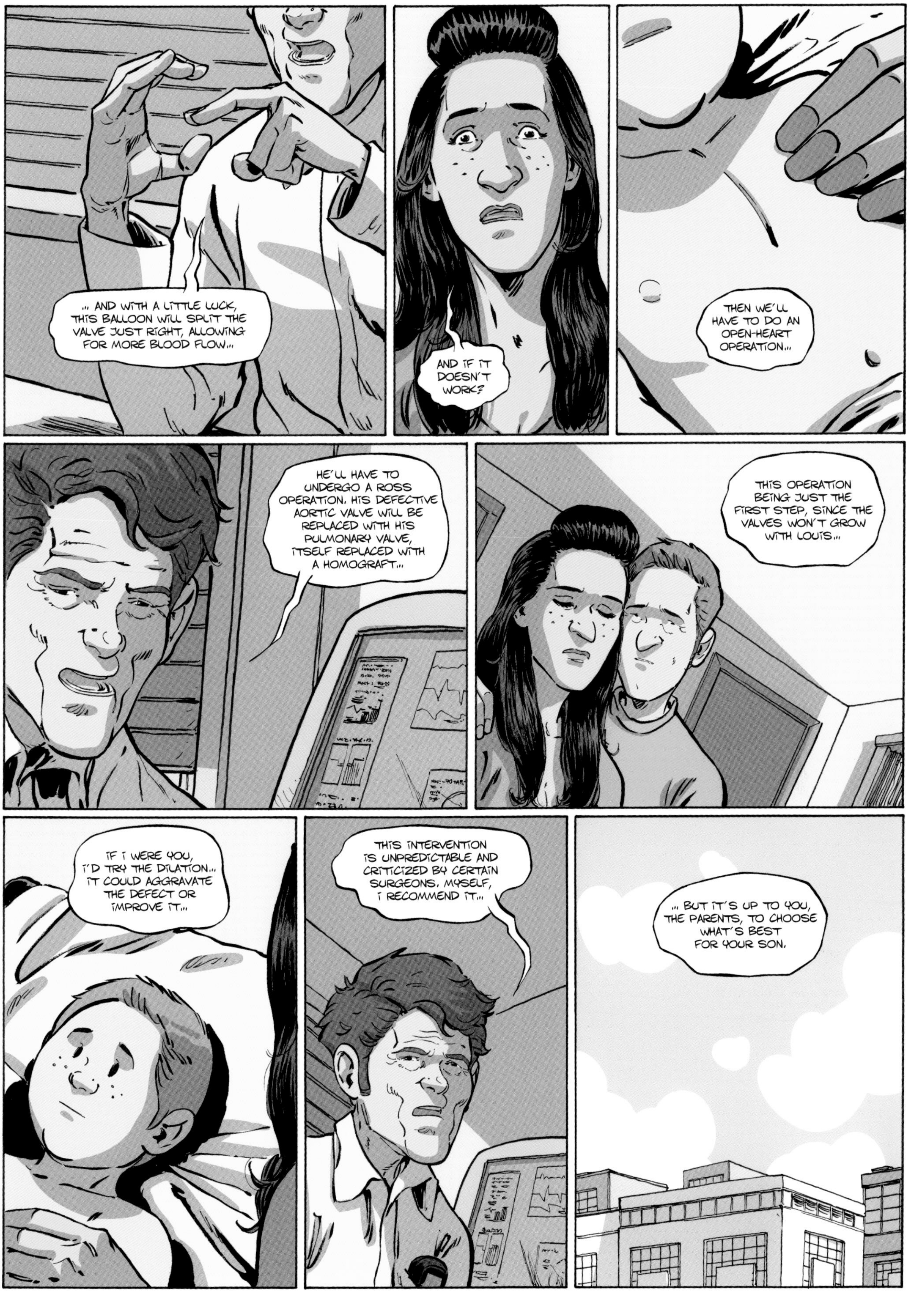
... AND WITH A LITTLE LUCK, THIS BALLOON WILL SPLIT THE VALVE JUST RIGHT, ALLOWING FOR MORE BLOOD FLOW...
AND IF IT DOESN'T WORK?
THEN WE'LL HAVE TO DO AN OPEN-HEART OPERATION...
HE'LL HAVE TO UNDERGO A ROSS OPERATION. HIS DEFECTIVE AORTIC VALVE WILL BE REPLACED WITH HIS PULMONARY VALVE, ITSELF REPLACED WITH A HOMOGRAFT...
THIS OPERATION BEING JUST THE FIRST STEP, SINCE THE VALVES WON'T GROW WITH LOUIS...
IF I WERE YOU, I'D TRY THE DILATION... IT COULD AGGRAVATE THE DEFECT OR IMPROVE IT...
THIS INTERVENTION IS UNPREDICTABLE AND CRITICIZED BY CERTAIN SURGEONS. MYSELF, I RECOMMEND IT...
... BUT IT'S UP TO YOU, THE PARENTS, TO CHOOSE WHAT'S BEST FOR YOUR SON.

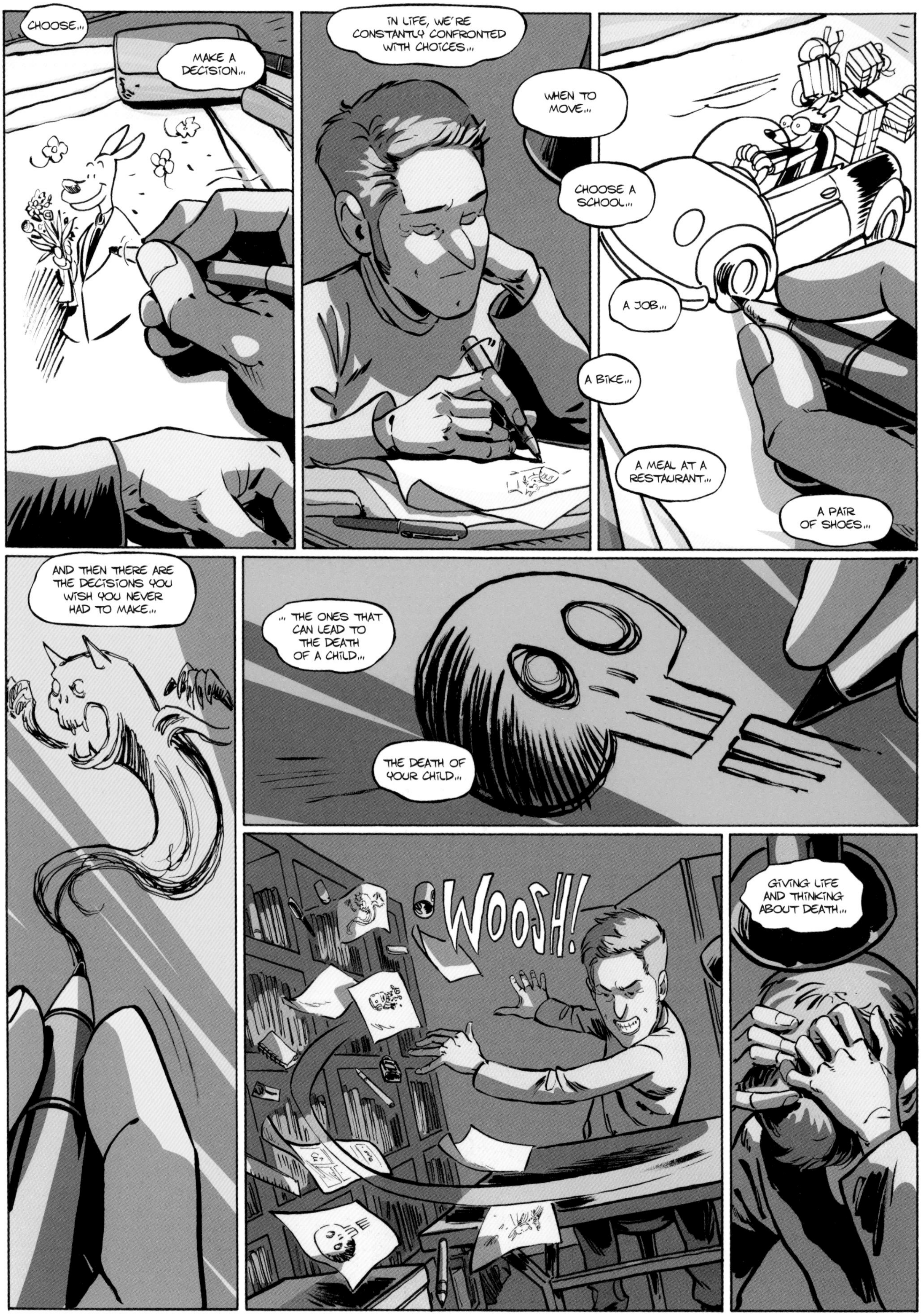
CHOOSE...
MAKE A DECISION...
IN LIFE, WE'RE CONSTANTLY CONFRONTED WITH CHOICES...
WHEN TO MOVE...
CHOOSE A SCHOOL...
A JOB...
A BIKE...
A MEAL AT A RESTAURANT...
A PAIR OF SHOES...
AND THEN THERE ARE THE DECISIONS YOU WISH YOU NEVER HAD TO MAKE...
... THE ONES THAT CAN LEAD TO THE DEATH OF A CHILD...
THE DEATH OF YOUR CHILD...
WOOSH!
GIVING LIFE AND THINKING ABOUT DEATH...

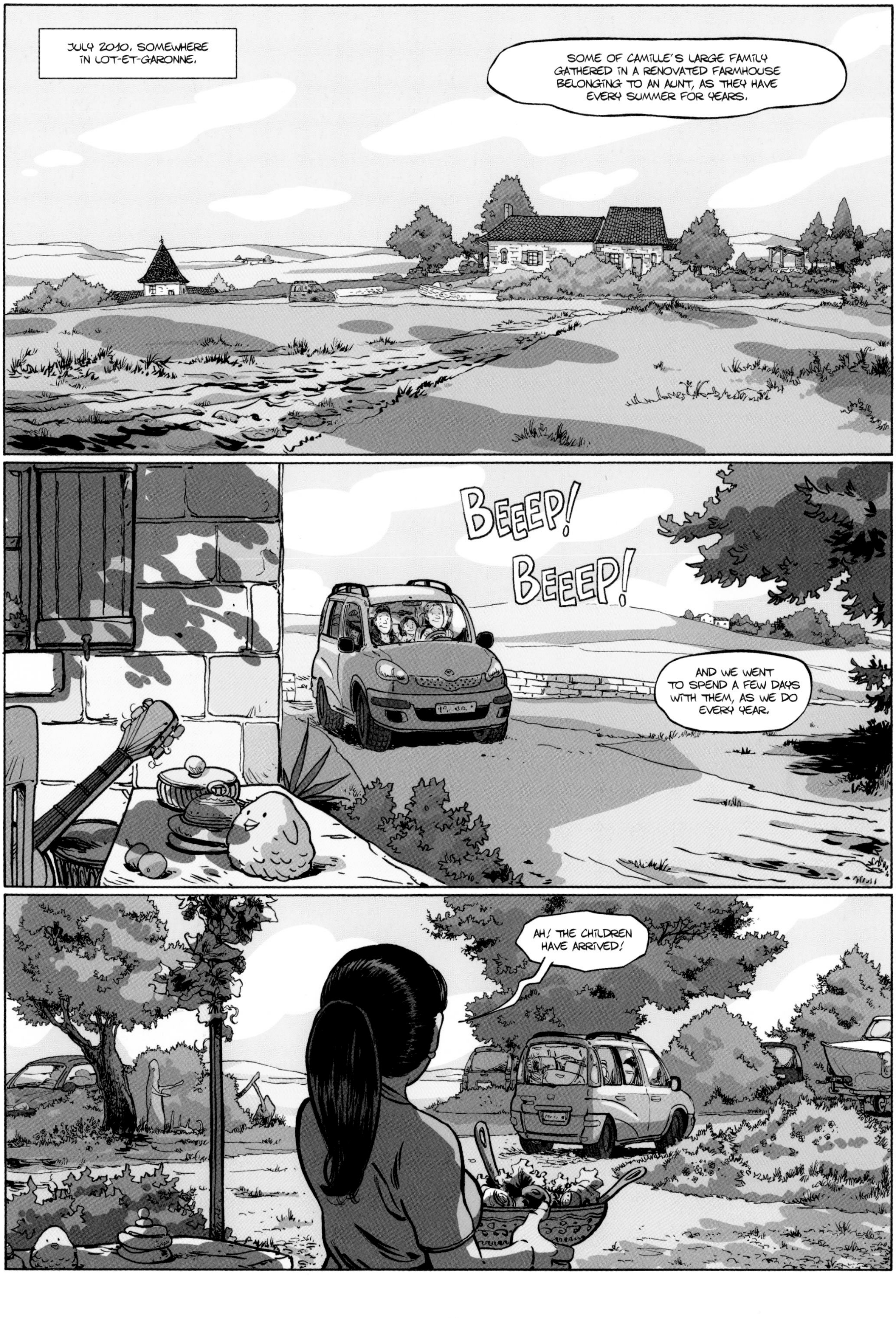
JULY 2010, SOMEWHERE IN LOT-ET-GARONNE.
SOME OF CAMILLE'S LARGE FAMILY GATHERED IN A RENOVATED FARMHOUSE BELONGING TO AN AUNT, AS THEY HAVE EVERY SUMMER FOR YEARS.
BEEEP! BEEEP!
AND WE WENT TO SPEND A FEW DAYS WITH THEM, AS WE DO EVERY YEAR.
AH! THE CHILDREN HAVE ARRIVED!

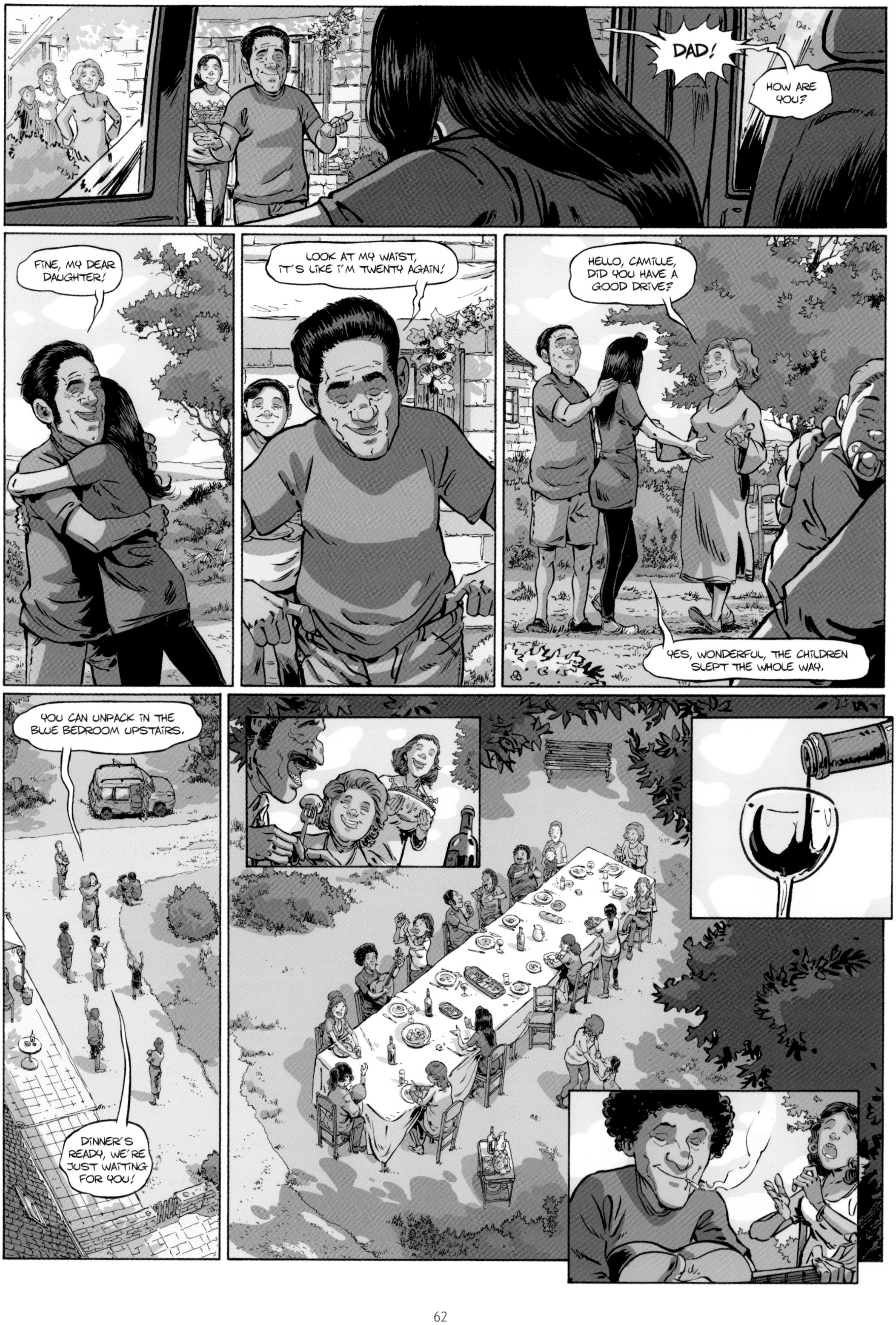
DAD!
HOW ARE YOU?
FINE, MY DEAR DAUGHTER!
LOOK AT MY WAIST, IT'S LIKE I'M TWENTY AGAIN!
HELLO, CAMILLE, DID YOU HAVE A GOOD DRIVE?
YES, WONDERFUL, THE CHILDREN SLEPT THE WHOLE WAY.
YOU CAN UNPACK IN THE BLUE BEDROOM UPSTAIRS.
DINNER'S READY, WE'RE JUST WAITING FOR YOU!

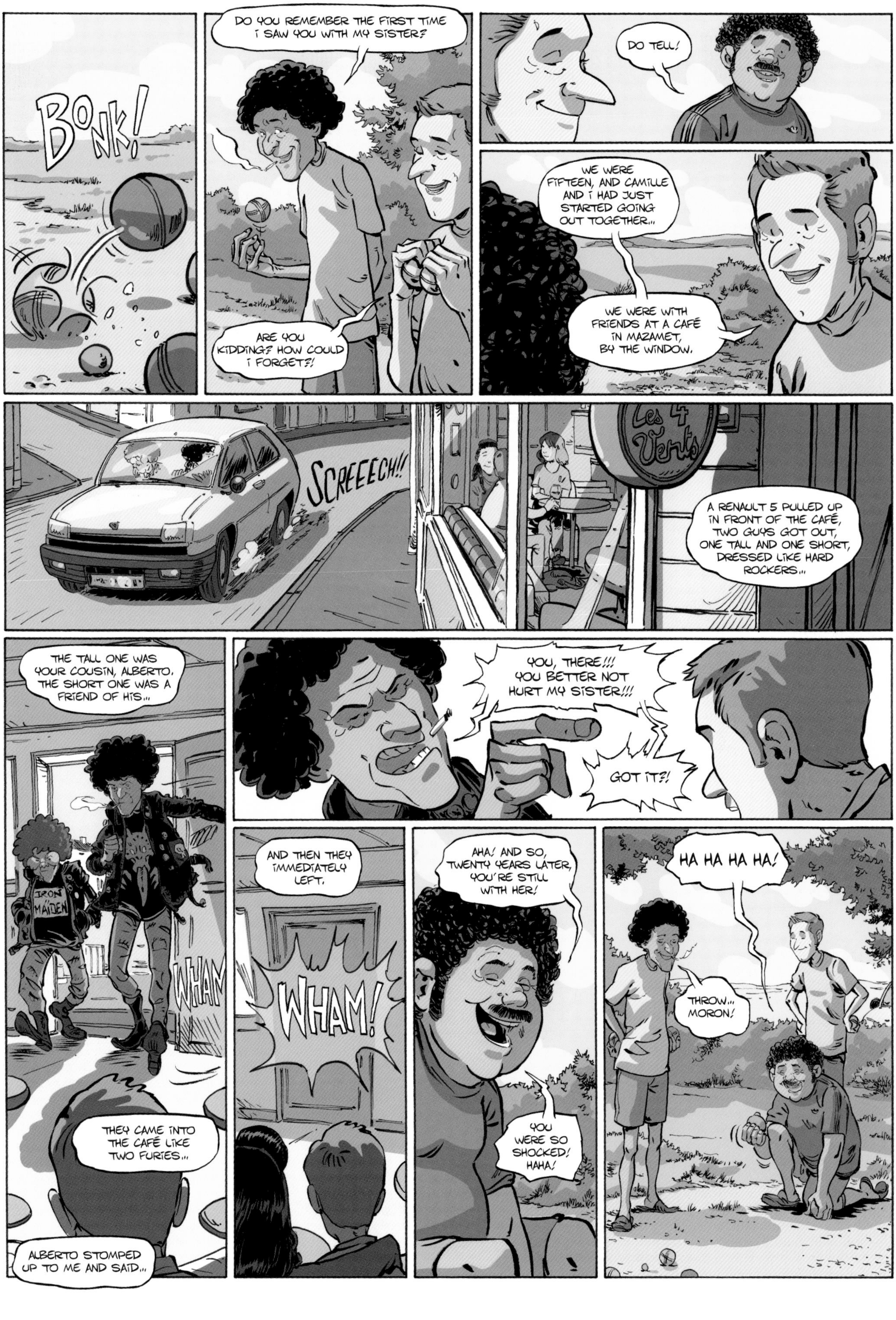

BONK!
DO YOU REMEMBER THE FIRST TIME I SAW YOU WITH MY SISTER?
ARE YOU KIDDING? HOW COULD I FORGET?!
DO TELL!
WE WERE FIFTEEN, AND CAMILLE AND I HAD JUST STARTED GOING OUT TOGETHER...
WE WERE WITH FRIENDS AT A CAFÉ IN MAZAMET, BY THE WINDOW.
SCREEECH!!
Les 4 Vents
A RENAULT 5 PULLED UP IN FRONT OF THE CAFÉ, TWO GUYS GOT OUT, ONE TALL AND ONE SHORT, DRESSED LIKE HARD ROCKERS...
THE TALL ONE WAS YOUR COUSIN, ALBERTO. THE SHORT ONE WAS A FRIEND OF HIS...
IRON MAIDEN
WHAM
THEY CAME INTO THE CAFÉ LIKE TWO FURIES...
ALBERTO STOMPED UP TO ME AND SAID...
YOU, THERE!!! YOU BETTER NOT HURT MY SISTER!!!
GOT IT?!
AND THEN THEY IMMEDIATELY LEFT.
WHAM!
AHA! AND SO, TWENTY YEARS LATER, YOU'RE STILL WITH HER!
YOU WERE SO SHOCKED! HAHA!
HA HA HA HA!
THROW... MORON!

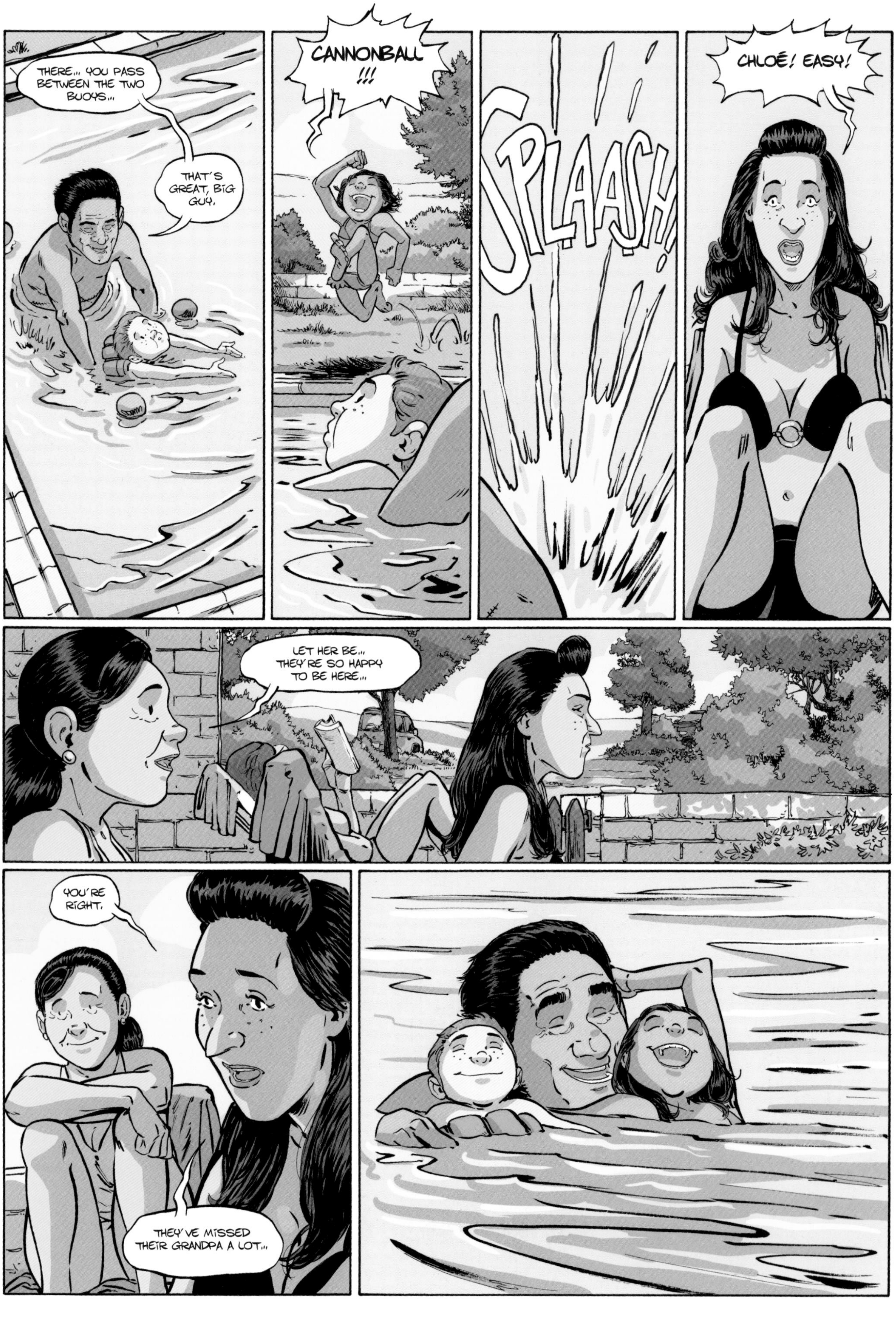
THERE... YOU PASS BETWEEN THE TWO BUOYS...
THAT'S GREAT, BIG GUY.
CANNONBALL !!!
SPLAASH!
CHLOÉ! EASY!
LET HER BE... THEY'RE SO HAPPY TO BE HERE...
YOU'RE RIGHT.
THEY'VE MISSED THEIR GRANDPA A LOT...

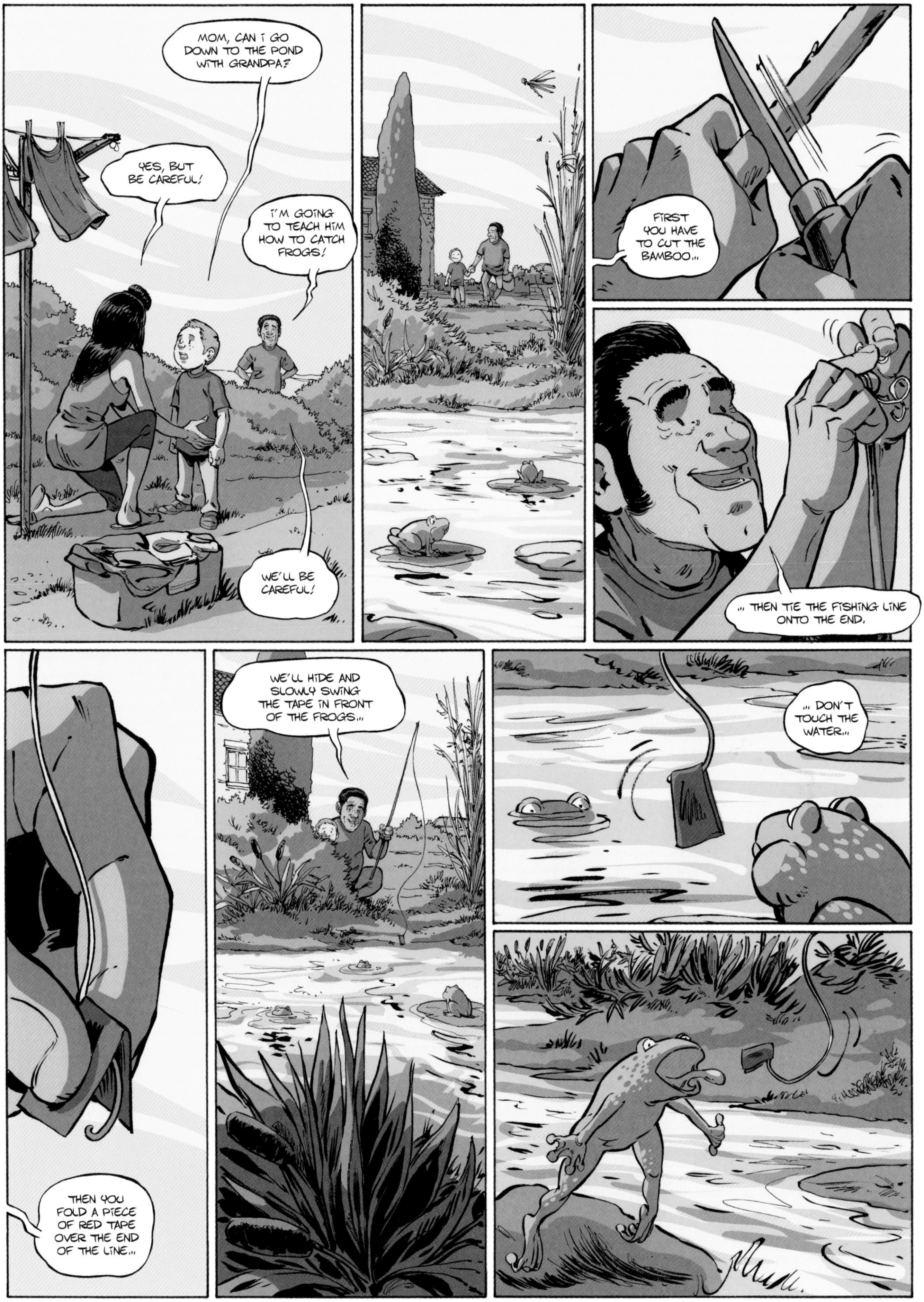

MOM, CAN I GO DOWN TO THE POND WITH GRANDPA?
YES, BUT BE CAREFUL!
I'M GOING TO TEACH HIM HOW TO CATCH FROGS!
WE'LL BE CAREFUL!
FIRST YOU HAVE TO CUT THE BAMBOO...
... THEN TIE THE FISHING LINE ONTO THE END.
THEN YOU FOLD A PIECE OF RED TAPE OVER THE END OF THE LINE...
WE'LL HIDE AND SLOWLY SWING THE TAPE IN FRONT OF THE FROGS...
... DON'T TOUCH THE WATER...

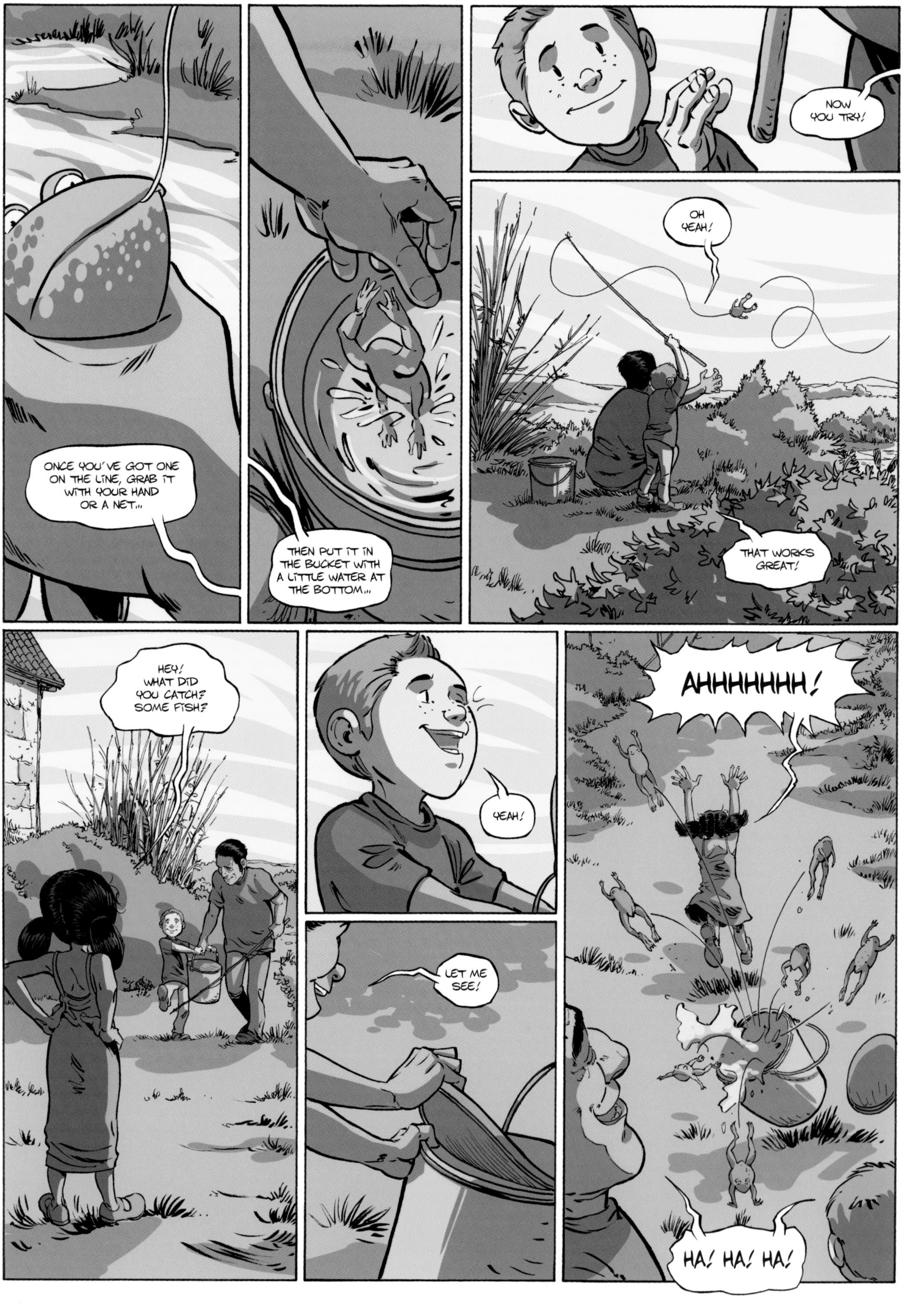

ONCE YOU'VE GOT ONE ON THE LINE, GRAB IT WITH YOUR HAND OR A NET...
THEN PUT IT IN THE BUCKET WITH A LITTLE WATER AT THE BOTTOM...
NOW YOU TRY!
OH YEAH!
THAT WORKS GREAT!
HEY! WHAT DID YOU CATCH? SOME FISH?
YEAH!
LET ME SEE!
AHHHHHHH!
HA! HA! HA!

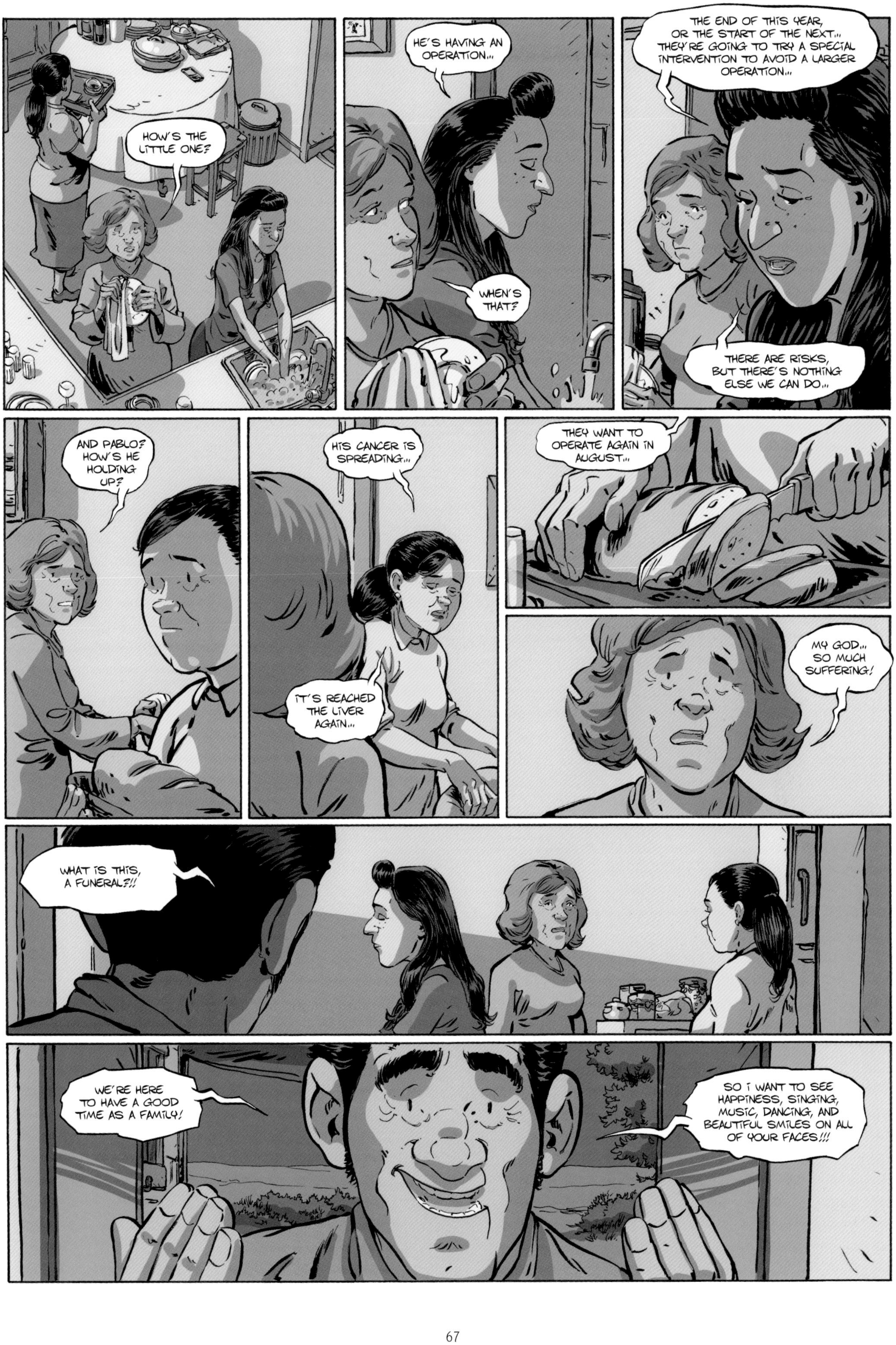
HOW'S THE LITTLE ONE?
HE'S HAVING AN OPERATION...
WHEN'S THAT?
THE END OF THIS YEAR, OR THE START OF THE NEXT... THEY'RE GOING TO TRY A SPECIAL INTERVENTION TO AVOID A LARGER OPERATION...
THERE ARE RISKS, BUT THERE'S NOTHING ELSE WE CAN DO...
AND PABLO? HOW'S HE HOLDING UP?
HIS CANCER IS SPREADING...
IT'S REACHED THE LIVER AGAIN...
THEY WANT TO OPERATE AGAIN IN AUGUST...
MY GOD... SO MUCH SUFFERING!
WHAT IS THIS, A FUNERAL?!!
WE'RE HERE TO HAVE A GOOD TIME AS A FAMILY!
SO I WANT TO SEE HAPPINESS, SINGING, MUSIC, DANCING, AND BEAUTIFUL SMILES ON ALL OF YOUR FACES!!!

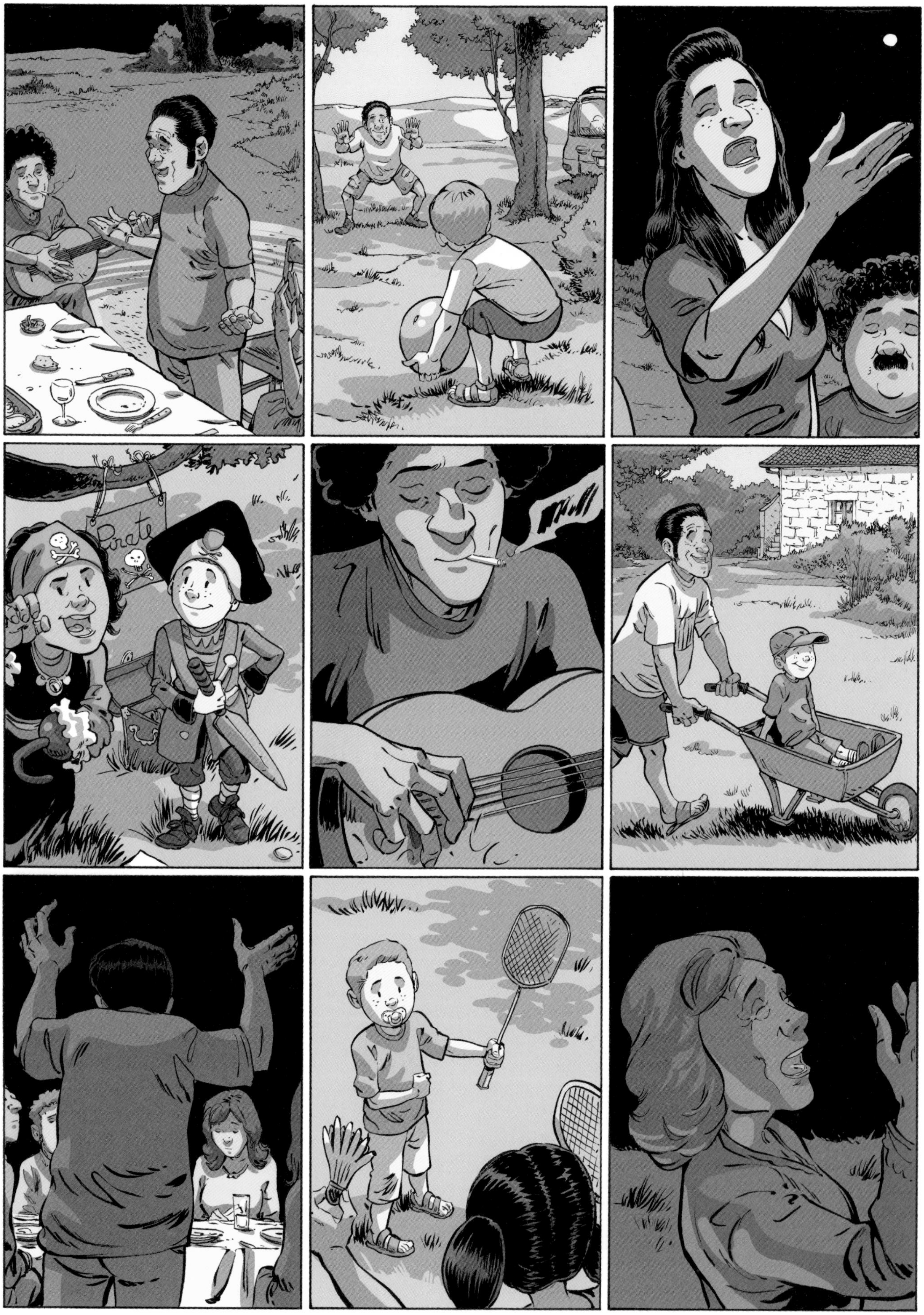
Pirate

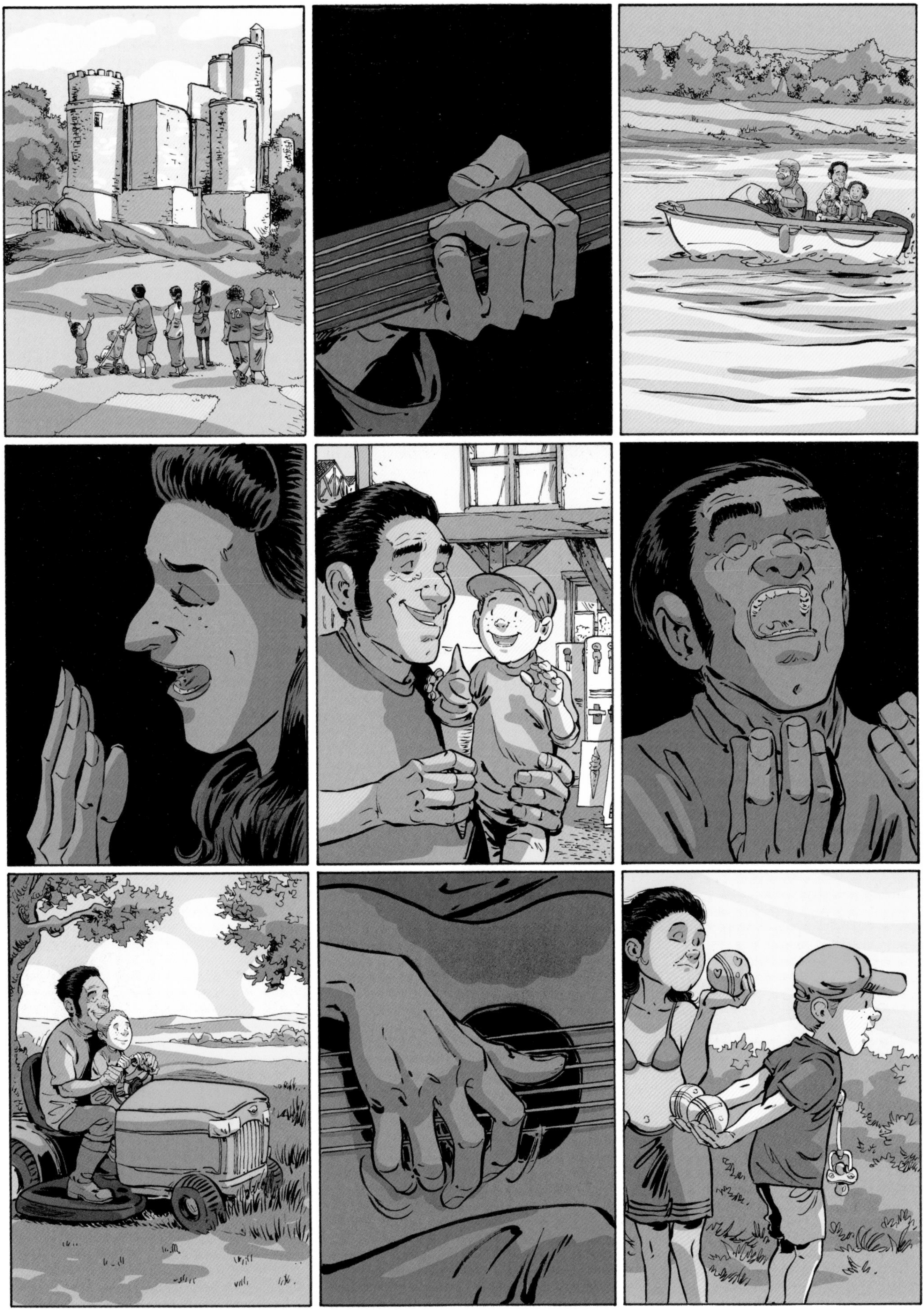

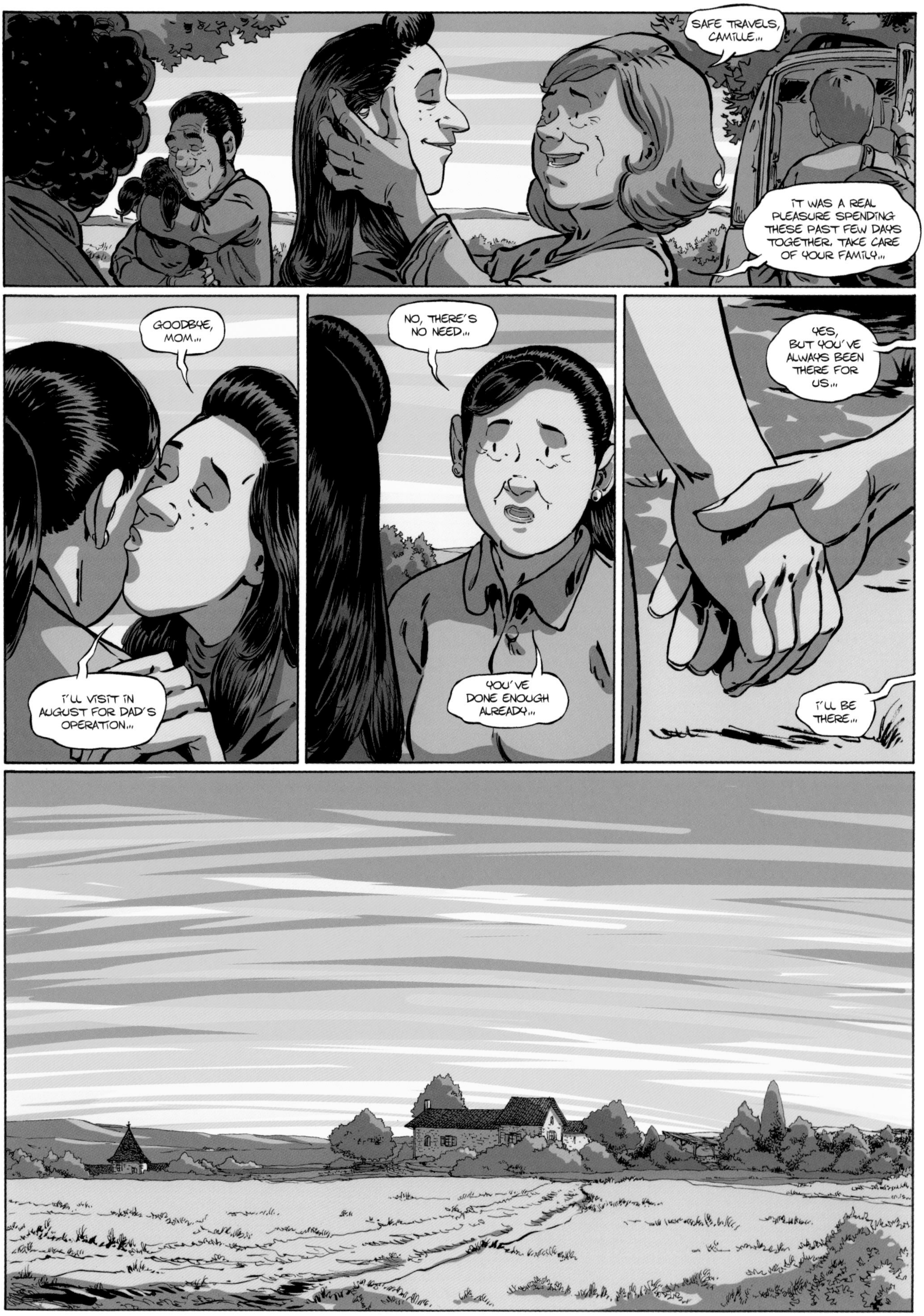
SAFE TRAVELS, CAMILLE...
IT WAS A REAL PLEASURE SPENDING THESE PAST FEW DAYS TOGETHER. TAKE CARE OF YOUR FAMILY...
GOODBYE, MOM...
I'LL VISIT IN AUGUST FOR DAD'S OPERATION...
NO, THERE'S NO NEED...
YOU'VE DONE ENOUGH ALREADY...
YES, BUT YOU'VE ALWAYS BEEN THERE FOR US...
I'LL BE THERE...

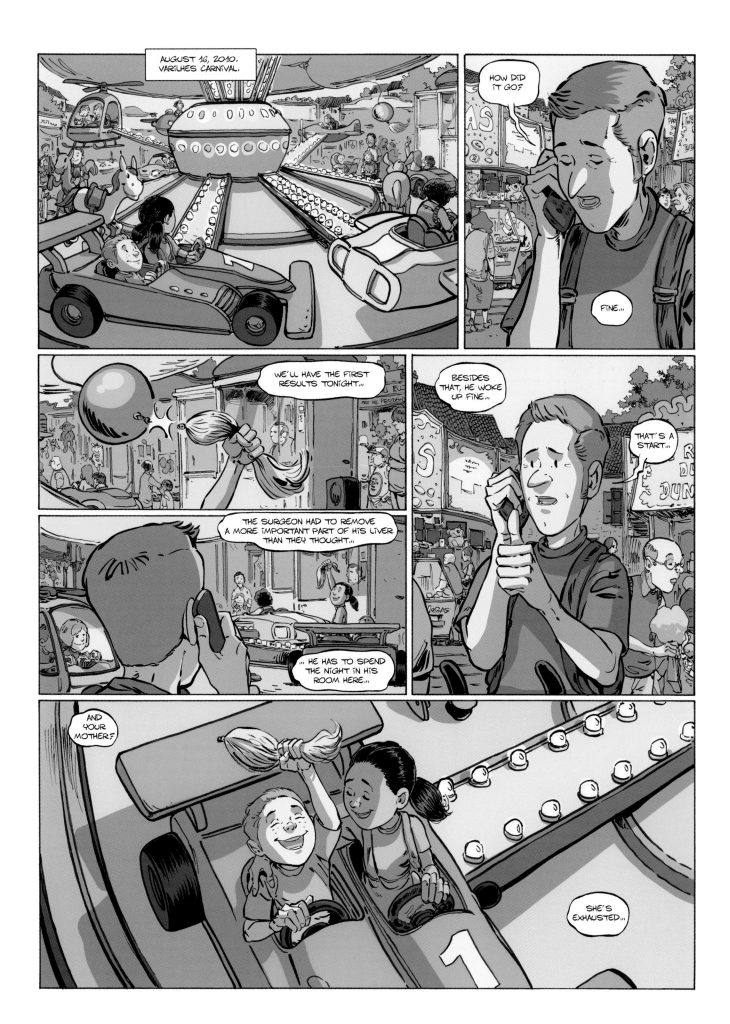

AUGUST 16, 2010.
VARILHES CARNIVAL.

HOW DID IT GO?

FINE...

WE'LL HAVE THE FIRST RESULTS TONIGHT...

THE SURGEON HAD TO REMOVE A MORE IMPORTANT PART OF HIS LIVER THAN THEY THOUGHT...

... HE HAS TO SPEND THE NIGHT IN HIS ROOM HERE...

BESIDES THAT, HE WOKE UP FINE...

THAT'S A START...

AND YOUR MOTHER?

SHE'S EXHAUSTED...

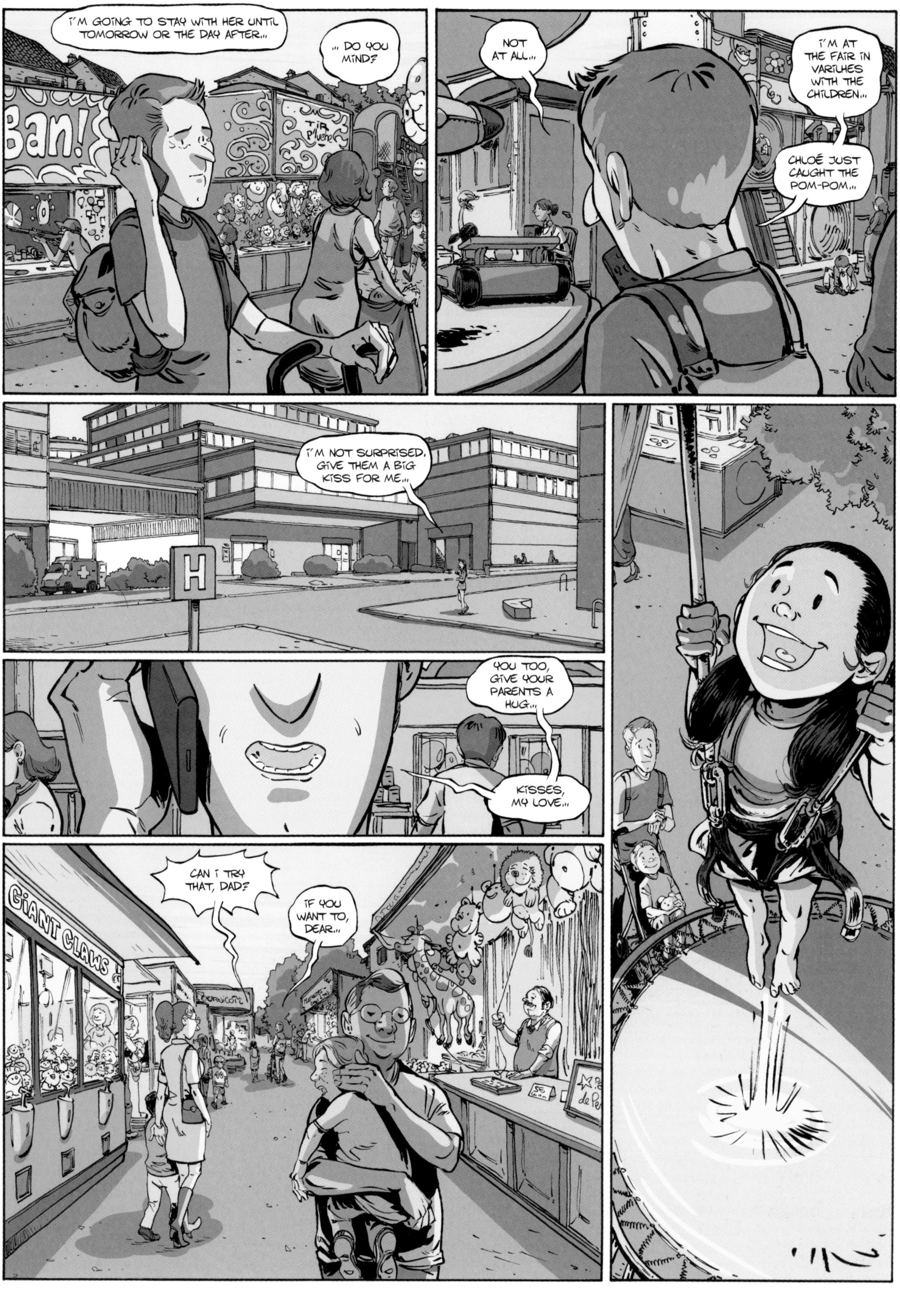
I'M GOING TO STAY WITH HER UNTIL TOMORROW OR THE DAY AFTER...
... DO YOU MIND?
Ban!
TIR
NOT AT ALL...
I'M AT THE FAIR IN VARILHES WITH THE CHILDREN...
CHLOÉ JUST CAUGHT THE POM-POM...
I'M NOT SURPRISED, GIVE THEM A BIG KISS FOR ME...
H
YOU TOO, GIVE YOUR PARENTS A HUG...
KISSES, MY LOVE...
CAN I TRY THAT, DAD?
IF YOU WANT TO, DEAR...
GIANT CLAWS

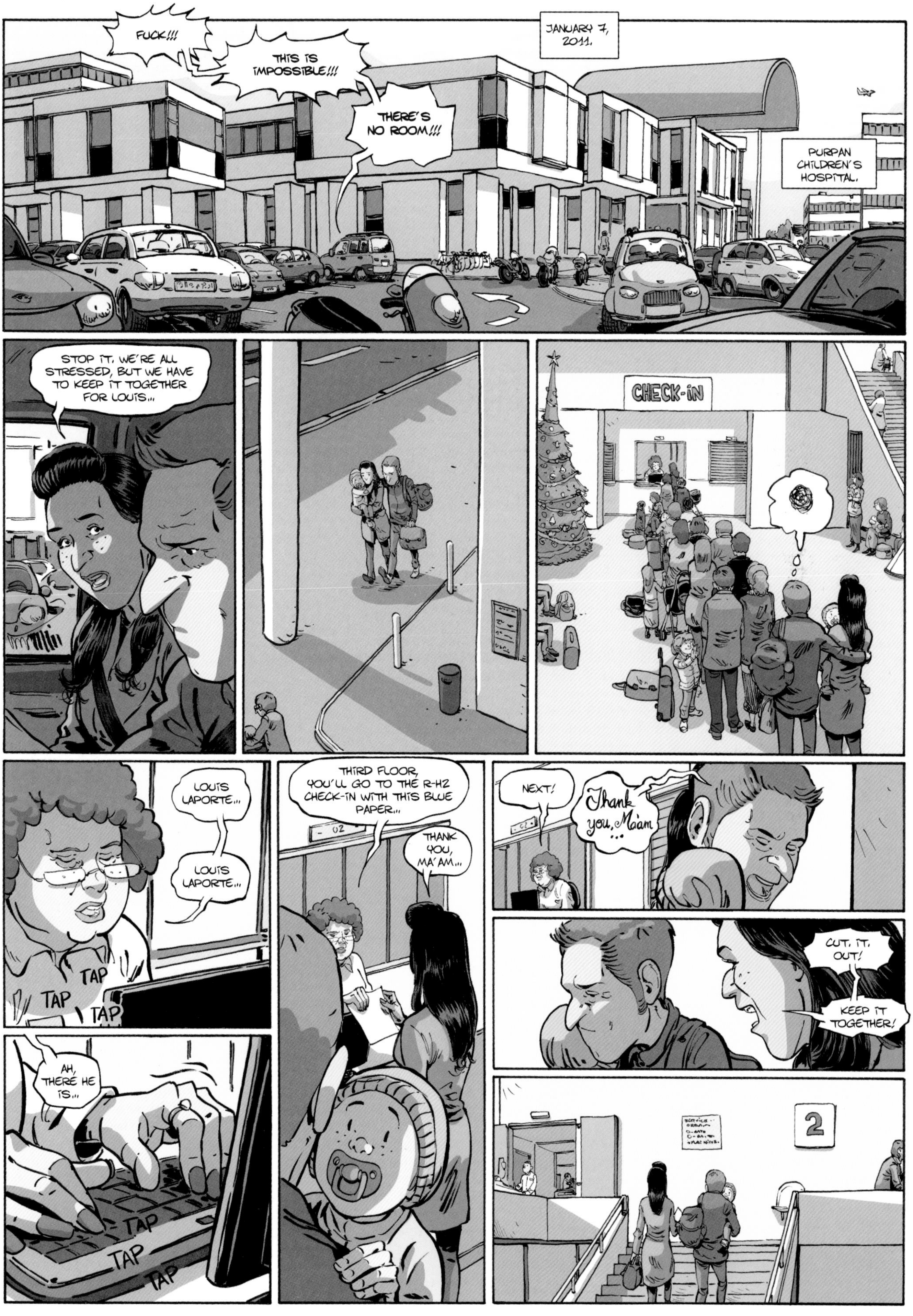

JANUARY 7, 2011.
FUCK!!!
THIS IS IMPOSSIBLE!!!
THERE'S NO ROOM!!!
PURPAN CHILDREN'S HOSPITAL.
STOP IT. WE'RE ALL STRESSED, BUT WE HAVE TO KEEP IT TOGETHER FOR LOUIS...
CHECK-IN
LOUIS LAPORTE...
LOUIS LAPORTE...
TAP
TAP
TAP
THIRD FLOOR, YOU'LL GO TO THE R-H2 CHECK-IN WITH THIS BLUE PAPER...
THANK YOU, MA'AM...
NEXT!
Thank you, Ma'am...
CUT. IT. OUT!
KEEP IT TOGETHER!
AH, THERE HE IS...
TAP
TAP
TAP
2

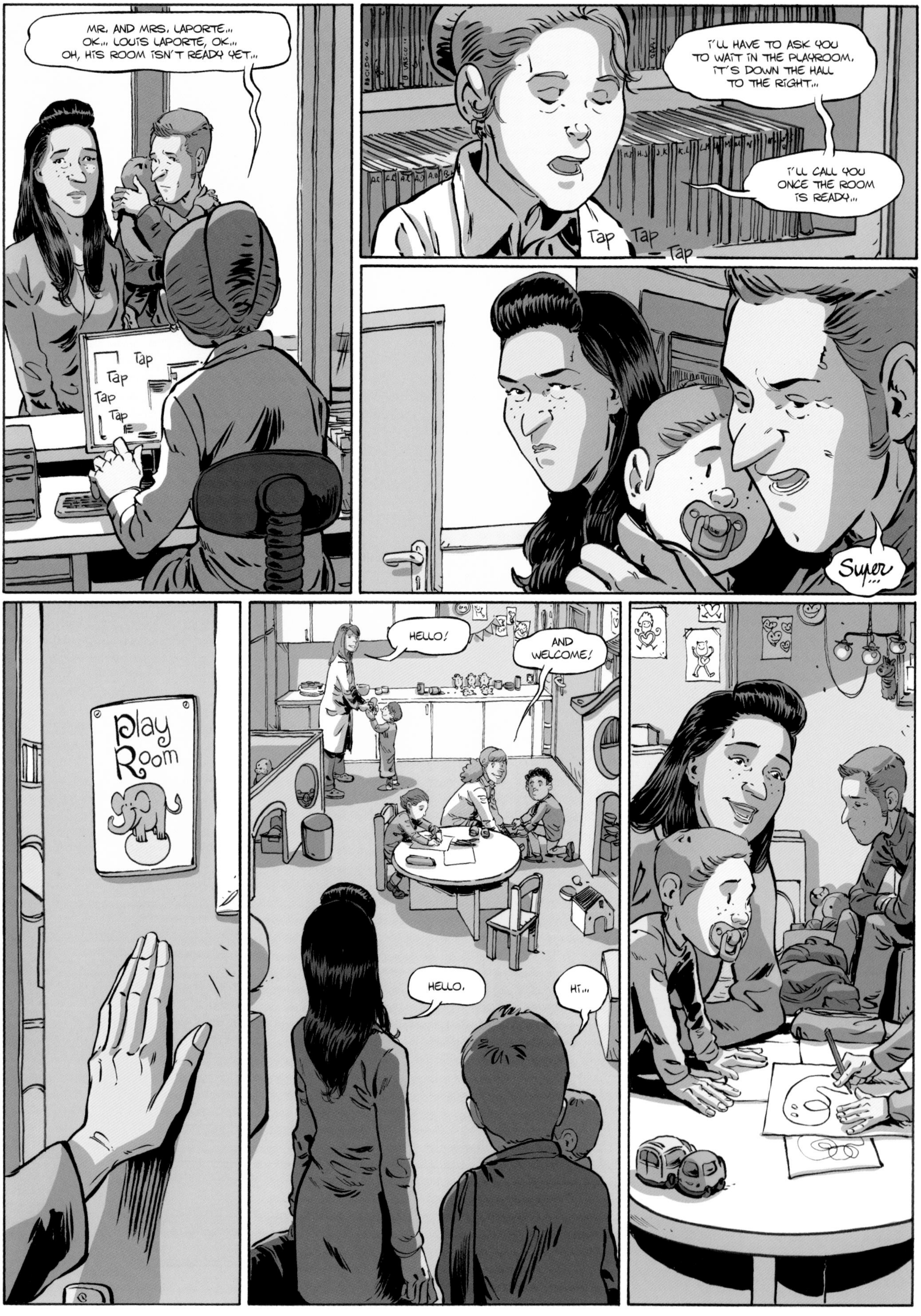
MR. AND MRS. LAPORTE... OK... LOUIS LAPORTE, OK... OH, HIS ROOM ISN'T READY YET...
Tap
Tap
Tap
Tap
I'LL HAVE TO ASK YOU TO WAIT IN THE PLAYROOM. IT'S DOWN THE HALL TO THE RIGHT...
I'LL CALL YOU ONCE THE ROOM IS READY...
Tap
Tap
Tap
Super...
Play Room
HELLO!
AND WELCOME!
HELLO.
HI...

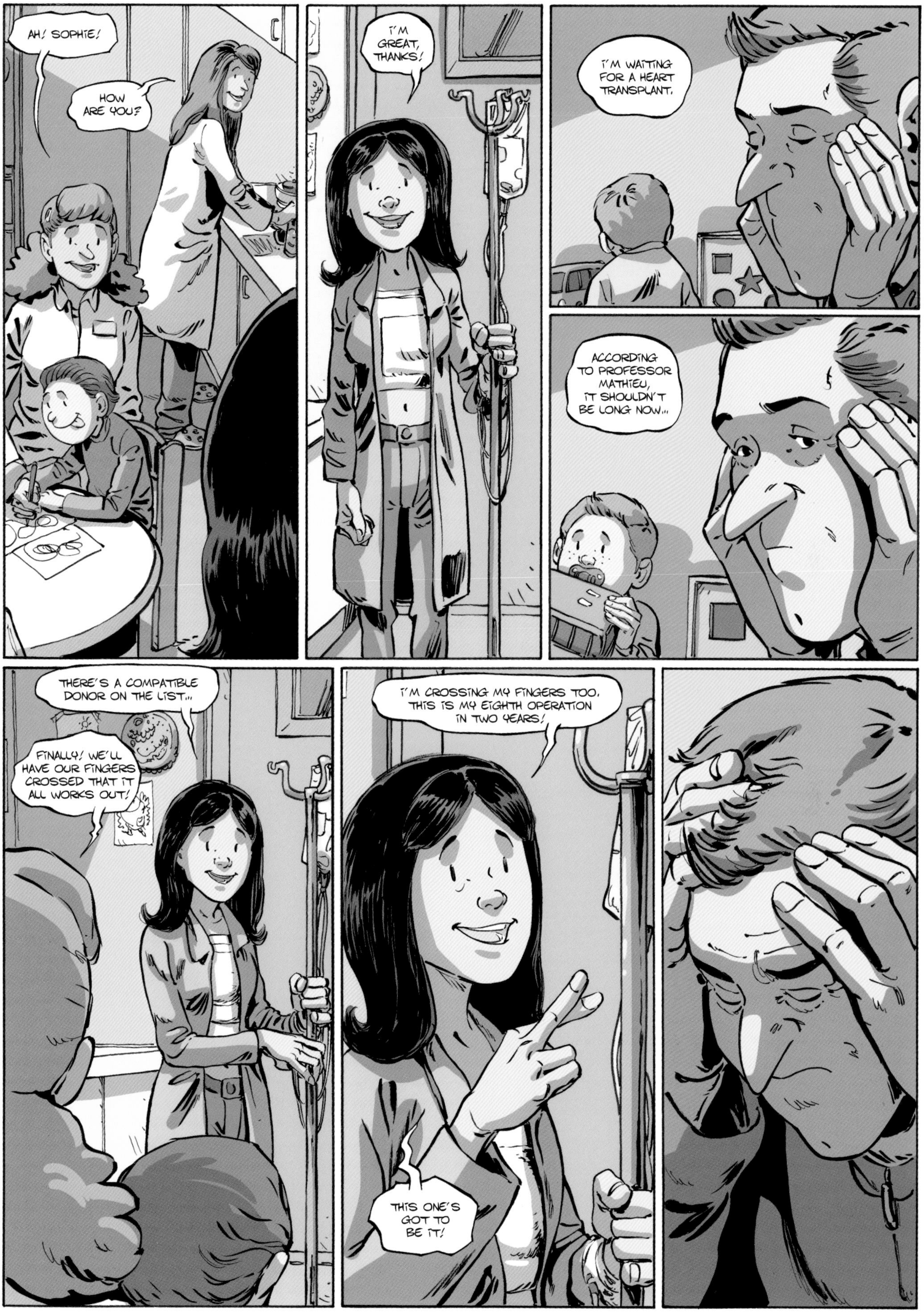
AH! SOPHIE!
HOW ARE YOU?
I'M GREAT, THANKS!
I'M WAITING FOR A HEART TRANSPLANT.
ACCORDING TO PROFESSOR MATHIEU, IT SHOULDN'T BE LONG NOW...
THERE'S A COMPATIBLE DONOR ON THE LIST...
FINALLY! WE'LL HAVE OUR FINGERS CROSSED THAT IT ALL WORKS OUT!
I'M CROSSING MY FINGERS TOO. THIS IS MY EIGHTH OPERATION IN TWO YEARS!
THIS ONE'S GOT TO BE IT!

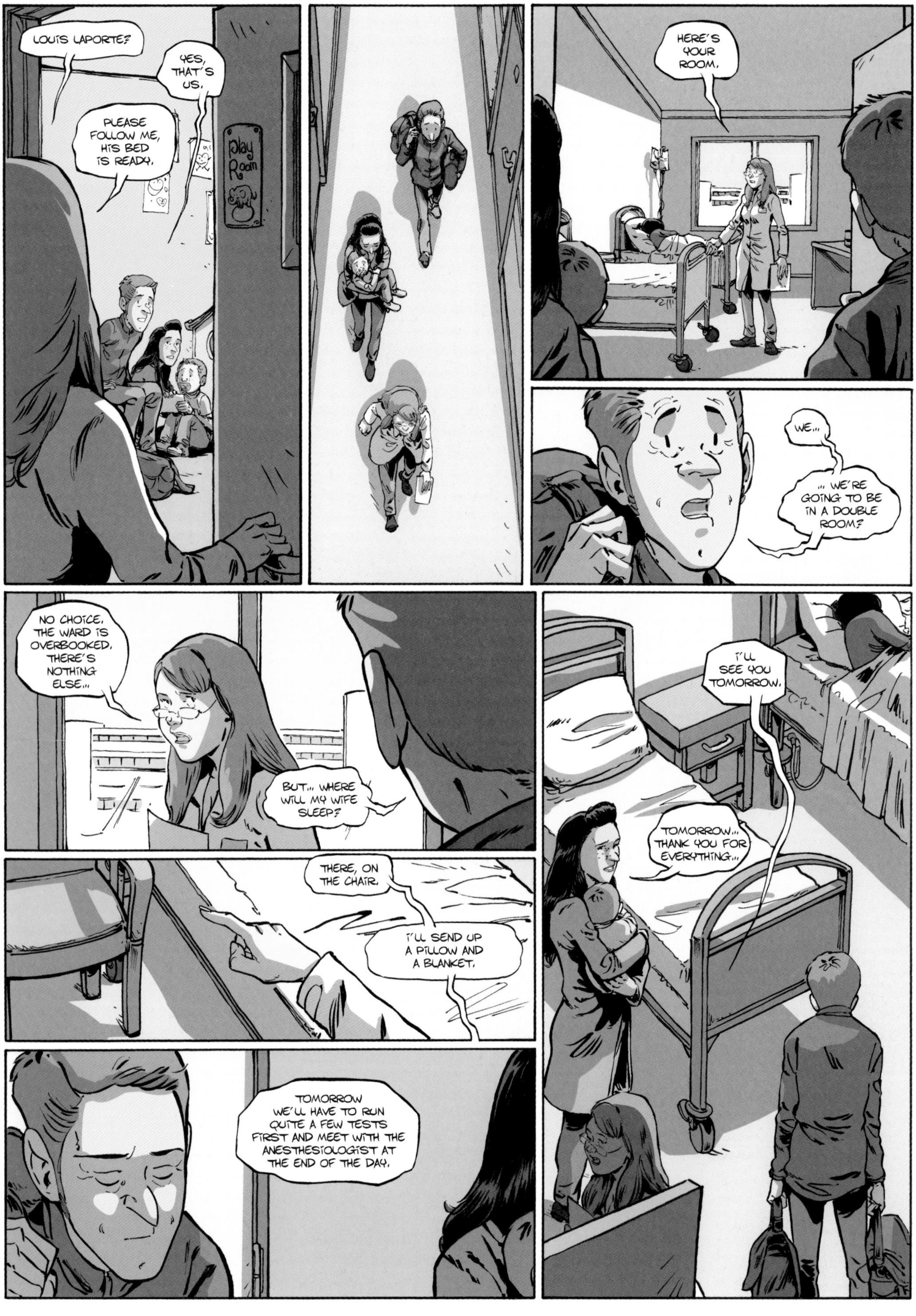
LOUIS LAPORTE?
YES, THAT'S US.
PLEASE FOLLOW ME, HIS BED IS READY.
Play Room
HERE'S YOUR ROOM.
WE...
... WE'RE GOING TO BE IN A DOUBLE ROOM?
NO CHOICE. THE WARD IS OVERBOOKED. THERE'S NOTHING ELSE...
BUT... WHERE WILL MY WIFE SLEEP?
THERE, ON THE CHAIR.
I'LL SEND UP A PILLOW AND A BLANKET.
TOMORROW WE'LL HAVE TO RUN QUITE A FEW TESTS FIRST AND MEET WITH THE ANESTHESIOLOGIST AT THE END OF THE DAY.
I'LL SEE YOU TOMORROW.
TOMORROW... THANK YOU FOR EVERYTHING...

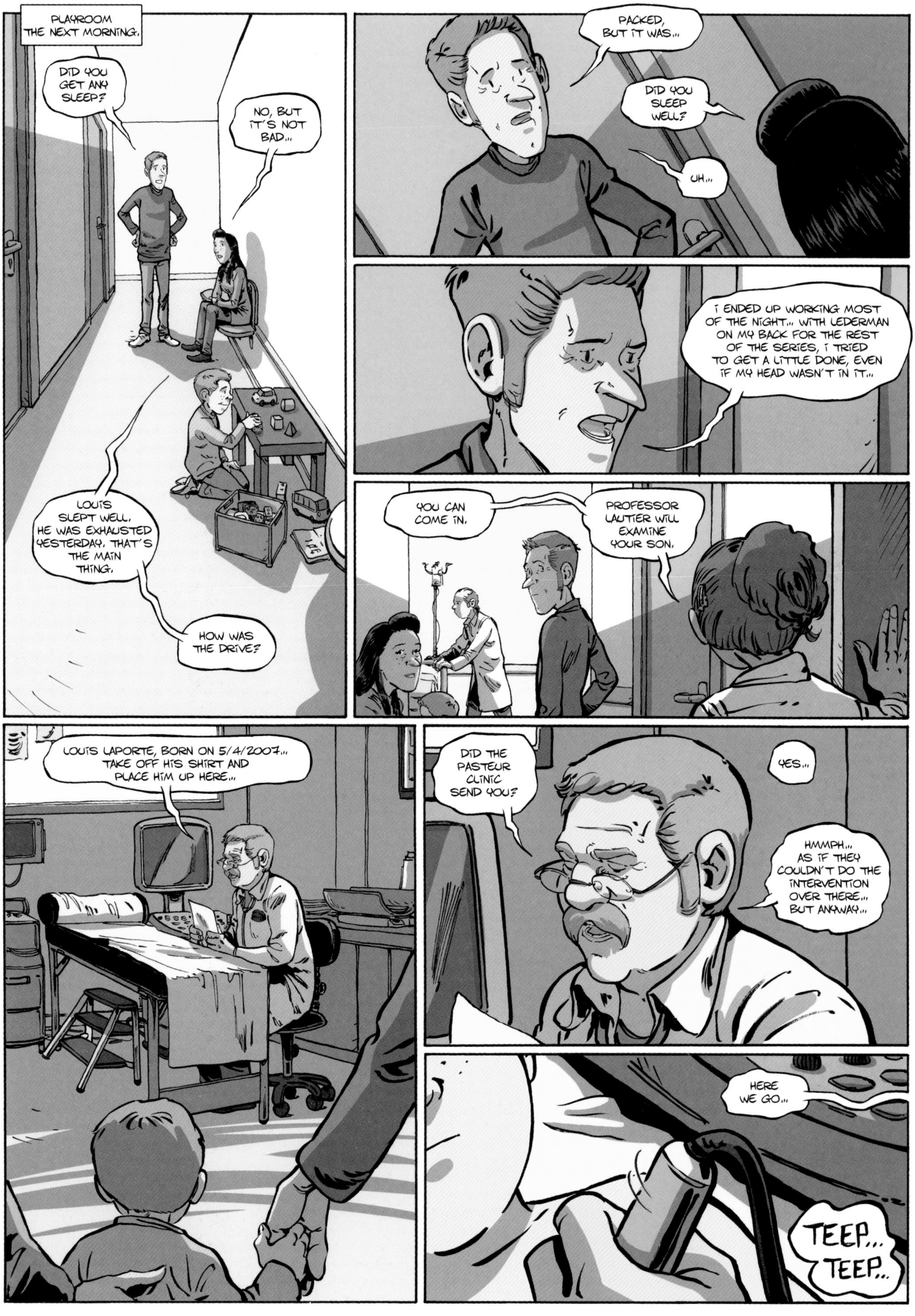
PLAYROOM THE NEXT MORNING.
DID YOU GET ANY SLEEP?
NO, BUT IT'S NOT BAD...
LOUIS SLEPT WELL. HE WAS EXHAUSTED YESTERDAY. THAT'S THE MAIN THING.
HOW WAS THE DRIVE?
PACKED, BUT IT WAS...
DID YOU SLEEP WELL?
UH...
I ENDED UP WORKING MOST OF THE NIGHT... WITH LEDERMAN ON MY BACK FOR THE REST OF THE SERIES, I TRIED TO GET A LITTLE DONE, EVEN IF MY HEAD WASN'T IN IT...
YOU CAN COME IN.
PROFESSOR LAUTIER WILL EXAMINE YOUR SON.
LOUIS LAPORTE, BORN ON 5/4/2007... TAKE OFF HIS SHIRT AND PLACE HIM UP HERE...
DID THE PASTEUR CLINIC SEND YOU?
YES...
HMMPH... AS IF THEY COULDN'T DO THE INTERVENTION OVER THERE... BUT ANYWAY...
HERE WE GO...
TEEP... TEEP...

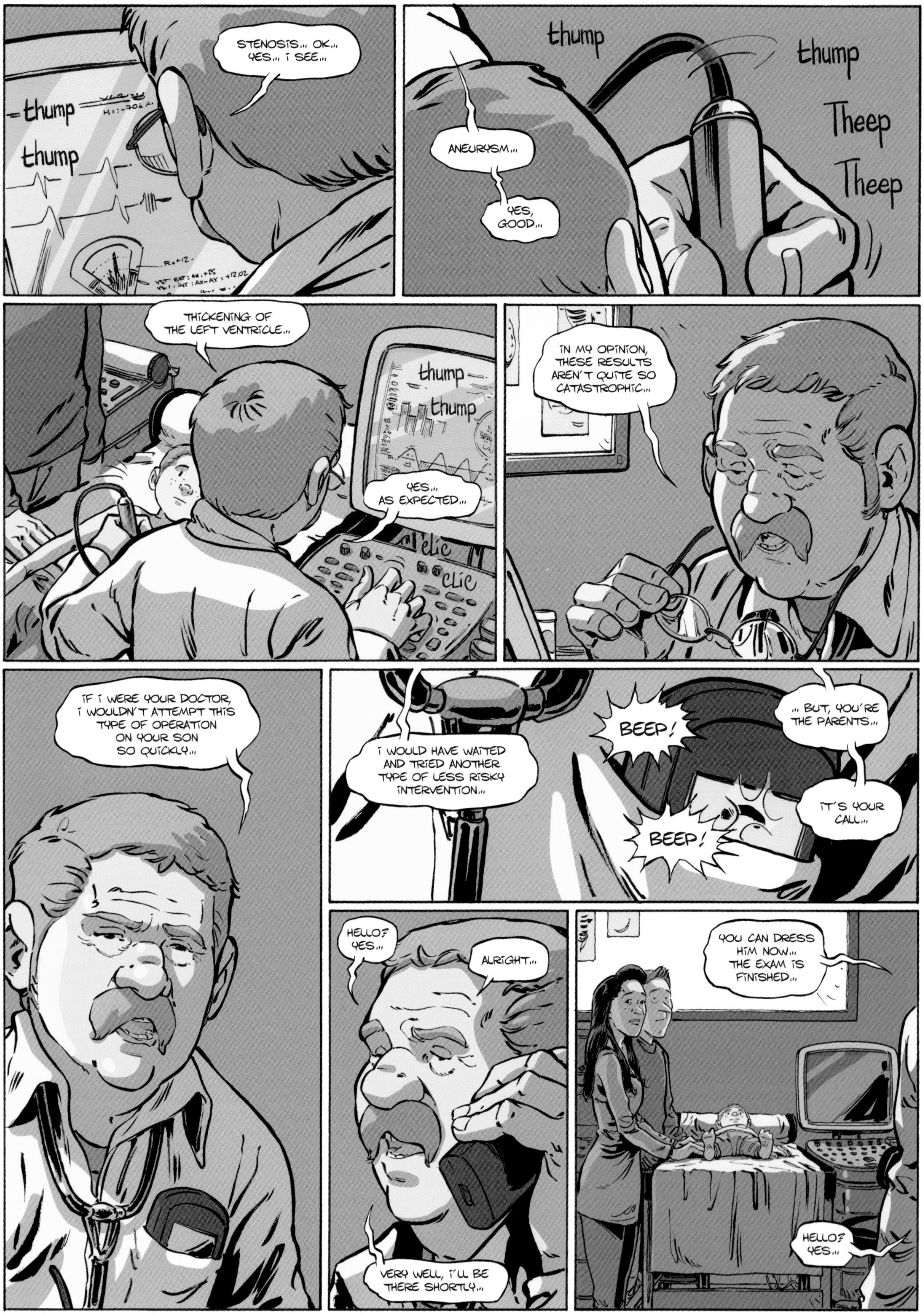

STENOSIS... OK... YES... I SEE...
thump
thump
thump
thump
Theep
Theep
ANEURYSM...
YES, GOOD...
THICKENING OF THE LEFT VENTRICLE...
thump
thump
YES... AS EXPECTED...
clic
clic
IN MY OPINION, THESE RESULTS AREN'T QUITE SO CATASTROPHIC...
IF I WERE YOUR DOCTOR, I WOULDN'T ATTEMPT THIS TYPE OF OPERATION ON YOUR SON SO QUICKLY...
I WOULD HAVE WAITED AND TRIED ANOTHER TYPE OF LESS RISKY INTERVENTION...
BEEP!
BEEP!
... BUT, YOU'RE THE PARENTS...
IT'S YOUR CALL...
HELLO? YES...
ALRIGHT...
VERY WELL, I'LL BE THERE SHORTLY...
YOU CAN DRESS HIM NOW... THE EXAM IS FINISHED...
HELLO? YES...

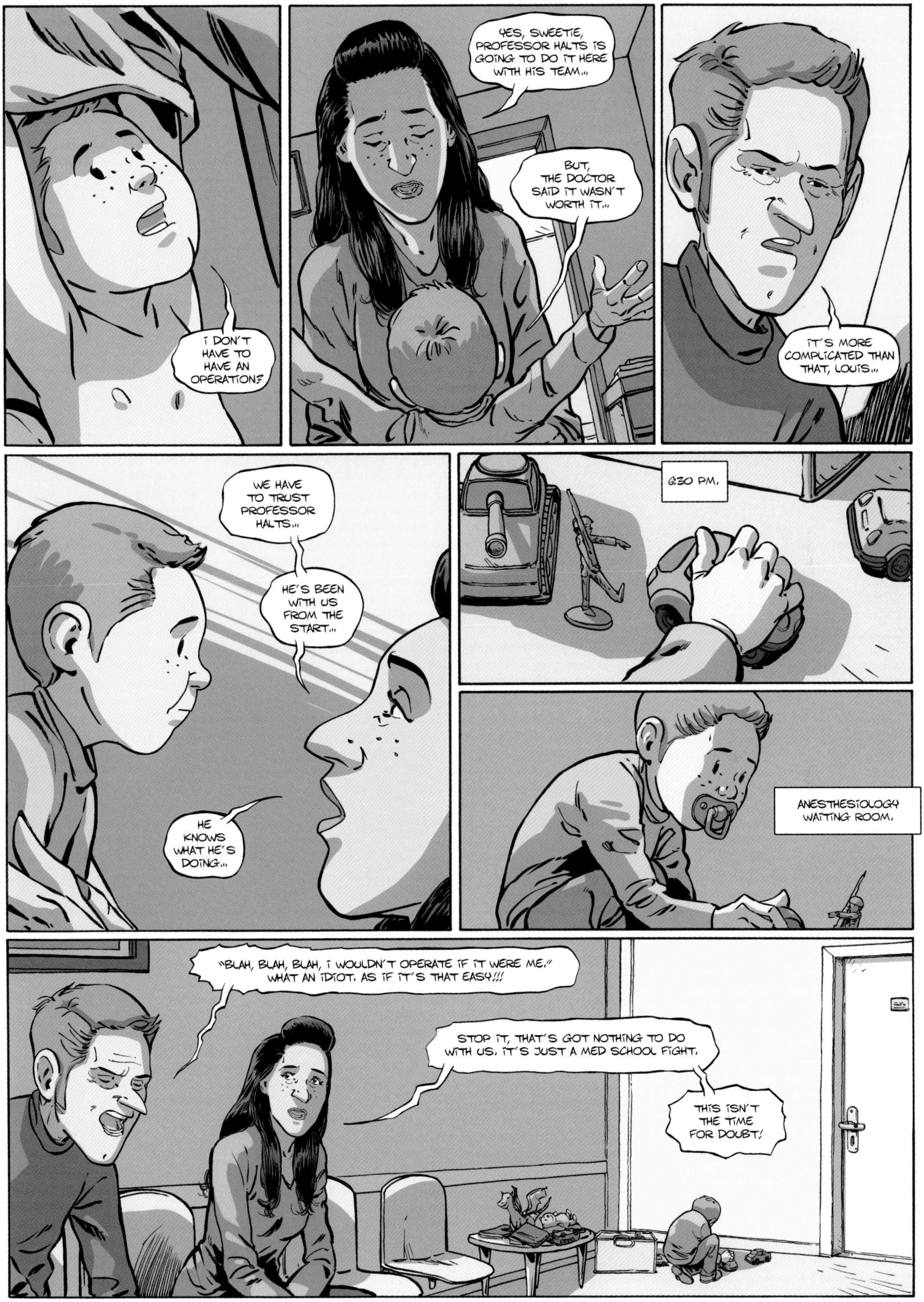
I DON'T HAVE TO HAVE AN OPERATION?
YES, SWEETIE, PROFESSOR HALTS IS GOING TO DO IT HERE WITH HIS TEAM...
BUT, THE DOCTOR SAID IT WASN'T WORTH IT...
IT'S MORE COMPLICATED THAN THAT, LOUIS...
WE HAVE TO TRUST PROFESSOR HALTS...
HE'S BEEN WITH US FROM THE START...
HE KNOWS WHAT HE'S DOING...
6:30 PM.
ANESTHESIOLOGY WAITING ROOM.
"BLAH, BLAH, BLAH, I WOULDN'T OPERATE IF IT WERE ME." WHAT AN IDIOT. AS IF IT'S THAT EASY!!!
STOP IT, THAT'S GOT NOTHING TO DO WITH US. IT'S JUST A MED SCHOOL FIGHT.
THIS ISN'T THE TIME FOR DOUBT!

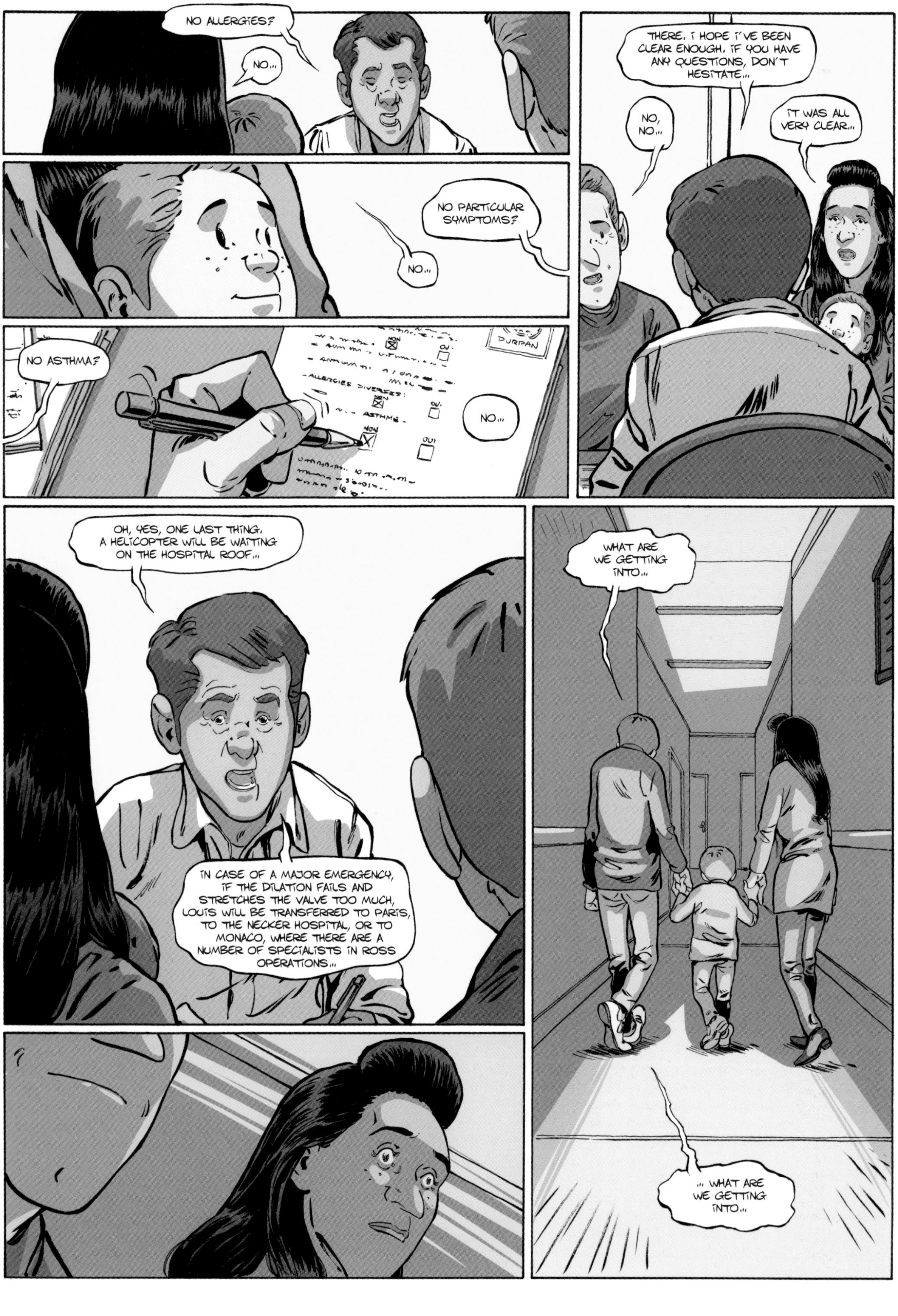
NO ALLERGIES?
NO...
THERE, I HOPE I'VE BEEN CLEAR ENOUGH. IF YOU HAVE ANY QUESTIONS, DON'T HESITATE...
NO, NO...
IT WAS ALL VERY CLEAR...
NO PARTICULAR SYMPTOMS?
NO...
NO ASTHMA?
NON
OUI
ALLERGIES DIVERSES:
ASTHME
PURPAN
NO...
OH, YES, ONE LAST THING. A HELICOPTER WILL BE WAITING ON THE HOSPITAL ROOF...
IN CASE OF A MAJOR EMERGENCY, IF THE DILATION FAILS AND STRETCHES THE VALVE TOO MUCH, LOUIS WILL BE TRANSFERRED TO PARIS, TO THE NECKER HOSPITAL, OR TO MONACO, WHERE THERE ARE A NUMBER OF SPECIALISTS IN ROSS OPERATIONS...
WHAT ARE WE GETTING INTO...
... WHAT ARE WE GETTING INTO...

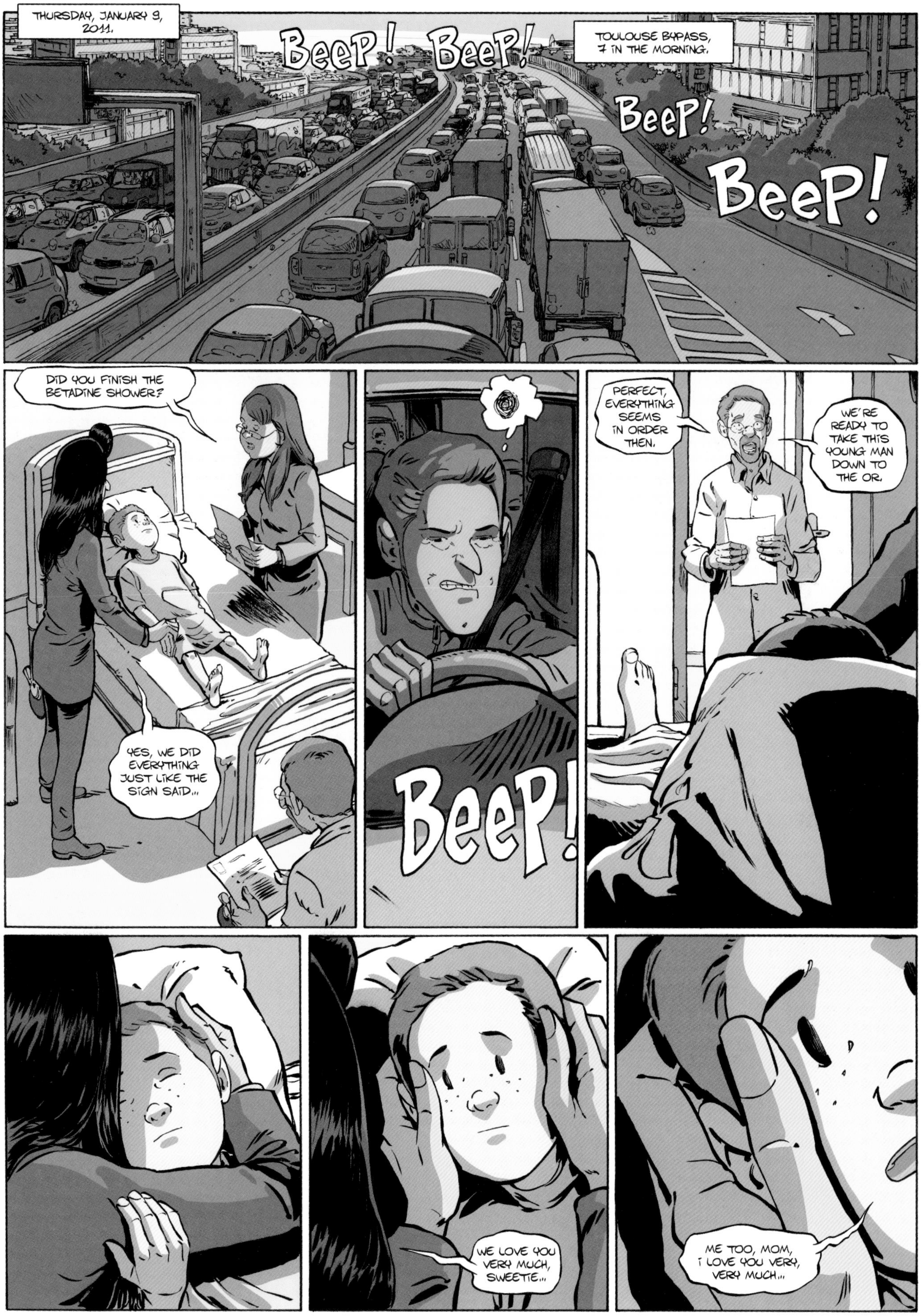
THURSDAY, JANUARY 9, 2011.
BEEP! BEEP!
TOULOUSE BYPASS, 7 IN THE MORNING.
BEEP!
BEEP!
DID YOU FINISH THE BETADINE SHOWER?
YES, WE DID EVERYTHING JUST LIKE THE SIGN SAID...
BEEP!
PERFECT, EVERYTHING SEEMS IN ORDER THEN.
WE'RE READY TO TAKE THIS YOUNG MAN DOWN TO THE OR.
WE LOVE YOU VERY MUCH, SWEETIE...
ME TOO, MOM, I LOVE YOU VERY, VERY MUCH...

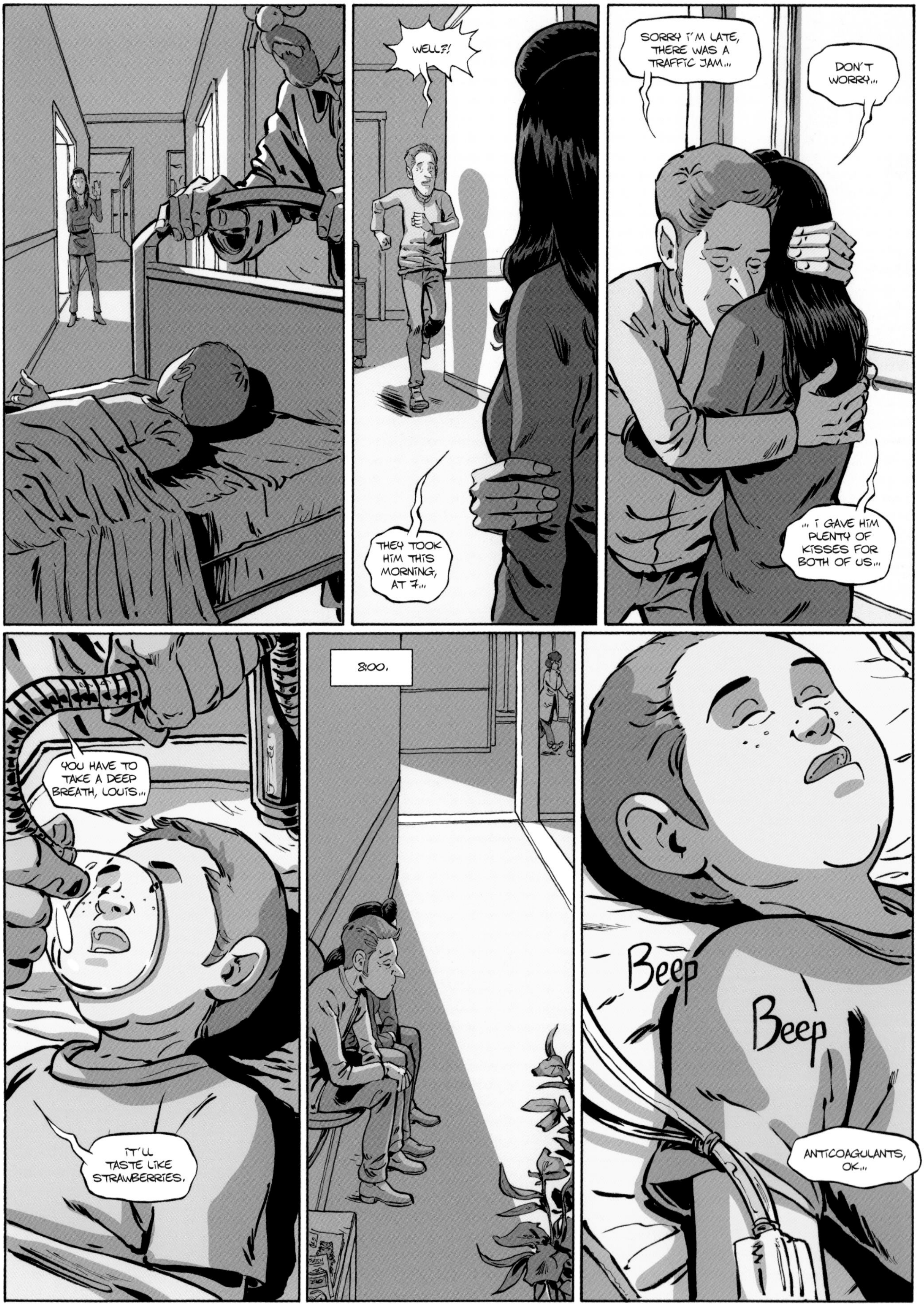
WELL?!
THEY TOOK HIM THIS MORNING, AT 7...
SORRY I'M LATE, THERE WAS A TRAFFIC JAM...
DON'T WORRY...
... I GAVE HIM PLENTY OF KISSES FOR BOTH OF US...
YOU HAVE TO TAKE A DEEP BREATH, LOUIS...
IT'LL TASTE LIKE STRAWBERRIES.
8:00.
Beep
Beep
ANTICOAGULANTS, OK...

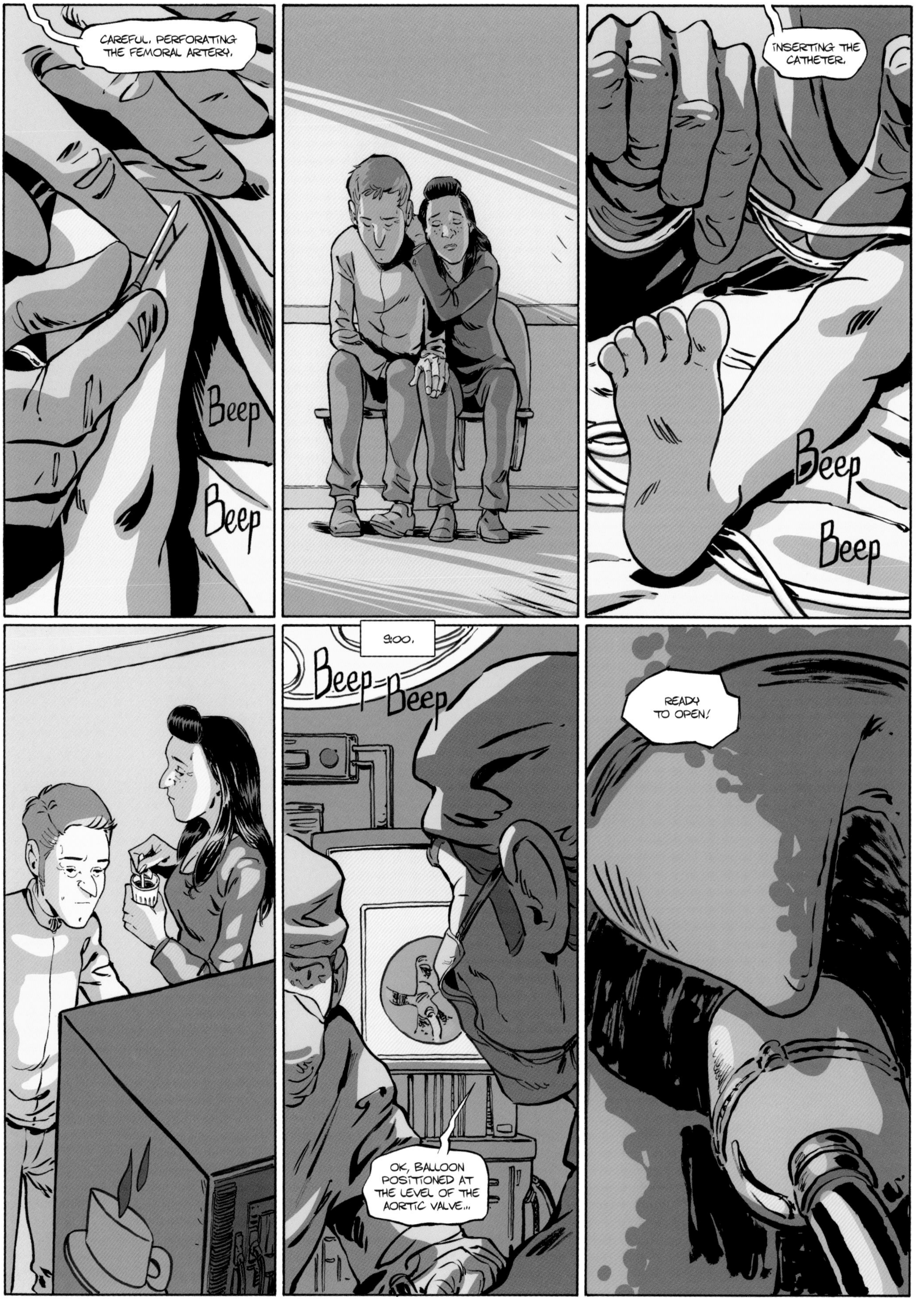
CAREFUL. PERFORATING THE FEMORAL ARTERY.
Beep
Beep
INSERTING THE CATHETER.
Beep
Beep
9:00.
Beep Beep
OK, BALLOON POSITIONED AT THE LEVEL OF THE AORTIC VALVE...
READY TO OPEN!

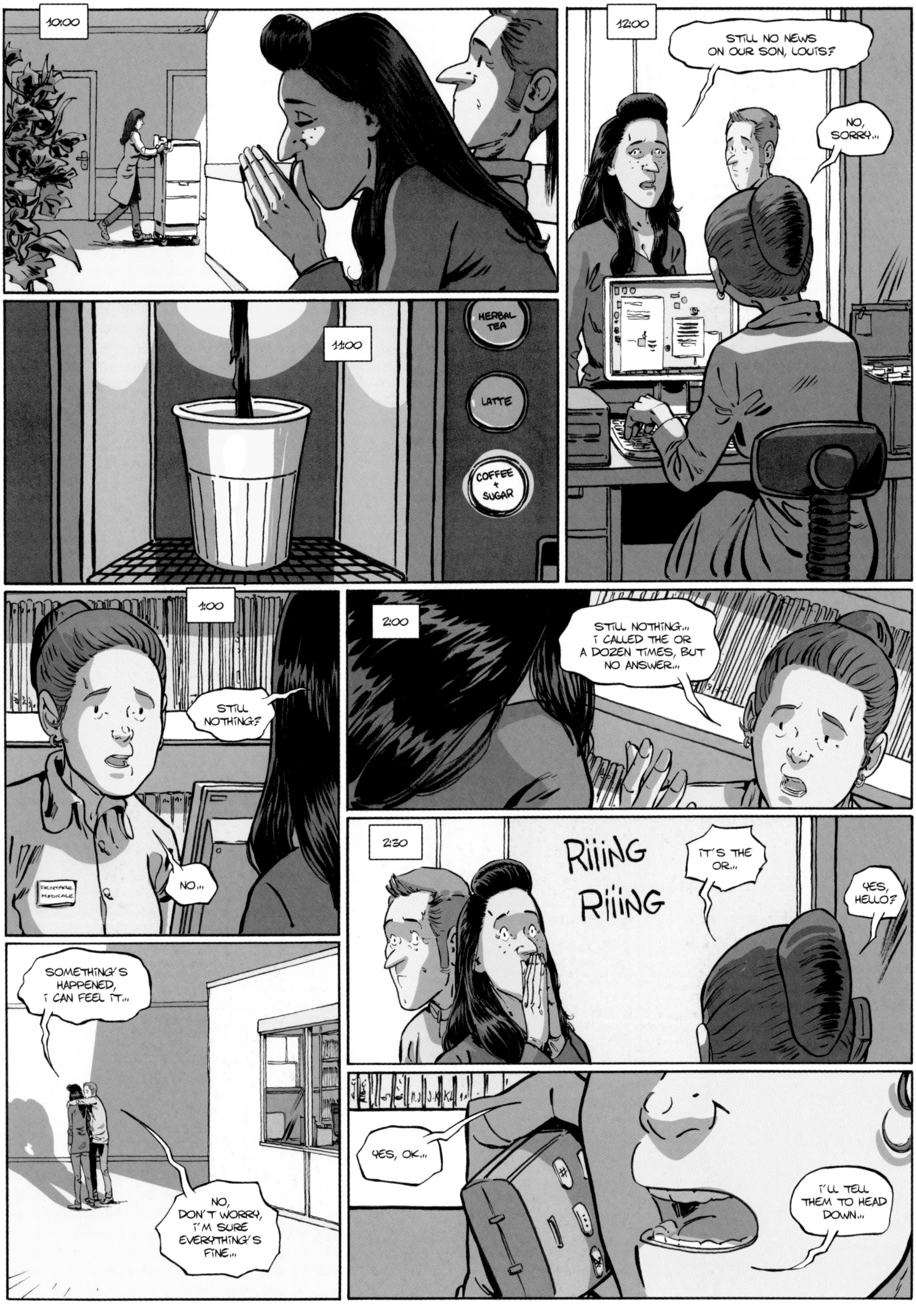
10:00
12:00
STILL NO NEWS ON OUR SON, LOUIS?
NO, SORRY...
11:00
HERBAL TEA
LATTE
COFFEE + SUGAR
1:00
STILL NOTHING?
SECRÉTAIRE MÉDICALE
NO...
2:00
STILL NOTHING... I CALLED THE OR A DOZEN TIMES, BUT NO ANSWER...
2:30
RIIING
RIIING
IT'S THE OR...
YES, HELLO?
SOMETHING'S HAPPENED, I CAN FEEL IT...
NO, DON'T WORRY, I'M SURE EVERYTHING'S FINE...
YES, OK...
I'LL TELL THEM TO HEAD DOWN...

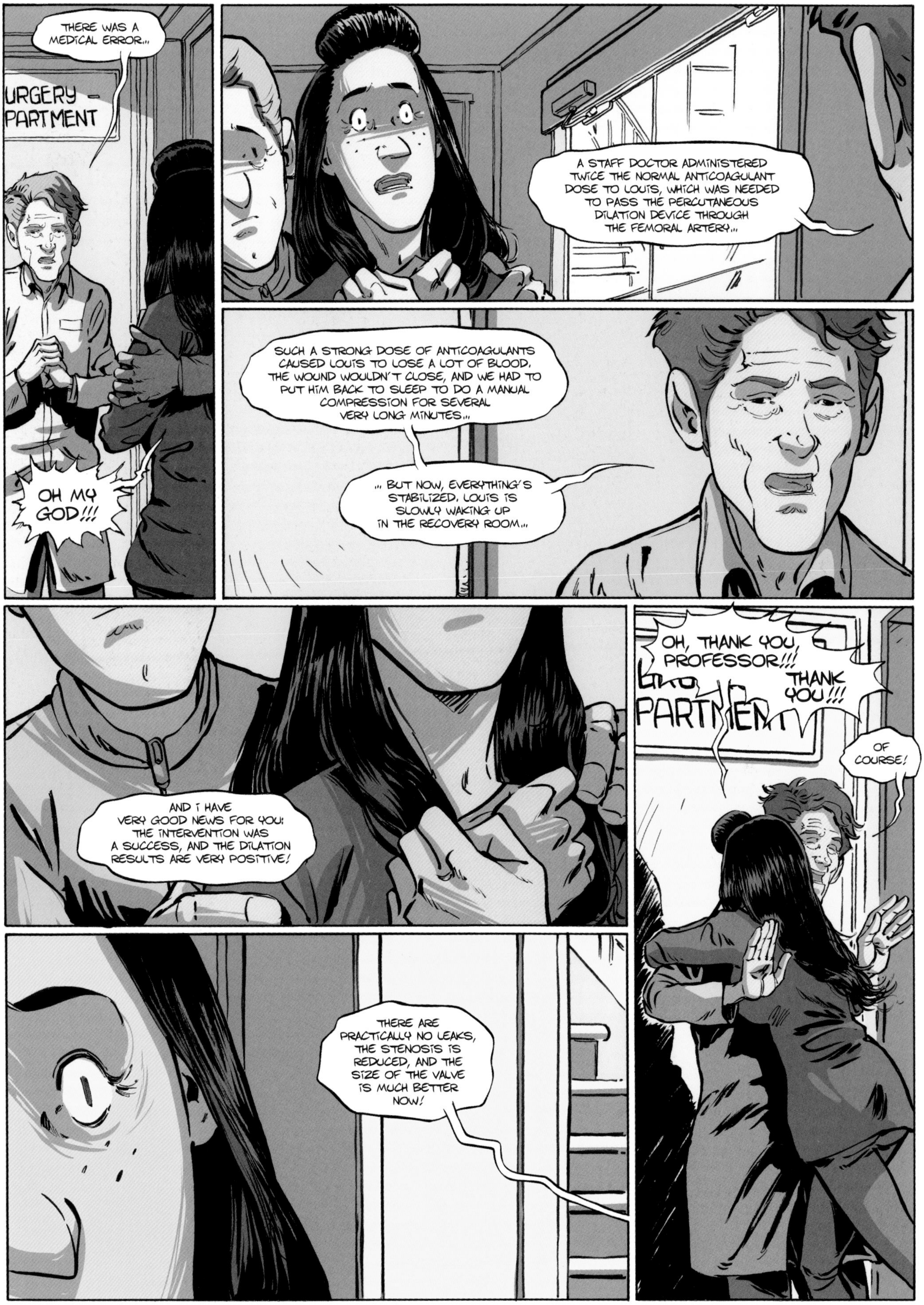
THERE WAS A MEDICAL ERROR...
URGERY - PARTMENT
A STAFF DOCTOR ADMINISTERED TWICE THE NORMAL ANTICOAGULANT DOSE TO LOUIS, WHICH WAS NEEDED TO PASS THE PERCUTANEOUS DILATION DEVICE THROUGH THE FEMORAL ARTERY...
SUCH A STRONG DOSE OF ANTICOAGULANTS CAUSED LOUIS TO LOSE A LOT OF BLOOD, THE WOUND WOULDN'T CLOSE, AND WE HAD TO PUT HIM BACK TO SLEEP TO DO A MANUAL COMPRESSION FOR SEVERAL VERY LONG MINUTES...
... BUT NOW, EVERYTHING'S STABILIZED. LOUIS IS SLOWLY WAKING UP IN THE RECOVERY ROOM...
OH MY GOD!!!
AND I HAVE VERY GOOD NEWS FOR YOU: THE INTERVENTION WAS A SUCCESS, AND THE DILATION RESULTS ARE VERY POSITIVE!
THERE ARE PRACTICALLY NO LEAKS, THE STENOSIS IS REDUCED, AND THE SIZE OF THE VALVE IS MUCH BETTER NOW!
OH, THANK YOU, PROFESSOR!!!
THANK YOU!!!
OF COURSE!

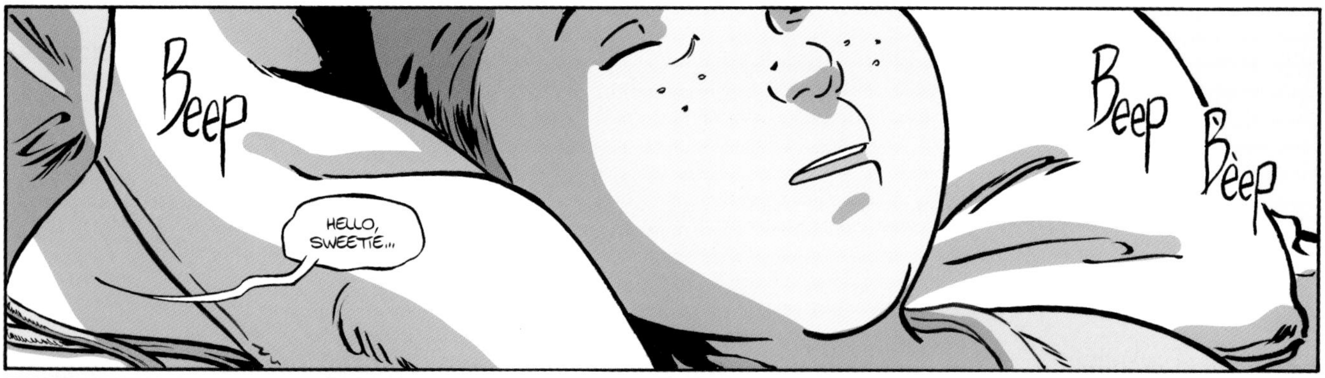
Beep
Hello, sweetie...
Beep
Beep

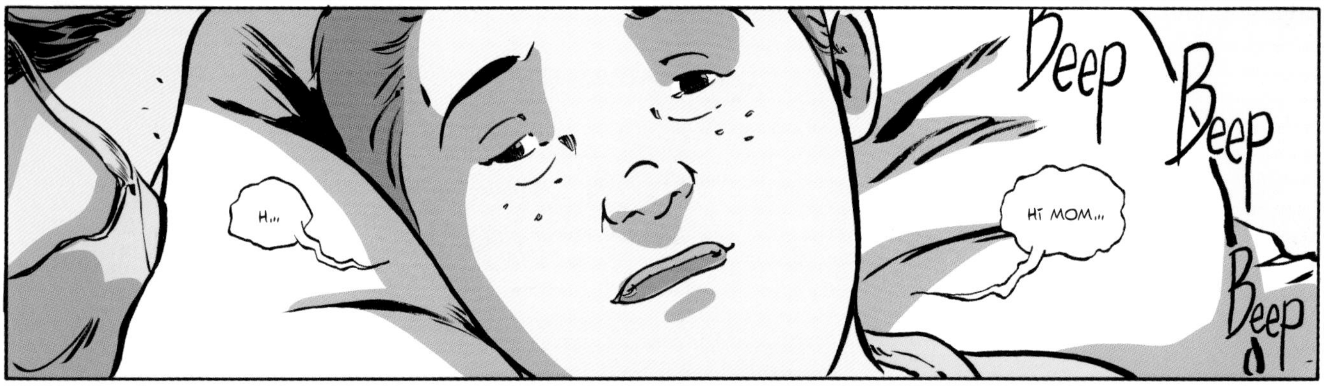
Beep
Beep
H...
Hi mom...
Beep

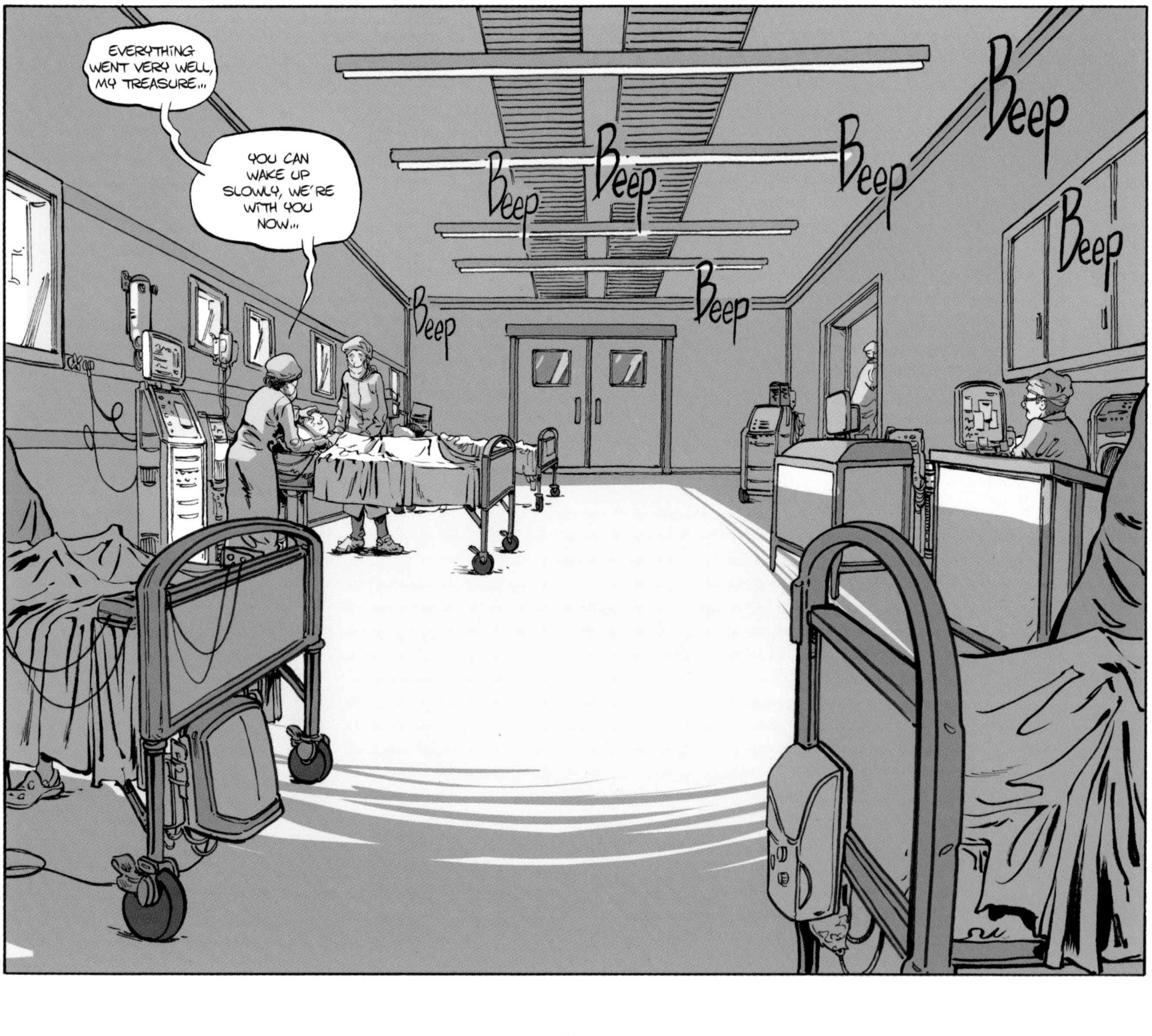
Everything went very well, my treasure...
You can wake up slowly, we're with you now...
Beep
Beep
Beep
Beep
Beep
Beep
Beep

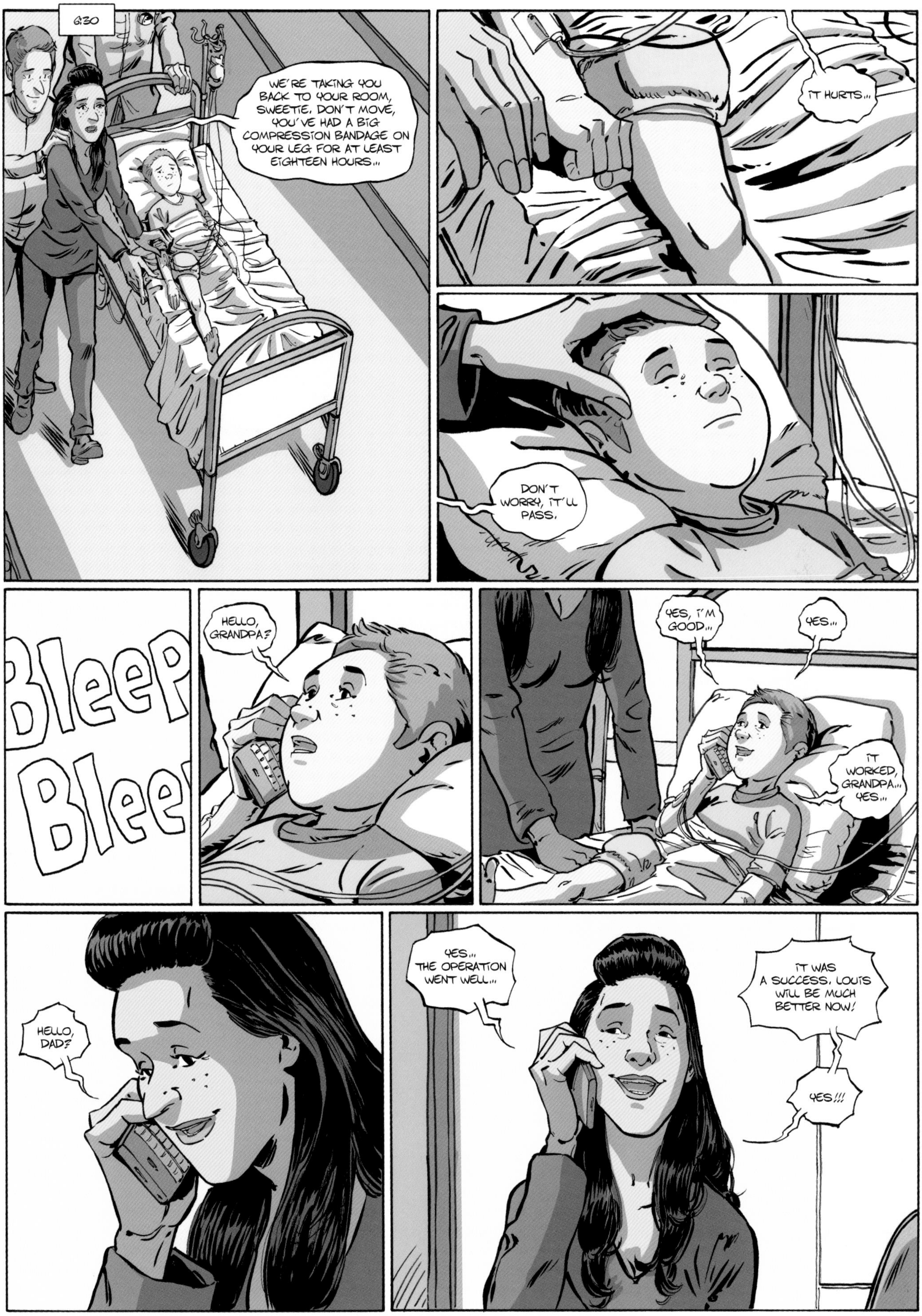
6:30
WE'RE TAKING YOU BACK TO YOUR ROOM, SWEETIE. DON'T MOVE, YOU'VE HAD A BIG COMPRESSION BANDAGE ON YOUR LEG FOR AT LEAST EIGHTEEN HOURS...
IT HURTS...
DON'T WORRY, IT'LL PASS.
Bleep Bleep
HELLO, GRANDPA?
YES, I'M GOOD...
YES...
IT WORKED, GRANDPA... YES...
HELLO, DAD?
YES... THE OPERATION WENT WELL...
IT WAS A SUCCESS. LOUIS WILL BE MUCH BETTER NOW!
YES!!!

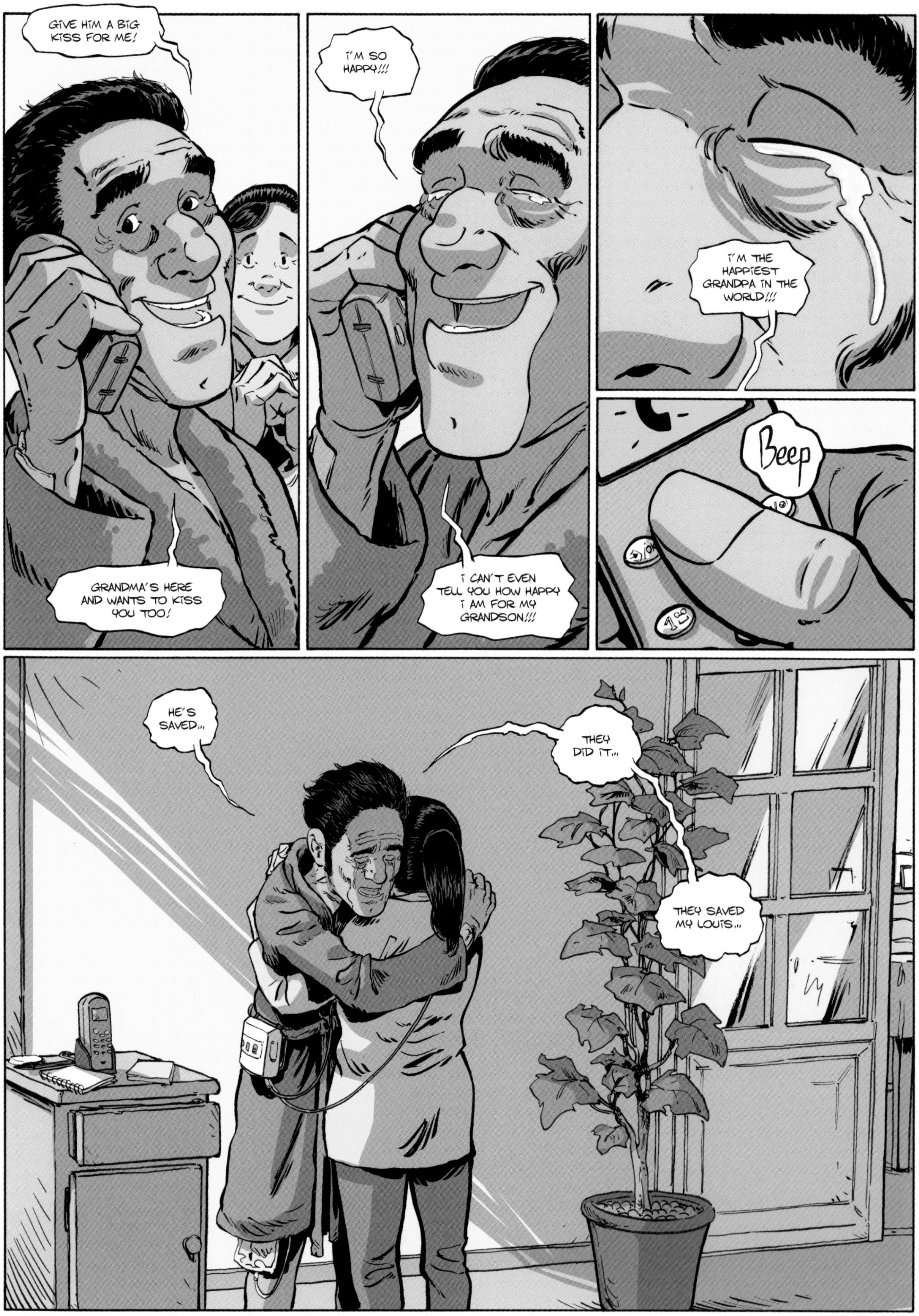
GIVE HIM A BIG KISS FOR ME!
GRANDMA'S HERE AND WANTS TO KISS YOU TOO!
I'M SO HAPPY!!!
I CAN'T EVEN TELL YOU HOW HAPPY I AM FOR MY GRANDSON!!!
I'M THE HAPPIEST GRANDPA IN THE WORLD!!!
Beep
HE'S SAVED...
THEY DID IT...
THEY SAVED MY LOUIS...

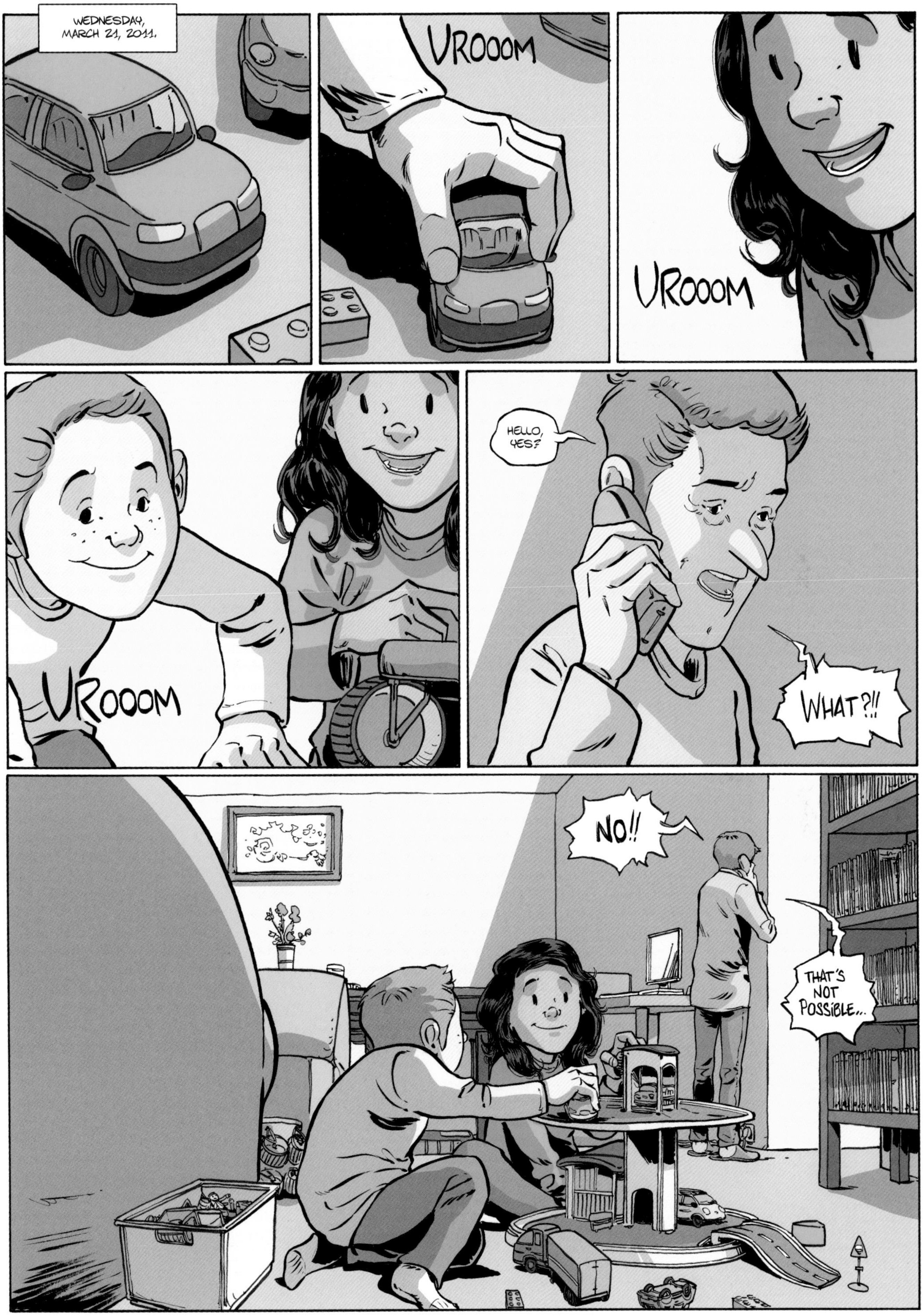

WEDNESDAY, MARCH 21, 2011.
VROOOM
VROOOM
VROOOM
HELLO, YES?
WHAT?!!
NO!!
THAT'S NOT POSSIBLE...

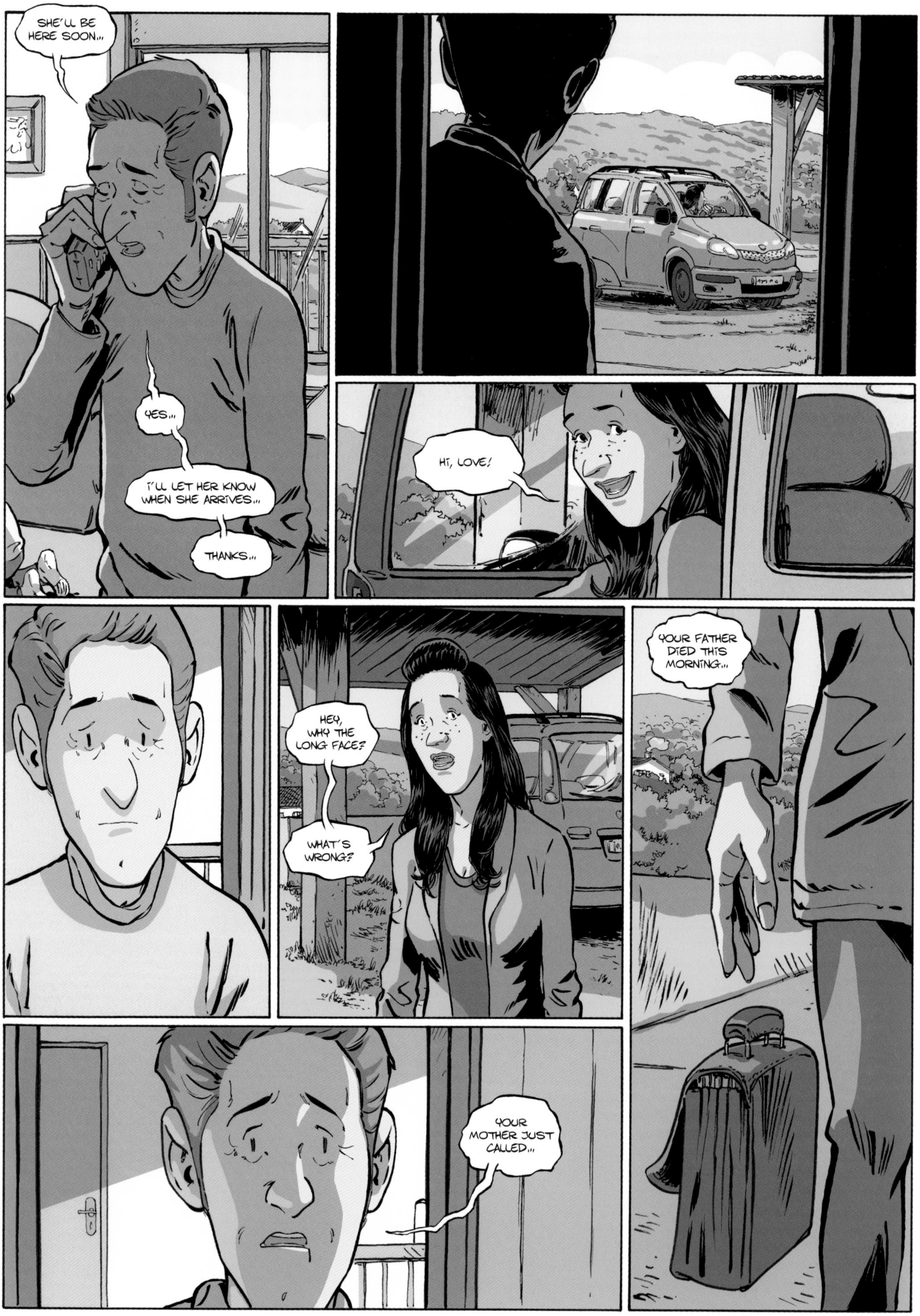
SHE'LL BE HERE SOON...
YES...
I'LL LET HER KNOW WHEN SHE ARRIVES...
THANKS...
HI, LOVE!
HEY, WHY THE LONG FACE?
WHAT'S WRONG?
YOUR MOTHER JUST CALLED...
YOUR FATHER DIED THIS MORNING...

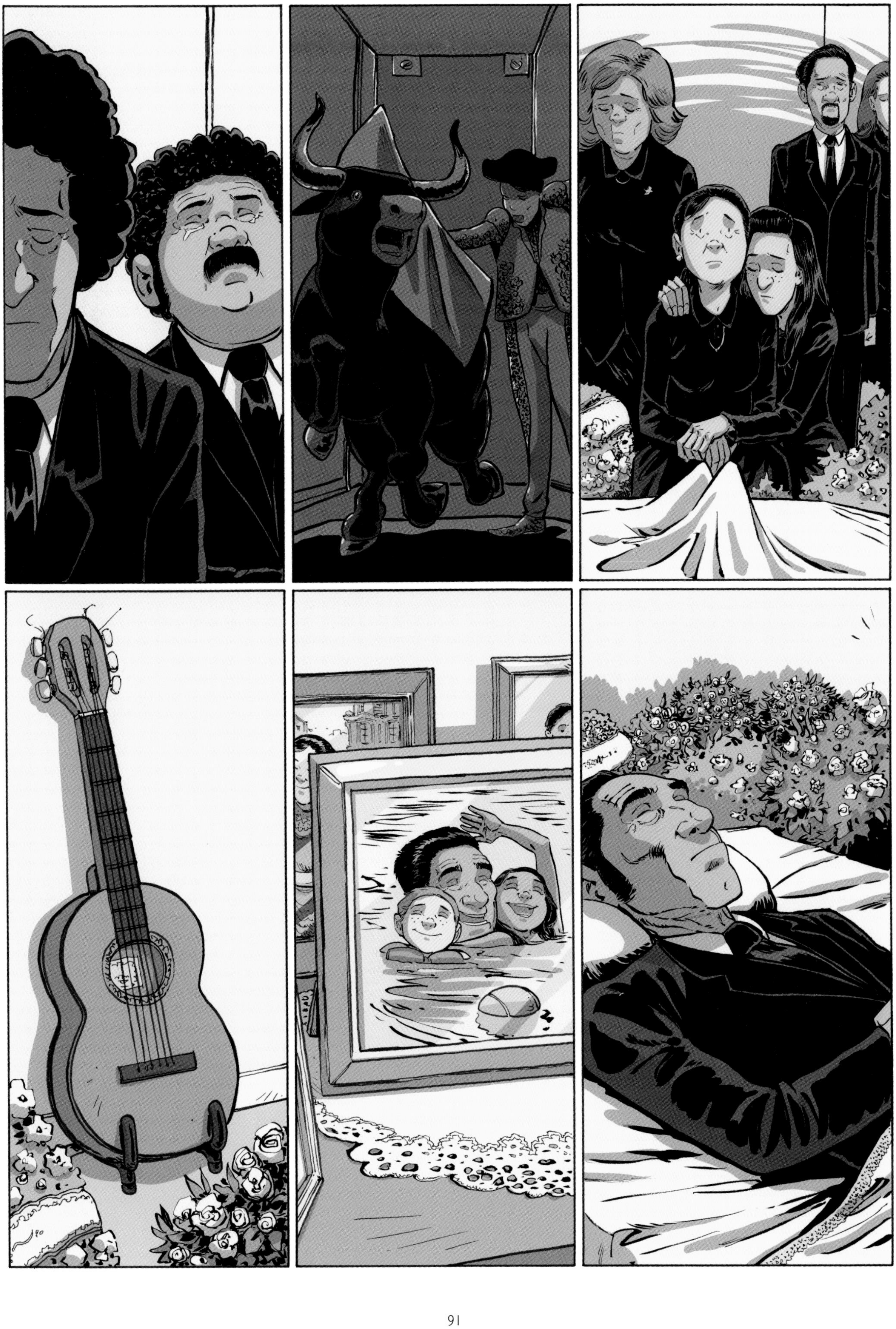

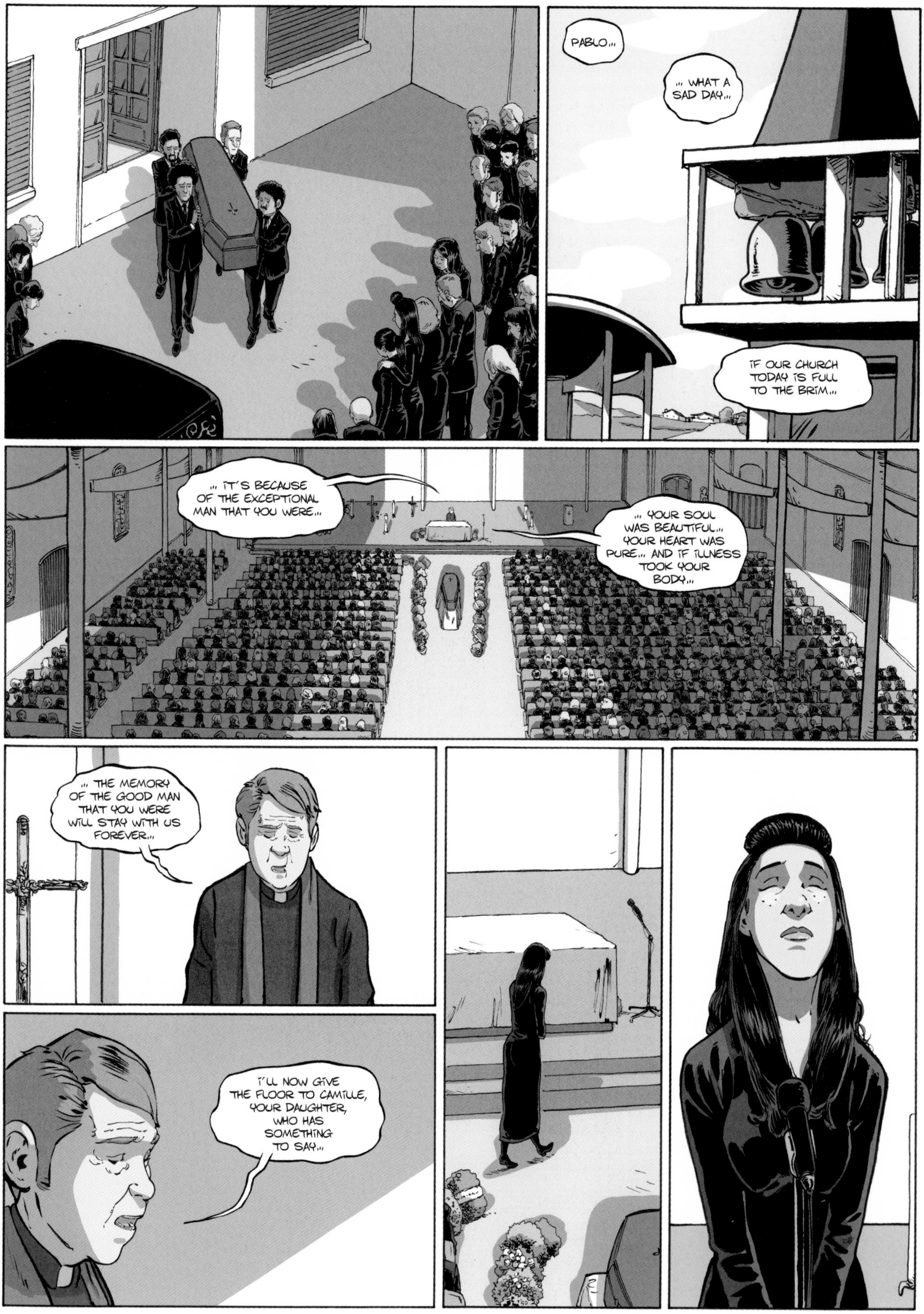
PABLO...
... WHAT A SAD DAY...
IF OUR CHURCH TODAY IS FULL TO THE BRIM...
... IT'S BECAUSE OF THE EXCEPTIONAL MAN THAT YOU WERE...
... YOUR SOUL WAS BEAUTIFUL... YOUR HEART WAS PURE... AND IF ILLNESS TOOK YOUR BODY...
... THE MEMORY OF THE GOOD MAN THAT YOU WERE WILL STAY WITH US FOREVER...
I'LL NOW GIVE THE FLOOR TO CAMILLE, YOUR DAUGHTER, WHO HAS SOMETHING TO SAY...

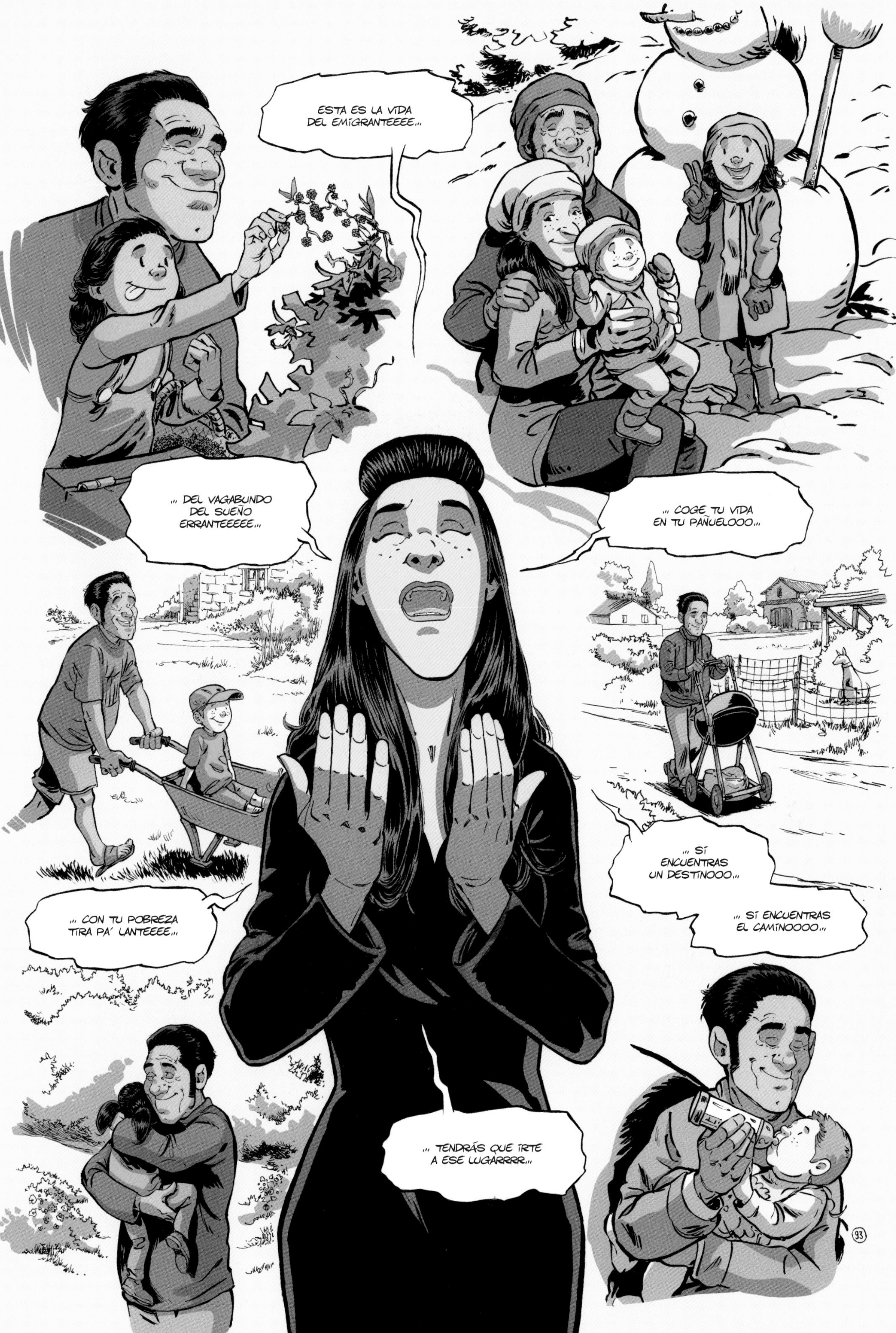
ESTA ES LA VIDA DEL EMIGRANTEEEE...
... DEL VAGABUNDO DEL SUEÑO ERRANTEEEEE...
... COGE TU VIDA EN TU PAÑUELOOO...
... CON TU POBREZA TIRA PA´ LANTEEEE...
... SI ENCUENTRAS UN DESTINOOO...
... SI ENCUENTRAS EL CAMINOOOO...
... TENDRÁS QUE IRTE A ESE LUGARRRR...

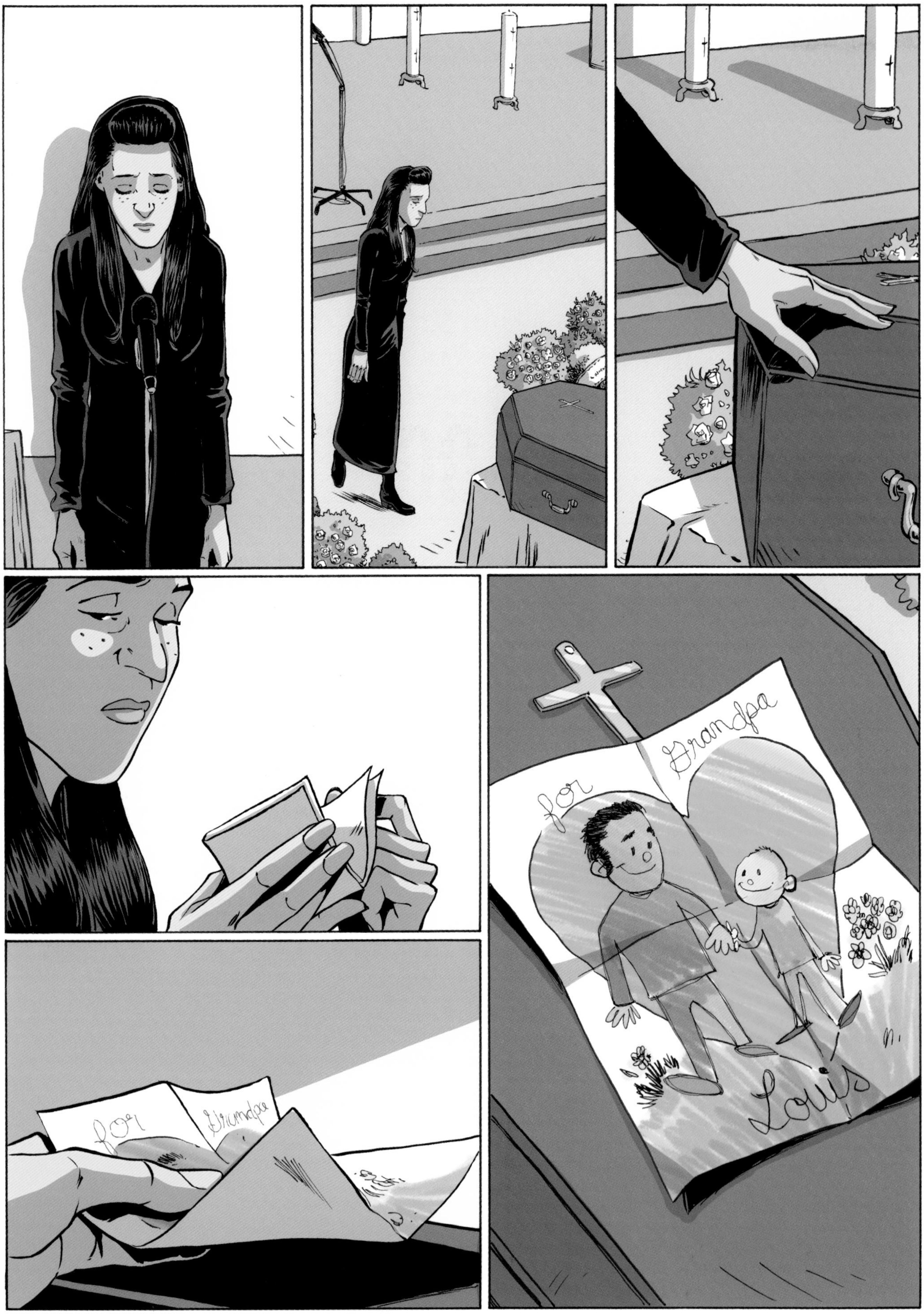
for
Grandpa
Louis

EPILOGUE

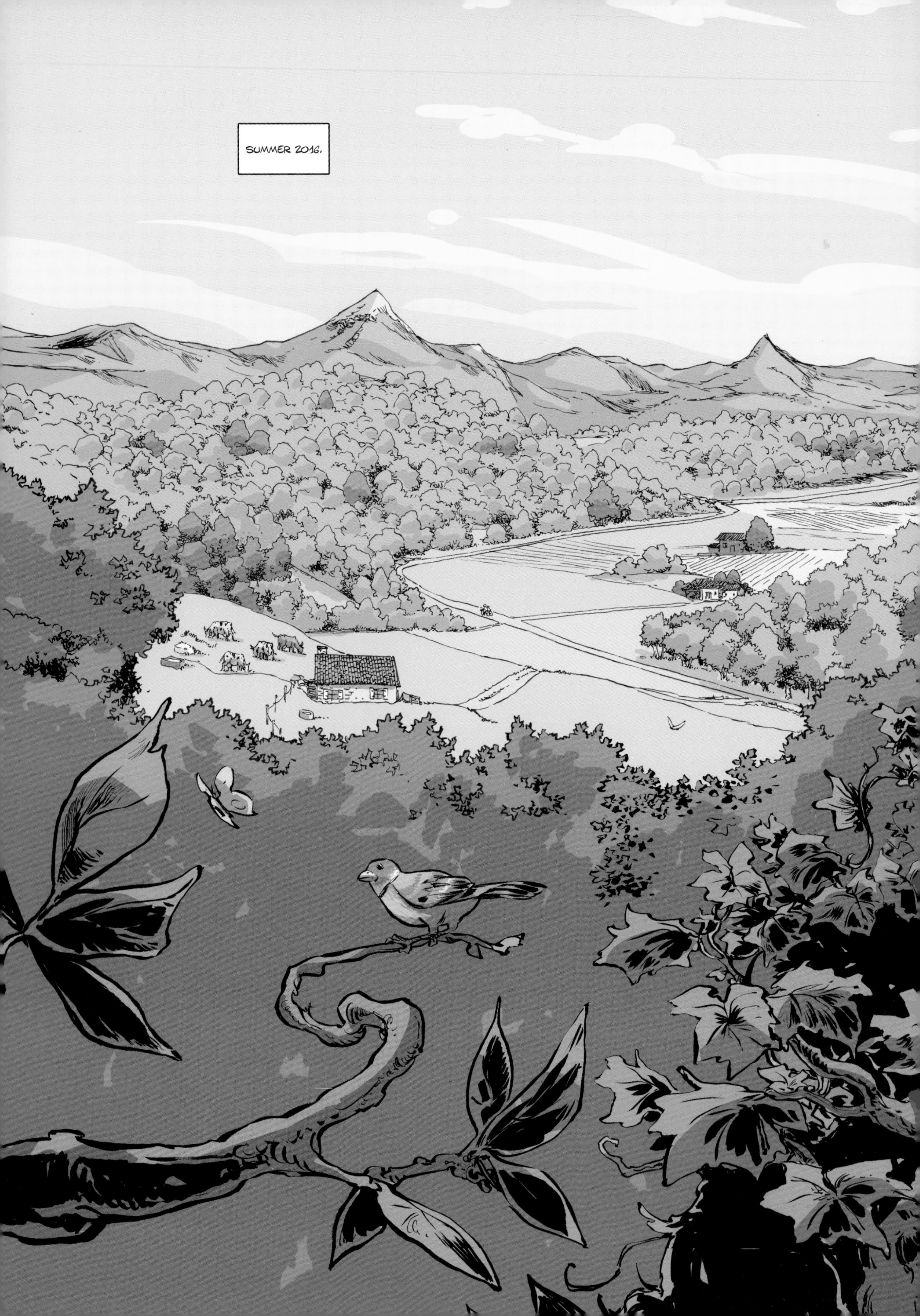
SUMMER 2016.

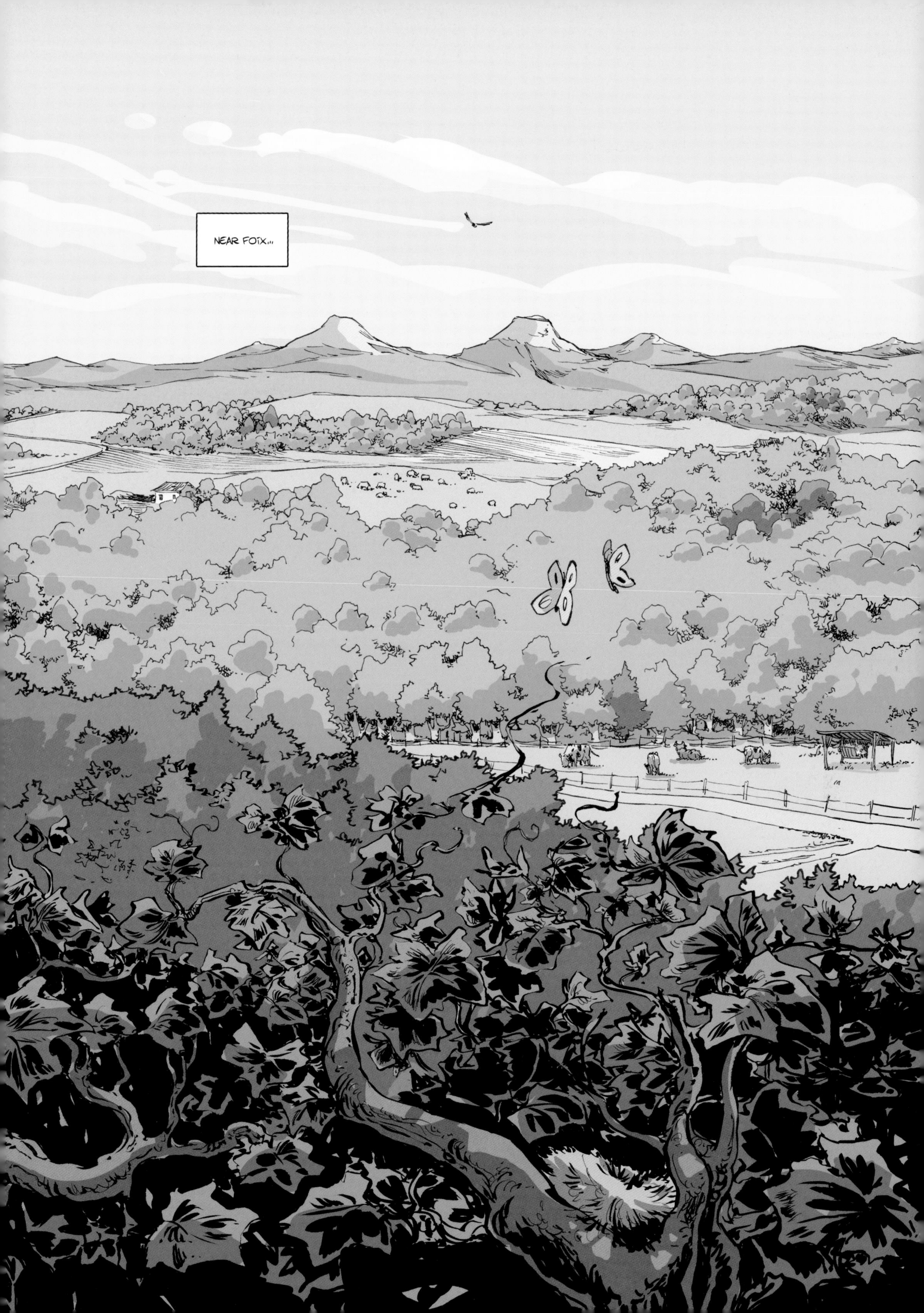
NEAR FOIX...

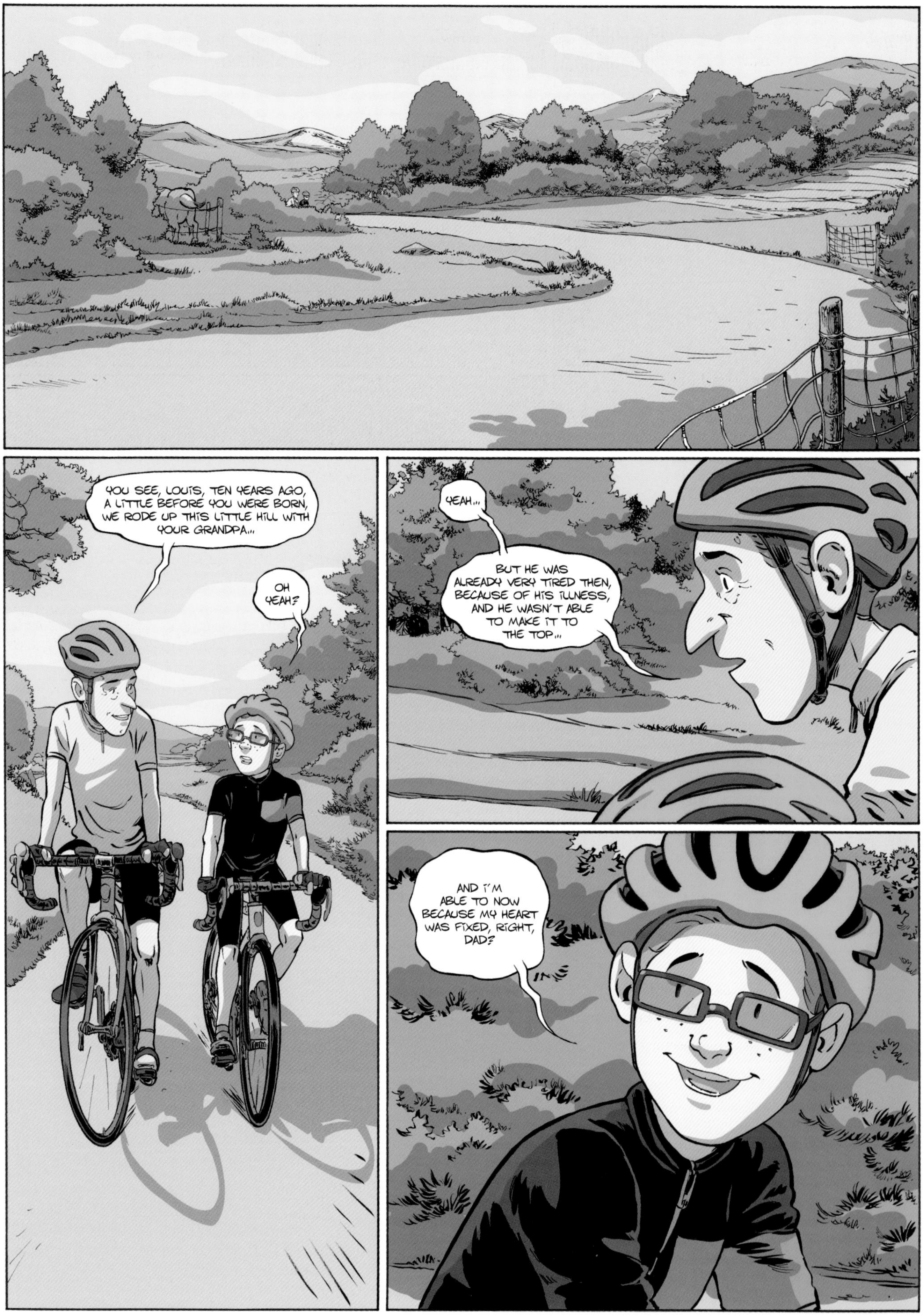
YOU SEE, LOUIS, TEN YEARS AGO, A LITTLE BEFORE YOU WERE BORN, WE RODE UP THIS LITTLE HILL WITH YOUR GRANDPA...
OH YEAH?
YEAH...
BUT HE WAS ALREADY VERY TIRED THEN, BECAUSE OF HIS ILLNESS, AND HE WASN'T ABLE TO MAKE IT TO THE TOP...
AND I'M ABLE TO NOW BECAUSE MY HEART WAS FIXED, RIGHT, DAD?

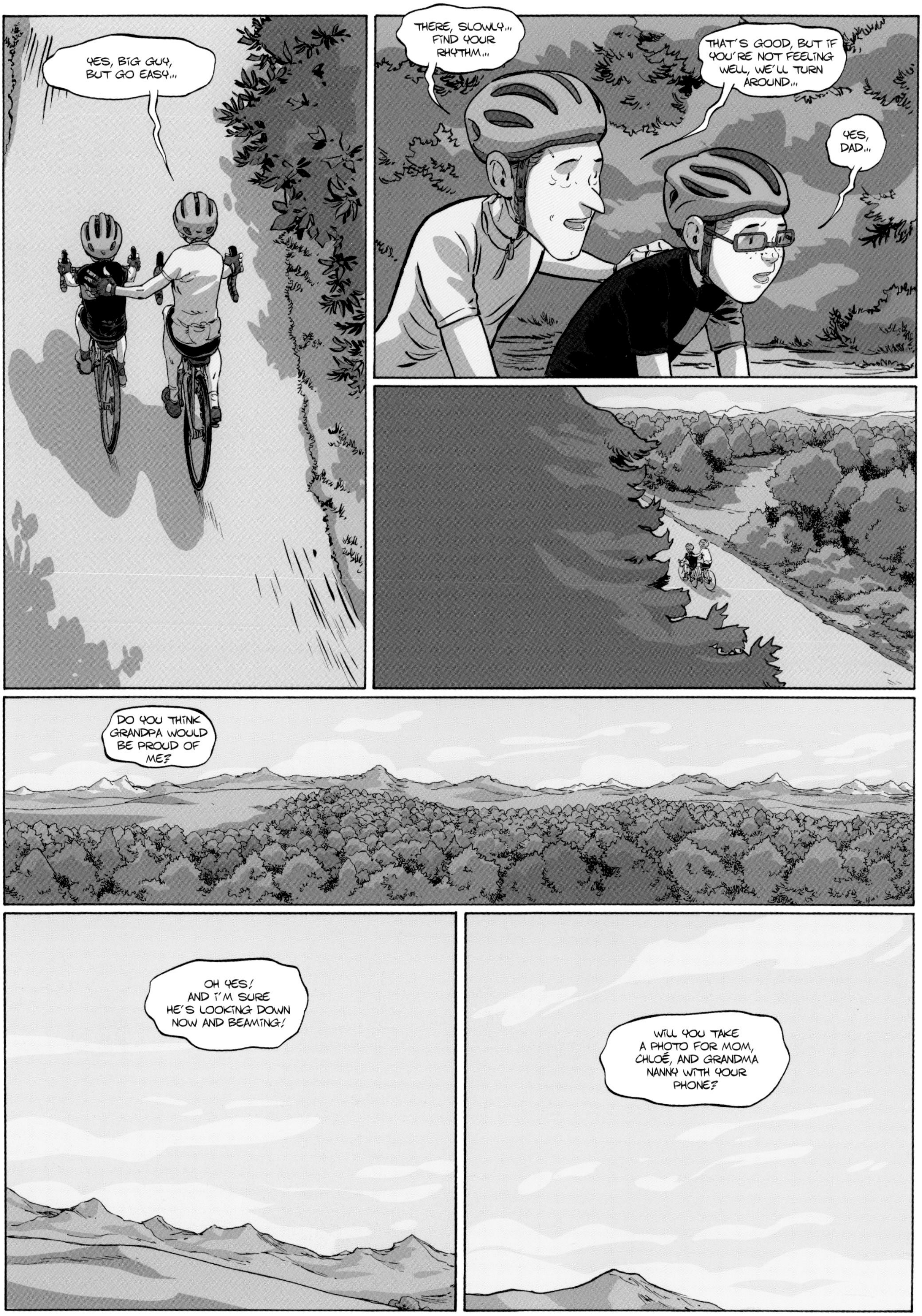
YES, BIG GUY, BUT GO EASY...
THERE, SLOWLY... FIND YOUR RHYTHM...
THAT'S GOOD, BUT IF YOU'RE NOT FEELING WELL, WE'LL TURN AROUND...
YES, DAD...
DO YOU THINK GRANDPA WOULD BE PROUD OF ME?
OH YES! AND I'M SURE HE'S LOOKING DOWN NOW AND BEAMING!
WILL YOU TAKE A PHOTO FOR MOM, CHLOÉ, AND GRANDMA NANNY WITH YOUR PHONE?

OK, TREASURE...

SNAP!

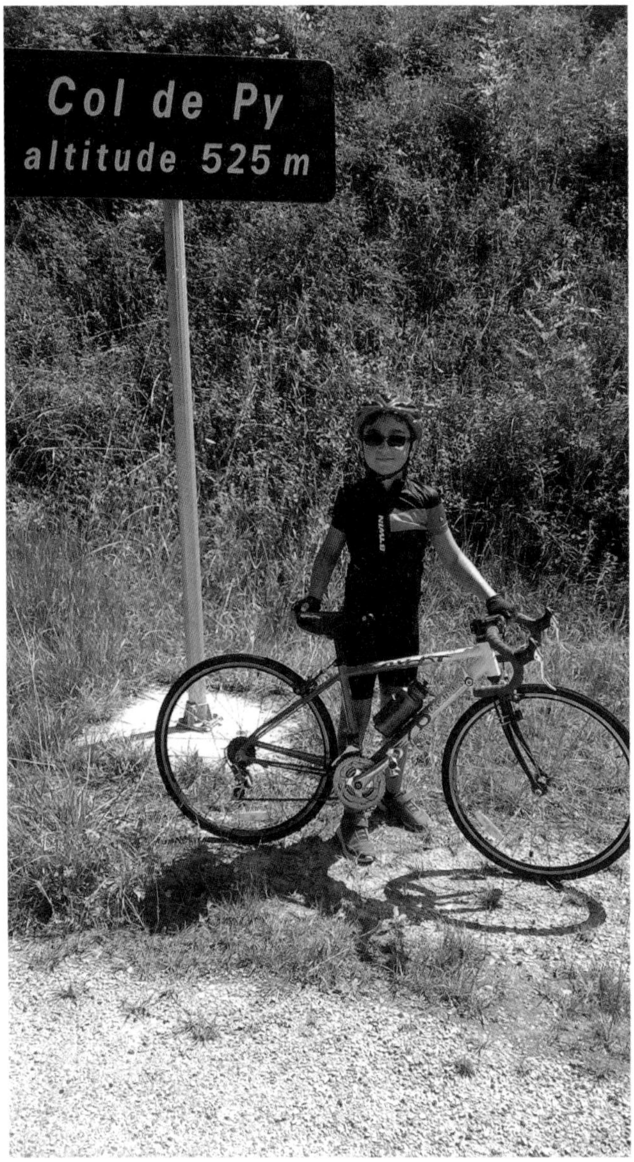
Col de Py
altitude 525 m